Civil Liberties and the Bill of Rights
Part I

Professor John E. Finn

THE TEACHING COMPANY ®

PUBLISHED BY:

THE TEACHING COMPANY
4151 Lafayette Center Drive, Suite 100
Chantilly, Virginia 20151-1232
1-800-TEACH-12
Fax—703-378-3819
www.teach12.com

ISBN 1-59803-198-8

John E. Finn, J.D., Ph.D.

Professor of Government, Wesleyan University

John E. Finn is Professor of Government at Wesleyan University. He received his B.A. in political science from Nasson College, a J.D. from Georgetown University, a Ph.D. in political science from Princeton University, and a degree in culinary arts from the French Culinary Institute. He has taught at Wesleyan since 1986, where his research focuses on constitutional theory, comparative constitutional law, the First Amendment, the legal regulation of terrorism and political violence, and cuisine and popular culture. He is the recipient of four distinguished teaching awards at Wesleyan: the Carol A. Baker `81 Memorial Prize for Excellence in Teaching & Scholarship, awarded in 1989; the Binswanger Prize for Excellence in Teaching in 1994; and on two occasions the Caleb T. Winchester Award for Teaching Excellence, first in 1997, and again in 2004. He was also the recipient of the Association of Princeton Graduate Alumni Teaching Award for distinguished teaching while a graduate student at Princeton. The American Political Science Association described his syllabus for American Constitutional Interpretation as "an ideal model."

Professor Finn is an internationally recognized expert on constitutional law and political violence. His public lectures include testimony in front of the U.S. House Judiciary Committee, as well as lectures in Chile, Bolivia, Spain, Italy, Canada, England, and France.

Professor Finn has published widely in the fields of constitutional theory and interpretation. Among his publications are *American Constitutional Law: Essays, Cases, and Comparative Notes*, 2nd edition (Rowman & Littlefield, 2004), with Donald P. Kommers of Notre Dame University and Gary Jacobsohn of the University of Texas, once described as "the Cadillac of constitutional law casebooks," and the highly regarded *Constitutions in Crisis: Political Violence and the Rule of Law* (Oxford University Press, 1991).

Professor Finn lives in Hartford, Connecticut, with his wife, Linda, and their two children.

Table of Contents
Civil Liberties and the Bill of Rights
Part I

Civil Liberties and the Bill of Rights

Scope:

This course is designed to introduce students to a uniquely American invention and, to some ways of thinking, a wonderfully naïve contribution to politics: The written specification of individual liberties and rights that citizens possess and can, through courts, enforce against the state. *Civil Liberties* is not, however, a course on law. It is, instead, a course that has as its subject the relationship of law to the most fundamental sorts of questions about politics, morality, and human nature.

In this course of 36 lectures, we shall see that most of the serious difficulties (and there are many) in the politics of civil liberties arise from conflicts between our commitments to two or more positive values. There are, for example, inevitable and recurrent conflicts (despite our attempts to ignore them) between the values of liberty and equality. As Felix Frankfurter once wrote, these and other such conflicts are "what the Greeks thousands of years ago recognized as a tragic issue, namely the clash of rights, not the clash of wrongs." We examine these clashes in light of the broader philosophical and institutional problems of the constitutional order. I hope to show that constitutional "answers" to problems like those of abortion, freedom of speech, and affirmative action require a coherent understanding of the U.S. Constitution and of the assumptions it makes about human nature and the proper ends of government and civil society.

We will, therefore, examine the doctrinal development of specific liberties and rights, such as due process and privacy, the ultimate denial of liberty entailed by the death penalty, freedom of speech and religion, and equal protection, but we shall consider them in a broader theoretical context. We shall want to know what overall conception of liberties, rights, and governmental powers most nearly reflects and promotes our best understanding of the Constitution and the polity it both constitutes and envisions.

The course is divided into three sections. We begin with the institutional and interpretive foundations of the American constitutional order. Our purpose here is to provide students with background on the U.S. Supreme Court and its role in the constitutional order, as well as an overview of the process of constitutional interpretation. In our first lecture, for example, we focus on the organization, composition, and decision-making authority of the Court. In our second lecture, we take up the "why" and the "what" of constitutional interpretation. We shall see that interpretation is both a choice and a necessity: a choice because we must choose among many diverse methods and strategies, and a burden because such choices are often difficult to justify or even to explain. In Lectures Three and Four, we take up the intersection of Lectures One and Two by considering how and why the power of constitutional interpretation—and, hence, the power to decide the most pressing issues of civil liberties—came to rest with the Supreme Court through the mechanism of judicial review.

In the second section of the course, we begin our inquiry into the Bill of Rights. In every case that arises under the Bill of Rights, we must reconcile our desire for individual liberty with the need for public order, personal autonomy with the needs of the community. Considered in its totality, and not simply provision by provision, a bill of rights sketches the broad outlines of the relationship between individual liberty and the needs of the community. In this larger sense, a bill of rights indicates how conflicts between liberty and community should be conceived and, to some extent, resolved. In our fifth lecture, we consider the history and theory of the Bill of Rights. Was a bill of rights really necessary? And why, initially, did its protections run only against the federal government, not the states? In the sixth lecture, we take up the fascinating doctrine of *incorporation*, or the torturous and winding road the Court followed to make the Bill of Rights applicable to state and local governments—arguably a constitutional revolution no less significant than the founding in Philadelphia.

In the third and, by far, the largest section of the course, comprising 30 lectures, we consider the individual provisions of the Bill of Rights and the development of several other specific liberties. In deference to the Founders, we begin with the constitutional right to property. The protection of private property, broadly defined, was a central purpose of the constitutional order, and the rise, fall, and possible resurgence of property as a constitutional right of magnitude has had important implications for civil liberties more generally. After property, we take up the fundamental rights of privacy and personhood, rights that cover a broad spectrum of liberty issues, including procreation and abortion, the definition of family, sexual orientation and preference, capital punishment, and the right to die.

We then devote a series of lectures to the speech and religion clauses of the First Amendment. We start with speech. Among the issues we will consider will be the definition of speech, hate speech and fighting words, indecency and pornography, and freedom of association. Our examination of the religion clauses likewise includes questions concerning the definition of religion, as well as consideration of the meaning of the establishment and free exercise clauses and how they interact.

In the final part of the course, we explore the many intricacies of the equal protection clause of the Fourteenth Amendment. When, if ever, does the equal protection clause allow the state to discriminate on the basis of race? Is there a constitutional difference between malignant discrimination, such as Jim Crow laws, and affirmative action, or so-called "reverse discrimination"? Should the Constitution be colorblind? The equal protection clause also applies to other forms of discrimination; thus, we will want to consider how the Supreme Court has addressed discrimination based on gender, sexual orientation, and national origin.

In addressing these issues, whether under the equal protection clause, the First Amendment, or the Eighth Amendment, we will confront a welter of difficult and controversial questions. It is unlikely that we will succeed in our attempts to answer them fully or finally. What we can hope to achieve, however, is an improved and more sophisticated appreciation of the importance of our commitment to civil liberties and of the sacrifices we must make if we choose to honor that commitment.

Lecture One
What Are Civil Liberties?

Scope:

This lecture introduces students to the overall themes of the course and to the methods and materials we will use in our study of civil liberties. We begin with a misleadingly simple question: What are *civil liberties*? There is not an easy or a single answer to this question. We will see, too, I hope, that most of the serious difficulties (and there are many) in civil liberties arise from conflicts between our commitments to two or more positive values. There are, for example, inevitable and recurrent conflicts between the values of liberty and equality. I hope to show that constitutional "answers" to such questions as abortion, freedom of speech, and affirmative action require a coherent understanding of the Constitution and of the assumptions it makes about human nature and the proper ends of government and civil society.

Outline

I. We begin with an overview of this course and the kinds of questions it will explore. As we shall see, the Constitution is a wonderfully sparse yet complex vision of the ideal polity.

   A. Part of that complexity results from the Founders' commitment to several complementary but sometimes conflicting goals. For example, there are inevitable tensions between the Founders' commitment to democracy and to the protection of individual liberties. The protection of civil liberties is one of the central purposes of the Constitution, but it is not the only one.

   B. In addition, a sophisticated understanding of the Constitution includes recognition of the assumptions it makes about human nature and the proper ends of government and civil society. We must ask: What overall conception of liberties, rights, and governmental powers most nearly reflects and promotes our best understanding of the Constitution?

   C. When we ask, "What are *civil liberties*?" we thus ask a number of different but related questions—some technical, some philosophical. In addressing them, we will consult a number of different sources, including the *Federalist Papers* and the occasional work of moral philosophy, but for the most part, our source material will be the decisions of the U.S. Supreme Court.

II. There are as many approaches to the field of civil liberties as there are professors who teach the material.

A. Some professors, for example, prefer to take a doctrinal approach to the material or an approach that focuses on the current state of the law.

B. Other professors are grounded more in political science than in law, and they are more inclined to teach about the Constitution and the Court as grounded fundamentally in politics or to treat the Court and constitutional interpretation as political constructs.

C. As suggested by my opening remarks, my approach is grounded fundamentally in political theory and the kind of critical inquiry that is the hallmark of a liberal arts education. In other words, I begin with the assumption that a course on civil liberties ought to draw on the skills and strengths that a liberal arts education promotes.

1. As taught in law school, constitutional law asks students to concentrate on technical rules and doctrines. In my view, a course on civil liberties and the Bill of Rights ought to help students to think critically about the fundamental principles and policies of the constitutional order. A liberal arts approach seeks to push such issues back to their foundation in social, moral, and political theory, thus prompting students to engage the great issues of political life addressed by the Constitution and constitutional interpretation.

2. Among these issues are questions about the meaning of justice and equality and, ultimately, the meaning of America itself.

III. The complexity of the topic, and the great number and variety of sources we might consult, means that we must make some difficult choices about what we can cover and what we must omit in this course.

    A. First, we will limit our coverage to the Bill of Rights and the other amendments to the Constitution, or to what are typically called *civil liberties*, not *civil rights*.

        1. By *civil rights*, we mean those rights established by legislation, not directly by the Constitution itself.

        2. For example, we will not have an opportunity to cover such areas as the Civil Rights Act of 1964 or the Voting Rights Act of 1975, even though both acts are of profound importance.

    B. Similarly, there are some provisions in the Bill of Rights, such as the Second Amendment and the Fourth, Fifth, and Sixth Amendments, that we will not address. These amendments, although obviously important, are typically covered in courses on criminal procedure and would require a full course of their own.

    C. Finally, we will not have room in this course to consider rights that trace their source to international law or international agreements, though, of course, many of those rights are similar in description and content to counterparts in the American Bill of Rights.

IV. On the other hand, there is much that we should and will cover in the next 35 lectures.

    A. We will begin with an overview of the Bill of Rights as a whole. As we will see, the Bill of Rights was not inevitable.

        1. The Philadelphia Convention, in fact, failed to submit a bill of rights to the states for ratification.

        2. There were multiple reasons for this failure, some grounded in political theory and others in political strategy.

    B. We will also spend some time exploring the development of *judicial review*.

        1. The concept itself is neither in the Bill of Rights nor in the Constitution more generally, at least explicitly, but it is central to understanding the relationship between the Supreme Court and the Bill of Rights.

2. We will also need to spend some time, therefore, discussing the history, composition, and functions of the U.S. Supreme Court.

C. Thereafter, we will begin to take up the specific liberties included in the Bill of Rights and other parts of the Constitution, such as the Fourteenth Amendment.

D. We begin, fairly conventionally, with an examination of the right to property.
   1. At the founding, property was perhaps the most significant of constitutional liberties.
   2. In addition, we begin with property because the significance of property has declined dramatically, or, I should say, its weight as a constitutional liberty has declined substantially.

E. Following property, I will take up the constitutional right to privacy. This shift is somewhat unusual, but there are good reasons for taking this approach.
   1. First, most of the Court's early privacy cases involved property rights as well.
   2. Second, I will argue that privacy means to our generation what property meant to earlier generations— that it serves the same kind of function in the constitutional order.

F. After privacy, we will take up the First Amendment. I have prepared several lectures just on the speech clauses and several on the religion clauses.
   1. These materials are exceptionally complex. We will spend a fair amount of time considering the doctrinal rules that govern speech, but in every case, I want to drive the materials back to larger questions of theory and principle.
   2. For example, we will consider not only specific issues, including hate speech and pornography, but also the larger issues these and other topics raise, such as: What is the definition of *speech*? When, if ever, is it permissible for the state to restrict speech, and for what reasons?
   3. We will spend an equal amount of time considering similar questions when we take up freedom of religion.

What is the definition of *religion*? Who should have the authority to decide? Is there a constitutionally relevant distinction between the freedom to believe and the freedom to act on belief?

G. After we conclude our treatment of the First Amendment, we will spend several lectures on the equal protection clause of the Fourteenth Amendment.

   1. First, we will consider the various problems in equal protection that are occasioned by racial discrimination.

   2. Second, we will take up other areas of discrimination, such as discrimination based on gender, age, wealth, and sexual orientation.

Essential Reading:

The Constitution of the United States, Article III.

Ralph Ketcham, ed., *The Federalist Papers*, No. 1.

Donald P. Kommers, John E. Finn, and Gary Jacobsohn, *American Constitutional Law: Essays, Cases and Comparative Notes*, Introduction.

Questions to Consider:

1. What assumptions does the Constitution make about human nature and the human condition?

2. Do you agree with those assumptions?

Lecture One—Transcript
What Are Civil Liberties?

Hello, my name is John Finn and for the past 20 years, I have had the great pleasure of teaching constitutional law and other courses on the Constitution at Wesleyan University. I'd like to start today by giving you a sense of the kinds of issues that we'll address as we continue throughout this course. As we shall see in our 36 lectures, the Constitution is a wonderfully sparse yet complex vision of the ideal polity. Part of that complexity results from the Founder's commitment to several different complementary, but sometimes conflicting, goals.

Consider, for example, the Preamble to the Constitution, which starts, "We the people of the United States, in order to form a more perfect union." Then it continues—we mean to establish justice. We hope to ensure domestic tranquility. We mean to provide for the common defense. We want to promote the general welfare. And finally, perhaps most importantly, we hope to secure the blessings of liberty. These are ambitious goals, and sometimes they work in tandem to help achieve that ideal polity. But sometimes, too, they conflict with each other. It may not always be possible to secure the common defense, for example, while respecting all of the blessings of liberty.

In order to understand the Constitution, we need to appreciate the kinds of assumptions it makes about human nature, and the kinds of assumptions it makes about the proper ends of government and civil society. We have to ask, what overall conception of liberties, rights, and governmental powers most nearly reflects and promotes our best understanding of the Constitution? I say "our best understanding" because there are at least several possible different ways to make sense of the Constitution and to make sense of the Bill of Rights. One of the recurrent themes of this course will be how difficult it is to justify one reading of the Bill of Rights in opposition to a different reading of the Bill of Rights. As we read the cases and other materials throughout our lectures, we will see again and again that there are few, if any, uncontested principles, or issues, or questions in the American constitutional order.

In our effort to make sense of that constitutional order, we will have to consult a great variety of sources. Before I elaborate on what those sources are, it is worth understanding that part of the reason we need to do that is because the Founders didn't set up a system committed simply to the protection of liberty, nor did they set up a system simply committed to the protection of rights that we might call self-governance rights. The founders didn't create a democracy. They didn't create a constitutional society. They created a society that remarkably tries to incorporate the principles of constitutionalism and the principles of democratic theory and it is a difficult, sometimes contentious, marriage.

In a constitutional democracy, we are committed, as a society, to two fundamental propositions. The first proposition is that we must, as a society, embrace the values of representative democracy. We are committed to the importance and to the realization of self-governance. We are simultaneously committed to the proposition, through our commitment to constitutionalism, that there are times when there are values, where there are goals that trump our commitment to majoritarian democracy. In a constitutional democracy, we try to reconcile our commitment to self-governance with our understanding that there are times when the majority must not be allowed to do certain kinds of things. The tension is irreducible. There are times when the majority must be permitted act; self-governance demands it. And, there are times when the majority must be prohibited from acting. Our commitment to constitutionalism—indeed, our commitment to the Bill of Rights—demands as much.

So, as we approach these questions, we will want to ask which understanding of the Constitution—and several are possible—best promotes the various and diverse goals that we, as a society, hope to achieve; the various and diverse goals that are hinted at in the Preamble to the Constitution itself.

There are as many approaches to the field of civil liberty as there are professors who teach the material. Some professors, typically professors who are in law schools, prefer to take what we might call a doctrinal approach to the material, or an approach that focuses on the current state of the law. The effort here is to teach students the various complex, verbal, sometimes mathematically inclined formulas that the court uses to decide particular constitutional issues. And, there are times in our course together where we will have to spend part of our lectures determining what the doctrine means and how it should be applied. But that is not our primary purpose together.

There are other professors, perhaps grounded more in political science than in law, who teach the Constitution as if the Constitution and the court are fundamentally and perhaps only political actors. They are inclined to treat the court and constitutional interpretation as political constructs. That, too, is an eminently sensible and perfectly legitimate way to understand the Constitution and to teach the Constitution. At various points in the course, we will see that politics seems, inevitably, to influence how we understand the Bill of Rights. Indeed, one of the things I shall try to do in most every case we take up is to situation that case in a larger political and social context.

As suggested by my opening remarks, however, my approach in this course is neither fundamentally political in nature nor even legal in nature. While we'll take up doctrine and while we will take up politics, neither is my primary purpose. My fundamental approach here, as it is in all of my courses, is to try to understand the Constitution in a way that is grounded in critical inquiry, in a way that takes advantage of the kinds of skills that we typically associate with a liberal arts education.

I begin with the assumption that a course on the Bill of Rights ought to draw on the kinds of skills and strengths that a liberal education promotes. Please let me elaborate on this just a little bit. As taught in law school, civil liberties, constitutional law—these kinds of courses asks students to concentrate on technical rules and doctrines that the court has developed in its examination of constitutional law. In my view, however, a course on civil liberties and the Bill of Rights—or at least this course—ought to help students to think critically about the fundamental principles and policies of the constitutional order more generally. A liberal arts approach, in contrast to the other approaches I have described, seeks to push constitutional issues back to their very foundation in social, moral, and political theory. I ask students when they address the Constitution to consider how the Constitution itself addresses the great issues of political life that have dominated American experience for the past two centuries. And among these issues are questions about the meaning of justice, questions about the meaning of equality, and questions about the meaning of America itself.

The complexity of our topic and the great number and variety of sources we must consult, means also that we must make some difficult choices about what we can cover and what we must omit. It pains me to make such choices. First, we will limit our coverage to the Bill of Rights itself and to a few other amendments to the Constitution, or to things that are typically called civil liberties, not civil rights. And the distinction is conventional and important. By civil rights, we typically mean those rights established by legislation, and not directly by the Constitution itself.

So, consider, for example, the Civil Rights Act of 1964, or the Voting Rights Act of 1965; or, alternatively, the Rehabilitation Act of 1973, or the Violence Against Women Act. All of these are profoundly important sources of liberty in the American constitutional order and, sadly, they are civil rights, not civil liberties. We will not have an opportunity to address them.

Unfortunately, there are also provisions in the Bill of Rights itself, such as the Second Amendment and the Fourth through Sixth Amendments, which we will not have an opportunity to address. I hope it is clear that we don't address them not because they are unimportant, but rather because our time is limited. Typically, these kinds of issues associated with the amendments I've just described are covered in courses on constitutional criminal procedure. They are, of course, interesting and important; but to cover them we would need an additional course.

Finally, we will not have room in this course to consider rights or sources of liberty that trace their origin to international law or to various international agreements. That, too, is unfortunate, in large part because many of these contemporary civil rights pacts draw their inspiration from counterparts in the American Bill of Rights; and in other cases, they go far beyond the kinds of protections that the American Bill of Rights includes.

That said, when it is appropriate, when we have an opportunity, we will sometimes consult the constitutions and the constitutional decisions of other constitutional democracies, not because they are source of American liberty—of course, they are not—but sometimes we best see ourselves through the eyes of others. And, our constitutional experience has had a profound impact on the constitutional experiences of other democracies.

Now, I've suggested the kinds of things that we might cover in the abstract, but I'd like to spend a little bit more time talking about what we will cover. Before I get there, I want to stress again that our coverage isn't dictated by the need or the desire to learn an enormous amount of sophisticated, complex doctrine, because I'm not concerned with that.

I want to spend just a sentence or two talking about why I have chosen the materials we have chosen. Most of the time, in most lectures, we will concentrate on a series of specific Supreme Court cases. There is an advantage to this in that it helps us to understand how the Bill of Rights has evolved over time. Most of the cases we will discuss are what scholars would call "canonical cases," by which we mean only that they are cases that almost every course on the Bill of Rights or civil liberties would necessarily choose to talk about.

Such cases include things that you might have heard of, such as *Marbury v. Madison,* or *Brown v. Board of Education,* or *Roe v. Wade*. These are cases that are a necessary part of any course on the Bill of Rights. On the other hand, because my interest is largely in the political theory of the Constitution, we will occasionally take up cases that are reasonably obscure or, to use the language of the academy, that are non-canonical.

One other point: most of the time the materials we take up will be decisions of the United States Supreme Court. I am a little uncomfortable with that focus. It is dictated, of course, by the need to understand the court's work; but we should not forget—and I will try to remind us at every place in the course—that it is not only the Court that makes the Constitution. It is not only the Court that makes constitutional meaning. Other branches of government, both federal and state, are routinely involved in the construction of constitutional meaning, which is perhaps an overly dramatic way of suggesting that if we want to know what liberties Americans possess, we need to concentrate on the work of other constitutional actors because they, too, are involved in giving the Constitution meaning.

Now, what kinds of things will we have an opportunity to cover? For the most part, as I've suggested, we will consider different parts of the Bill of Rights. But, we can't start with each or any individual provision. That would be inappropriate, if only because there are certain kinds of bedrock doctrines, certain kinds of essential constitutive principles, that we need to understand. So when we begin, we will begin with an overview of the Bill of Rights itself.

What do I mean by that? We will need to consider why we have a Bill of Rights. It will perhaps surprise you to learn that a Bill of Rights was not an inevitable part of the American constitutional order; and, as we shall see, the Founders who reported the Constitution out of the Philadelphia Convention either neglected or decided not to include one. There were good reasons for not including a Bill of Rights. Nevertheless, we have one and we will need to spend a certain amount of time considering why that happened and what the significance of that historical fact is.

I also mean to cover, when we've discussed this issue about an overview of the Bill of Rights, a second set of questions—what kind of a document is the Bill of Rights?

I hope we'll see in later lectures that there is room for disagreement about what the Constitution is. By that I mean, first, that there is room for disagreement about what the Constitution includes. Is it simply the words on the page? Those words contained in what lawyers like to call the "four corners of the document"? Does it include extra-textual understandings about what makes that document have meaning? Does it include, for example, the intention of the Founders? Does it include contemporary understandings about what cruel and unusual punishment might be? Or contemporary understandings about what the Equal Protection Clause refers to as the protection of the laws?

The meanings that those provisions have, the meanings that any provision of the Bill of Rights might have, is partly a construct of the words themselves, partly a construct of that piece of paper, but partly a construct of what each successive generation of Americans has determined the Constitution to mean. Consider that problem in its most straightforward sense—does the Constitution include the decisions of the United States Supreme Court itself?

Now, I've asked what kind of document is the Constitution. What is the Constitution? One dimension of that problem is, what does it include? A second dimension, though, is what kind of document is it? Is it a document that is essentially a statement of legal principles, of legal rules, which govern specific cases?

There are certainly judges, certainly justices on the United States Supreme Court, who think that is how we should understand the Constitution. There are justices who think that we should approach the Bill of Rights as a set of legal principles. There are other justices, however, other scholars, who think that the Constitution, although it may in fact have the status of law, is not only and, perhaps, not even primarily a legal instrument. There are justices who think that the Constitution might be approached, say, as a biography; that it is a statement of faith; that it is a document that not only purports to govern law, but to govern our conception of ourselves. In the same way that some religious faiths have creeds, there are some scholars and some judges who think that the Constitution and the Bill of Rights should be approached primarily as a creed, as a statement of identity, as a statement about who we are as a people. Indeed, it might be the only statement of who we are as a people.

I don't mean to open up the difficult and contentious question about whether there is an America and, if so, what it looks like. That is a political question. I mean to ask a somewhat different kind of question. Is there some set of constitutional values—not constitutional rules, but constitutional values—principles that we all share? I'd like to return to that at the end of the lecture, but a few minutes on the kinds of issues that we will cover.

First, we begin with an overview of the Bill of Rights itself. After that, we turn to what it is one of the critical features of the American constitutional order and without which, probably, we can't understand any part of the Bill of Rights; and that is the origins of judicial review. As we shall see, judicial review might be the distinctive feature of the American Bill of Rights. Certainly, when we turn our eyes to the impressions that other constitutional democracies have of the United States, we will see that almost every other constitutional democracy assumes that a critical part, perhaps *the* critical part of the American constitutional order, is the institution of judicial review itself. All the more amazing that this doctrine of judicial review, so fundamental to the American constitutional order, is not in the Constitution and, I think I can say with some confidence, cannot be found in the Constitution.

After we cross these boundaries, after we understand these fundamental premises of the constitutional order, we will begin to take up specific provisions in the Bill of Rights—or if you prefer, specific civil liberties. The first of these will be property. There are good reasons to begin with property. There are good analytical reasons, there are good philosophical reasons, but perhaps the best reason is that the Founders themselves gave priority to property.

As we shall see, the protection of property was a central purpose of the constitutional order. When I say it was a central purpose, I mean it was part of the driving force for the repudiation of the Articles of Confederation, part of the driving force for a convention at Philadelphia. But just as importantly, property is critical to any intellectual understanding about what the Bill of Rights—or the Constitution, more generally—means. It might be the case that nothing in the Constitution makes sense without understanding how fantastically important property was, not to the founder's conception of what constitutes good government—or not only that—but rather the importance of property to the Founder's conception of what made human beings virtuous. Property isn't critical to the political order; property is critical to any understanding—or at least it was for the Founders—to any understanding of human dignity and autonomy.

That understanding is what drives my decision to turn later in the course from property to a consideration of the constitutional right of privacy. I think I owe you an explanation. It is not a normal part of a civil liberties course to move from property to privacy. That is a very unconventional transition; but I think that you can probably see why I have chosen to make it. If property was critical to the Founder's understanding about the relationship of individuals to society, of individuals to government, then it may be that privacy fulfills the same role for contemporary American society. It may be, in other words—and this is simply an argument, not a conclusion—that in the same way that property was a "fence for liberty" in Madison's words at the Founding generation; the fence for liberty in our generation may be privacy. Privacy, in other words, may mark the point, just as property once did, between the self and society.

After we take up the privacy cases—and we shall address those cases in lectures Nine through Sixteen—we will take up the First Amendment. We have scheduled 11 lectures on the First Amendment. Lectures Eighteen through Twenty-Three will concern speech; Lectures Twenty-Four through Twenty-Nine will concern religion. Together, that takes up nearly one-third of our time together. That is, of course, an enormous investment of resources on just this one—or perhaps two, if you want to divide up religion and speech—topics. I think it's worth that investment. I'm more worried that we need a greater investment of time.

Surely, we could spend an entire 36 lectures on the problems of speech and religion. Consider just for a moment the kinds of issues that we'll have to address. Does our society's commitment to freedom of speech extend to speech that is subversive? To speech that threatens the integrity of the state itself—by integrity not its emotional, or spiritual, or intellectual integrity, but its physical integrity. I mean, does it really, really threaten our very survival? Or, consider speech that is fundamentally noxious because it offends or is meant to offend other citizens. Or, consider speech that might happen to be offensive. Consider, for example, problems associated with indecency or obscenity. And this takes us only to speech.

Consider the kinds of problems that we will have to address when we consider freedom of religion in Lectures Twenty-Four through Twenty-Nine. Consider this first, perhaps most difficult, of problems: How do we define religion? I ask that question because we might ask it of any other part of the course. We might ask, what's property? We might ask, what is speech? Or, what is equality?

You'll recall that I began by noting that the Constitution is a remarkably sparse document. Its economy of words means that the Constitution itself, the Bill of Rights itself, tells us nothing about what the definition of speech actually is. The Constitution tells us nothing at all about what religion is. This hints at a recurrent theme throughout the course; or, I should say that it hints at several recurrent themes throughout the course.

First, in the absence of any clear, textual, constitutional definition for words such as religion, speech, property; or for phrases such as cruel and unusual, or due process of law, or equal protection; in the absence of any textual guidance, where do we find constitutional meaning? Do we look at what the Founders intended? Do we consult dictionaries? Perhaps we should consult earlier Supreme Court cases that may have addressed these issues.

What I'm trying to suggest here, is that part of what we will do in this course is not simply read cases and try to discern meaning; we will try to figure out how it is that we find meaning in the first place.

I am sorry to have been so oblique about that. I mean only this: constitutional law doesn't exist; what exists is constitutional interpretation. And what we need to do is to find out how, why, and when judges use other sources to interpret, to give meaning to, the vague provisions of the Constitution.

After that, after religion, we will take up the intractable problems of equal protection. Equal protection will take up Lectures Thirty to Thirty-Five. What kinds of issues do we address with equal protection? Profoundly important issues, profoundly controversial issues.

We will want to know, for example, what kinds, if any, of racial discrimination are permissible under the Constitution. We will want to know when, if ever, the state may discriminate on the basis of gender or sexual orientation and preference. All of these are the sorts of issues that we will take up when we address the Equal Protection Clause, recognizing all the while that behind our inquiry must be the most fundamental of inquires. What does it mean to be a society protected, or that is committed to the protection of equality? Now, those are the kinds of issues and, to some extent, the kinds of themes and questions we will take up more generally.

I want to remind you that as we take up these materials, we are not looking for clear, unequivocal answers, and rarely, if ever, will we find them, even if only by misdirection. The point of our inquiry is not to memorize cases, it is not to memorize rules; it is to open up the most fundamental questions that drive American politics, that drive any consideration of the Bill of Rights. And, that said, there is one such question that I have not yet addressed. It will be implicit in everything we do. We should not assume, necessarily, that the highest order, that our highest obligation as citizens, is actually to promote the Bill of Rights or to respect the Constitution. The Constitution represents a set of choices; the Bill of Rights represents a set of choices. And those choices cannot be assumed to be correct; they must be defended. And in order to be defended, they must be understood.

Lecture Two
The Bill of Rights—An Overview

Scope:

The document produced by the Philadelphia Convention and submitted to the states for ratification did not include a bill of rights. Some of the Founders, as we shall see in this lecture, believed that a bill of rights was, at best, unnecessary and, at worst, even a threat to liberty. In this lecture, we explore the history of the Bill of Rights, considering, first, whether and why a bill of rights was necessary and, second, why it took the form it did. As we saw in Lecture One, we will not be able to consider every provision of the Bill of Rights, and, sadly, we will not be able to address any single provision in as much depth as we might like. The First Amendment's provisions on speech alone would merit an entire course, as might the religious freedom clauses of the same amendment. And many of the topics we shall consider are not, strictly speaking, a part of the Bill of Rights proper. We shall, for instance, spend a fair amount of time with the due process and equal protection clauses of the Fourteenth Amendment. Like the First Amendment, the Fourteenth is a staple of modern constitutional litigation.

Although it may seem peculiar to modern sensibilities, one of the most important issues surrounding the Bill of Rights concerns its application: Does it protect citizens against the federal government only or also against the actions of state governments? This was the issue in the seminal case of *Barron v. Baltimore* (1833), in which Chief Justice John Marshall, writing for the Court, concluded that the Bill of Rights did not apply to the states. We then consider whether and to what extent that decision was effectively overturned by the passage of the Fourteenth Amendment and how the Court approached that question in the years immediately following the Civil War. We conclude by considering the *doctrine of incorporation*, or the process by which the Supreme Court, over time, finally made individual provisions of the Bill of Rights applicable to the states by incorporating, or including, them in the due process clause of the Fourteenth Amendment.

Outline

I. The Constitution produced in Philadelphia did not contain a bill of rights. Indeed, the subject came up hardly at all at the convention.

    A. Its omission became an important part of the ratification debates. Eventually, several states made the addition of a bill of rights a key condition to their decision to ratify—known as *conditional ratification.*

    B. In other words, several states insisted that they would not ratify the new Constitution without a bill of rights. A bill of rights thus became a precondition for the new Constitution.

II. The demands for a bill of rights gave rise to an important and sophisticated discussion about the nature and limits of rights in the American constitutional order.

    A. Alexander Hamilton and James Madison, writing in the *Federalist Papers,* argued that a bill of rights was unnecessary, because the Constitution itself was a limited document of enumerated powers. Hamilton went so far as to suggest that a bill of rights "would even be dangerous…. For why declare that things shall not be done which there is not power to do?"

    B. Madison argued, in addition, that no list of liberties could ever hope to be complete, and this might lead governments to abridge liberties that were not explicitly listed as protected. Moreover, mere "parchment barriers," he wrote, could not protect liberty.

        1. This is an interesting argument. If taken to an extreme, its logic—that words alone will not limit power—undercuts the constitutional enterprise.

        2. On the other hand, perhaps it is a mistake to think of the Constitution or the Bill of Rights as "mere parchment barriers."

    C. In contrast, anti-Federalists argued that a bill of rights would do no harm, and Jefferson, in particular, argued that such a document might have an important educational purpose. In addition, Jefferson argued that a bill of rights might put "a legal check … in the hands of the judiciary."

1. This is a little ironic—Jefferson was quite skeptical of judicial power, as we shall see when we take up *Marbury v. Madison* (1803).
2. Jefferson's first argument—that a bill of rights might constitute a public reminder of our commitment to liberty—hints at a conception of the Bill of Rights grounded in civic education.

III. As he had promised in the ratification debates, Madison submitted a bill of rights to the very first Congress, and an amended version was submitted to the states shortly thereafter and ratified in 1791. Before we consider the individual provisions of the Bill of Rights, we need to look at it as a whole.

A. Considered in its totality, a bill of rights sketches the broad outlines of the relationship between liberty and community. A bill of rights is a blueprint—less a list of liberties than a vision of the ideal relationship between liberty and community.

B. In every case that arises under the Bill of Rights, we must reconcile our desire for individual liberty with the need for public order, personal autonomy with the needs of the community.

C. In this course, we will address those provisions in the Bill of Rights that have tended to generate the most controversy and case law.
1. In particular, we will spend a fair amount of time with the First and Eighth Amendments.
2. In addition, we will spend a great deal of time on provisions that are not, strictly speaking, a part of the Bill of Rights proper, such as the due process and equal protections of the Fourteenth Amendment.

IV. Passage of the Bill of Rights did not quiet all controversy. The language of the amendments seemed to leave open the question of whether they applied to the federal government alone or also to the states.

A. Inherent in this unresolved question were two very different conceptions of liberty and community.

B. Madison, for example, thought the Bill of Rights ought to apply to both, because the federal and state governments were equally likely to threaten liberty.

C. Most anti-Federalists, however, were more fearful of threats by a remote federal government. They believed the proximity of state and local governments to their citizens made those governments less likely to abuse power.

V. The Supreme Court took up this issue in the very important case of *Barron v. Baltimore* (1833).

A. Writing for the Court, Chief Justice John Marshall concluded that the Bill of Rights applied only to the national government.

    1. The Bill of Rights reflected the Founders' fears that the new government might exceed its powers. "The Constitution was ordained and established by the people of the United States for themselves ... and not for the government of the individual states."

    2. Implicit in Marshall's decision is a particular understanding about the relationship among the national government, state governments, and citizens.

B. *Barron* is an important case, in part because it made clear that the liberties contained in the Bill of Rights did not protect citizens against actions taken by state governments.

VI. Following the Civil War, Congress ratified the Thirteenth, Fourteenth, and Fifteenth Amendments, or the Reconstruction Amendments. Some judges soon began to ask whether those amendments, in particular the Fourteenth, should be understood as making the Bill of Rights applicable to states, thus overruling, at least in consequence, *Barron*.

A. The Court rejected the philosophy behind this claim in the important Slaughter-House Cases (*Butchers' Benevolent Association v. Crescent City Livestock*, 1873). Here, the Court gave a restricted reading to the privileges and immunities clause of the Fourteenth Amendment, thus denying the proposition that the clause had made the Bill of Rights applicable to state governments.

B. But only 30 years later, the question resurfaced in a series of cases concerning the First Amendment and the criminal procedure provisions of the Bill of Rights.

VII. Under the so-called *incorporation doctrine*, the Supreme Court began to apply individual provisions of the Bill of Rights to the states. In a series of cases, the Court began to conclude that the due process clause of the Fourteenth Amendment includes, or *incorporates*, parts of the Bill of Rights. The states were, thus, bound to observe those amendments as part of due process of law.

> **A.** The Court considered four different approaches to incorporation:
> 1) the fundamental fairness doctrine; 2) total incorporation; 3) total incorporation "plus"; 4) selective incorporation.
>
> **B.** Eventually, in the critical case of *Palko v. Connecticut* (1937), the Court settled on the selective incorporation approach, which meant that some parts of the Bill of Rights would be incorporated—those "implicit in the concept of ordered liberty"—and others would not.

Essential Reading:

Barron v. Baltimore (1833).

Butchers' Benevolent Association v. Crescent City Livestock (1873) (The Slaughter-House Cases).

Palko v. Connecticut (1937).

Kommers, Finn, and Jacobsohn, *American Constitutional Law*, chapter 4.

Ralph Ketcham, ed., *The Federalist Papers*, Nos. 10, 45, 78, 80, 84, 89.

Supplementary Reading:

Theodore Becker, *The Declaration of Independence: A Study in the History of Political Ideas*.

Neal Cogan, *The Complete Bill of Rights: The Drafts, Debates, Sources, and Origins*.

Leonard Levy, *Origins of the Bill of Rights*.

Questions to Consider:

1. Is a bill of rights necessary? Is there a vision of human nature implicit in both the purpose of the Bill of Rights and the specific liberties it singles out for protection?

2. Should we consider the Ninth and Tenth Amendments as part of the Bill of Rights? Is there any practical consequence to doing so?

Lecture Two—Transcript
The Bill of Rights—An Overview

The document produced by the Philadelphia Convention did not include a bill of rights. Hence, when the Constitution was sent to the states for ratification, there was no bill of rights to be ratified. Some of the Founders, as we shall see in this lecture, thought that a bill of rights itself was unnecessary. I suppose, in that sense, they might have said that a bill of rights was trivial. Others agreed that the question wasn't trivial, but nevertheless were opposed to a bill of rights because they thought a bill of rights might actually be a threat to liberty itself. In this lecture, we take up the argument surrounding the ratification of the Bill of Rights. We'll consider, first, whether and why a bill of rights was necessary and, second, why it took the form it did.

Now, I've used the word "ratification" twice already, and there's a reason why I did that. The reason we have a bill of rights is because of a process known as "conditional ratification." Conditional ratification simply refers to this: as I said, the Constitution was submitted to the states without a bill of rights. Several states insisted that they would only ratify that document if they received a promise in return. In other words, it was a condition of their acceptance that the first congress would adopt a bill of rights. We'll consider the process of conditional ratification and, in particular, we'll begin with the arguments that were addressed on both sides of the issues.

I think the first place we need to begin is with Alexander Hamilton and James Madison. Both wrote in *The Federalist Papers* that a bill of rights would be unnecessary in the American constitutional order because, as Madison once said, "The Constitution itself is a bill of rights." He meant by that that the Constitution was a creation, a document, a conception of a constitutional order in which a government, the federal government, would have only those powers enumerated in the constitutional text itself—a document of enumerated powers. All that means is that the government didn't have some great residual authority to act; it could only act. The new national government was only authorized to act in those specific places where the constitutional text said so.

Consider this issue: Did the new government have the authority to impinge upon freedom of speech? No provision in the text said that it could; no provision in the text said that it could not. Madison's argument was that in the absence of any explicit, or perhaps implicit, authorization for the government to act, it could not touch speech. There is an important sense in which a bill of rights on such a theory would be utterly redundant. It would simply say that government may not do things that that government was already not permitted to do. This is the argument, in other words, that a bill of rights would be unnecessary.

Hamilton went a bit further. Hamilton said, "A bill of rights would even be dangerous.... For why declare that things shall not be done which there is not power to do?" All he means is that, in the absence of any explicit constitutional authorization permitting government to infringe upon this liberty or that liberty, the government was possessed of no such authority. Why say it again?

Now, we might be worried simply about redundancy here, but Hamilton does have another point. He was greatly concerned that if we constructed a list that government may not interfere with speech, or religion, or the sanctity of your home; or may not abolish trial by jury, nor impose cruel and unusual punishments, that everyone eventually would assume that government may not do those things, but it might be permitted to do anything else. The claim here is simply this: no list of liberties, no bill of rights, could ever hope to be complete, and this might lead governments to abridge liberties that were not explicitly protected in the bill of rights.

Madison had another claim as well. Madison sometimes wrote of "parchment barriers," of paper barriers. Parchment barriers, he argued, could not protect liberty. Think about the importance, the extraordinary importance, of this claim. Madison wanted to argue that a government intent on violating civil liberties would hardly be restrained from doing so by the mere existence of a piece of paper. Parchment barriers, he argued, would have no profound limiting effect on a government intent on doing mischief.

That is a fascinating proposition. If we take it seriously, then we probably ought to ask Madison, if governments may not be restrained by parchment barriers that we call bills of rights, then why would they be restrained by parchment barriers that we call constitutions?

Perhaps, Madison did not have this faith, but most of the Founders did. By this faith, I mean, most of the Founders believed—perhaps this is naïve—that paper limitations, whether expressed in bills of rights or in constitutions more generally, might actually constrain governments. What a remarkable thing to believe, that saying a thing makes it so, that reducing it to paper transforms it from an idea to a legal rule. It is well to remember that most of the Founders were products of the Enlightenment, and the idea itself that constitutional rules on a piece of paper might somehow influence human beings intent on governing is probably only possible in an Enlightenment era.

Now, there were other arguments for a bill of rights as well. Perhaps the most important, if only politically, was advanced by Thomas Jefferson, who argued that even if a bill of rights might only be parchment barriers, they might still be important for two reasons. First, Jefferson argued that a bill of rights might "put a legal check in the hands of the judiciary." Great foresight hides behind such a quote. We wouldn't be here; we couldn't have this course if Jefferson's prediction had not come true. Or, if we did have this course, we would be talking about a bill of rights routinely interpreted and applied by state governments, or by congress, or by the president. We would not have a course that considers the Bill of Rights in the hands, as Jefferson said, of the judiciary. There's something a little ironic about this quote. As it turns out, Jefferson was no great lover of judicial authority; and as we shall see just a short time from now, Jefferson routinely combated judicial efforts to give meaning or application to the Constitution.

Jefferson advanced another argument, however, as well. It's one that I think we will have to take seriously throughout our time together. Jefferson argued that there might be a kind of educational value to a bill of rights. His claim here is very simple. A bill of rights might teach citizens, might teach governmental actors, about the meaning and the importance of liberty. In other words, a bill of rights might be a nice posted reminder about basic principles that we are all supposed to respect.

Eventually, conditional ratification won because it was politically powerful. There would be no Constitution if the process of conditional ratification had not finally persuaded Madison and the other Founders that a bill of rights was simply the price of the

Constitution. And, true to his word, as he had promised in the ratification debates, Madison did submit a bill of rights to the very first congress. And, ultimately, an amended version of his bill of rights was submitted to the states and ratified in 1791. I say it was ratified in 1791 only because the requisite number of states ratified it; some states didn't get around to ratifying the Bill of Rights for a very long time. My home state of Connecticut, for example, did not actually ratify the Bill of Rights until 1939.

Before we look at the individual provisions included in the Bill of Rights, we need to look at it as a whole. Considered in its totality—not point by point, not as a laundry list—considered as an entire document, the Bill of Rights sketches the broad outline of the relationship between liberty and community. In this sense, a bill of rights is a blueprint; it's less a list of liberties than a vision of what my relationship is to the state, of what your relationship is to the state, perhaps a vision about the relationship between the state and civil society itself. Because it is that, in every case that arises under the Bill of Rights, in every single case we will take up, we must reconcile our desire for liberty with the need for public order. We will have to reconcile personal autonomy with the needs of the community.

Now, when we take up these particular cases we will see that the Bill of Rights rarely, if ever, tells us how to mediate those controversies. The Bill of Rights is typically written in great abstraction. And, as I said in our first lecture, the Bill of Rights rarely, if ever, tells what a specific, correct, single, right answer is to any constitutional controversy. Because the Bill of Rights speaks in the grandest of terms, because it speaks, as lawyers like to say, in concepts rather than conceptions, making sense of the Bill of Rights is partly about learning rules, partly about memorizing doctrine—and those are important things and we will do them. But, it is also partly about the larger process of constitutional interpretation, of trying to understand what the basic values and commitments are that give meaning to, that rest behind, that animate the Bill of Rights more generally.

Now, the Bill of Rights was ratified in 1791. Partly because it speaks with a voice that talks in generalities rather than specifics, passage of the Bill of Rights didn't end an era in American constitutional history; it opened up an era in constitutional history; it opened up the kinds of questions that we will consider in our remaining lectures.

One particular controversy, however, we need to address now. This controversy is difficult, I think, for most of us to understand. It requires an act of imagination on my part and an act of imagination on your part as well.

The language of the Bill of Rights, the specific language in this great collection of provisions left unresolved, or at least seemed to leave unresolved, a question of extraordinary importance. That question was this: Against whom did the Bill of Rights apply? It is all well and good to say that the state government may not interfere with your freedom of speech, or owes you fundamental obligations concerning the sanctity of your home, or must provide to you a fair trial with a jury; but which government?

Remember, in the United States we have several levels of government and, as odd as it may seem, the first question to be resolved under the Bill of Rights was whether or not the Bill of Rights applied to every level of government—city, county, state—or to only one level of government—the federal government.

Imagine a world, for example, in which the Bill of Rights protects you against the federal government, but does not protect you against your state or local government. Imagine, more specifically, a world in which you can go to a street corner and criticize the president on almost any ground you like and be reasonably confident that if your criticisms are not violent in nature, not intended to incite a riot or to harm anyone, that your criticisms are protected by the First Amendment's provisions regarding freedom of speech. And, imagine in that same speech, as you work yourself up into a fit, as the spittle begins to fly, that you no longer concentrate your ire on the president, but instead, brush everybody in the president's political party with the same set of criticisms.

Or, imagine that your criticisms now extend to your governor, or to your state representative, or to your mayor, or to the local police, or to a public school teacher—does the Bill of Rights protect you regarding those actors? That was an open question at the Founding. It was an open question, in other words, about whether the Bill of Rights protected you not only against the national government, but also against the state governments.

The reason I say that this probably requires an active imagination is because, surely, the answer must be for our time, of course it protects you against all governments. It must be difficult to imagine that we care where our threat to liberty comes from. Surely, our liberty is equally threatened if we are thrown in a federal prison or if we are thrown in a state prison, because we had the unmitigated gall to criticize some public official. And yet, that was the world the Founders lived in.

This is not a small, technical problem. This is a problem of the first order. The Supreme Court took up this problem in the celebrated case of *Barron v. Baltimore* decided in the year 1833. I can't resist mentioning that it was the year 1833. We are now 30 years past the passage of the Bill of Rights and yet, still this most fundamental of questions is unresolved, or at least, unresolved judicially.

Here's a little bit about the facts in this case. Barron owned a wharf in the city of Baltimore and a public works improvement project rendered his wharf unusable. His dock, his wharf, no longer had the depth necessary to discharge its function. This case involves, obviously, what I called the most important of constitutional liberties in the first lecture, the right to property—Barron's right to property.

Now, imagine you are Barron. Does it really matter to you if it is the federal government that has rendered your wharf useless? Or a state government that has rendered your wharf useless? In either event, your property has been harmed. In either event, your ability to make a living has been diminished by some governmental action.

As it turns out, however, it did matter who harmed Barron's wharf. John Marshall, taking up the question, concluded—and we will reach his conclusion first and then explain the reasoning—that the Bill of Rights did not apply to the state of Maryland, much less to the city of Baltimore. As a consequence, because the Constitution's Bill of Rights protected only against federal action, Barron's wharf was harmed and Barron would receive no compensation. It did matter, in other words, who hurt Barron. If the federal government had dredged the harbor and deposited the silt that made his wharf unusable, he'd be entitled to compensation. That isn't what happened, unfortunately.

Writing for the Court and reaching the conclusion that that the Bill of Rights applied only to the national government, John Marshall argued that the Bill of Rights reflected the Founder's fear that the new government might exceed its powers. "The constitution was ordained and established by the people of the United States for themselves," he wrote, "and not for the government of the individual states."

Barron is a critically important case because it made clear that the liberties contained in the Bill of Rights did not necessarily protect citizens against actions taken by their own state governments. Now, let me just backtrack for a second. This does not mean, necessarily, that you had no liberty claim, no right of any kind—be it speech, religion, or anything else—against state governments. You might well be protected by your own state constitution, but you were not entitled to any federal comfort.

Following the Civil War, Congress ratified the Thirteenth, Fourteenth, and Fifteenth Amendments to the Constitution, sometimes called the Reconstruction Amendments. Why have I made the transition from *Barron* in 1833 to post-Civil War America? Some judges, as soon as these amendments were passed, began to ask whether something in those amendments, and in particular whether one phrase in the Fourteenth Amendment, should be understood as overruling, at least in consequence, *Barron v. Baltimore*.

Here's what I mean by this—the Fourteenth Amendment begins, "No state shall deny the privileges and immunities of citizenship." And, if you took that clause out of context, out of the context of this lecture, and just ask, what does that clause mean, you would ask, what are the privileges and immunities of citizenship? The Fourteenth Amendment does not answer that question. And you can just try to make them up, or you might try to find meaning somewhere else in the Constitution. It shouldn't be any great surprise, I think, that judges and some scholars began to argue that the privileges and immunities of citizenship are those things that are listed in the Bill of Rights.

So, we might rephrase the Fourteenth Amendment to say, "No state shall deny the privileges and immunities of citizenship. Parenthetically those privileges and immunities are listed in the Bill of Rights." Then, we would have the Bill of Rights applicable to the states; no state shall deny.

This is an eminently sensible reading of the Fourteenth Amendment. It's not the only possible reading, however; and in an important case known as the Slaughter-House Cases decided in 1873, the Court rejected that interpretation. It said, instead, that the privileges and immunities of citizenship are not co-extensive with the Bill of Rights. Well, then, what are they? Such unimportant things as the right to travel the navigable waters of the United States and to travel to capitals. Now, those are not unimportant. I was being sarcastic, of course. They're not unimportant, but they hardly attain or reach the significance of the Bill of Rights itself.

The Court understood in Slaughter-House that it had in front of it something that might amount to a constitutional revolution. The majority opinion acknowledged that the Fourteenth Amendment might fundamentally have transformed American society by making the Bill of Rights applicable against every government. Faced with that possibility, with something that truly amounted to a constitutional revolution, the majority backed off and said, surely, if Congress had meant to affect such a radical transformation, it would have said so in clearer terms, prompting one of the dissents to argue that that is precisely what Congress had intended, and that the new amendments—the Thirteenth, Fourteenth, and Fifteenth—amounted, in effect, to a new Magna Carta.

So, now we exist in the 1870s and the 1890s, and the Bill of Rights still does not apply against state governments. Eventually, however, something changed. Right around the turn of the century, the Court began to reopen not the broad question of does the Bill of Rights apply to the states, but rather a more specific set of questions. Does this particular provision apply to the states?

These cases started with the First Amendment, and what happened in these cases was that courts began to ask themselves, perhaps some parts of the Bill of Rights are so important that they are an elemental part of due process, more generally. What happened, in other words, is that over time the Supreme Court began to pick out individual provisions of the Bill of Rights and make them applicable to the states under the Due Process Clause of the Fourteenth Amendment. Let me say that again: The Fourteenth Amendment provides, as we saw, "No state shall deny the privileges and immunities of citizenship;" it goes on to say, "nor shall any state deny to persons due process of law or equal protection of law."

Do you see what's happened? The Bill of Rights might have been made applicable to the states through the Privileges and Immunities Clause. Slaughter-House foreclosed that—one door closed, another opened—and over time the Supreme Court began to make parts of the Bill of Rights applicable to the states under the Due Process Clause. This is known as the incorporation doctrine. Parts of the Bill of Rights were incorporated by the Due Process Clause.

This process didn't occur overnight. It began, as I mentioned, with the Fourteenth Amendment, around the turn of the century, and continued up until the 1930s, when the Court was asked whether or not the Due Process Clause incorporated, included, as against the states, the Fifth Amendment's provisions on double jeopardy. The justice entrusted with writing a majority opinion in this case, *Palko v. Connecticut* in 1937, Justice Cardozo, looked at the line of cases in front of him and was confronted with a mess. In some cases, the Court had said, "Yes, this provision is incorporated." In other cases, it had said, "But this provision is not incorporated." What do you make of two lines of cases, some of which say yes, some of which say no? Cardozo wrote, "If we look behind the cases, we will see an organizing principle."

Now, there were a number of organizing principles that would make sense not only of these cases, but of the entire problem we have been discussing. The first of these principles that might have made sense was the principle of total incorporation. We might argue, in other words, that the Due Process Clause totally incorporates every part of the Bill of Rights. It's just a done deal; one shot, that's it. The Due Process Clause makes the Bill of Rights applicable to the states.

Other justices rejected that approach and argued that, instead, we need to consider a doctrine known as the "fundamental fairness doctrine." What that means in the incorporation controversy, is that the Due Process Clause of the Fourteenth Amendment incorporates only those parts of the Bill of Rights that are central to our notions of fundamental fairness. Those are two organizing principles.

Here's a third: you might say, as some justices did, that the Fourteenth Amendment's Due Process Clause incorporates every part of the Bill of Rights, plus something else—maybe a fundamental commitment to justice, or to liberties that are not actually included in the text of the Bill of Rights. Or, you might take a fourth approach. The fourth approach is known as "selective incorporation"—some parts of the Bill of Rights will be selected as incorporated; other parts won't. How would you know which ones should be selected and which ones ought not to be selected? *Palko* gives us the answer.

As it turns out, no majority on the Court between, say, 1900 and 1937, could be found to agree upon any one of these approaches. In *Palko*, Justice Cardozo advanced the doctrine, finally, of selective incorporation and argued that there is a way to know which parts of the Bill of Rights should be incorporated. Here is his answer: We incorporate those parts of the Bill of Rights that "are implicit in the concept of ordered liberty." If a liberty protected in the Bill of Rights is not implicit in the concept of ordered liberty, then it does not apply to the states.

Just so you know, as it turns out, in *Palko* a majority of the Court concluded that the double jeopardy provisions of the Fifth Amendment were not implicit in the concept of ordered liberty, and, as a consequence, did not apply to *Palko*. What did that mean for Palko? Palko was executed.

Now, why spend all this time on these alternative methods of making the Bill of Rights applicable to the state? As it turns out, our description of methodology doesn't necessarily tell us what the result is. All I mean is this—the justices used, in the end, the method of selective incorporation and, in that process, eventually came to a position where we are today of total incorporation.

I hope that's not confusing. All I mean to say is that through the process of selective incorporation, nearly all of the provisions of the Bill of Rights were eventually made applicable to the states. That is where we are now, with two minor trivial exceptions. Every provision in the Bill of Rights is applicable to every level of government in the United States. That is a remarkably recent phenomenon, a mid-to-late-20th-century development.

Two more things: I think it's worth asking why the justices spent so much time trying to fight over method. I don't think we have the tools yet to be able to begin to answer that question, but I want to put it on the table for future lectures. Why do justices sometimes fight over methodology even if it seems to have no immediate impact on the result, which is how we might describe the entire incorporation controversy? Second, *Palko*'s notion that there are some liberties that are implicit in the concept of ordered liberty and, hence, must be protected, and some that are not, suggests that there are two kinds of constitutional liberties—those in the language of *Palko* that are fundamental, and those that are not. That idea, that some constitutional liberties might be more important than others, is one that we will wrestle with throughout the entire course.

Finally, the Bill of Rights is a remarkably complex document, a remarkably simple document. I hope that you will engage it with me with as much enthusiasm as we can all muster.

Lecture Three
Two Types of Liberty—Positive and Negative

Scope:

In the last lecture, we considered questions concerning the breadth of the Bill of Rights. We continue that topic here, although in a somewhat different fashion. In this lecture, we will focus heavily on one Supreme Court case—*DeShaney v. Winnebago County* (1989). *DeShaney* is important because it teaches about two other issues concerning the breadth and scope of the Bill of Rights. Our first topic concerns the *state action doctrine*—a principle that holds that the Constitution applies only to public action, or the actions of state actors, and does not apply to the actions of private individuals or organizations. As we shall see, the state action doctrine is an essential part of the constitutional order. Our second question concerns the nature of the rights included in the Constitution. What does it mean to say that a right is guaranteed? Does it mean only that the government may not interfere with the right, save on certain conditions? Or does it mean that the government must make efforts to help citizens realize and exercise those rights? The former, we shall see, are commonly called *negative rights*. The latter are so-called *positive rights*. This lecture will explore which version of the two doctrines of the Bill of Rights the Constitution protects. Finally, *DeShaney* introduces a theme that will run throughout the remainder of this course: What role should the Court play in the protection of civil liberties?

Outline

I. In our last lecture, we saw that through the doctrine of selective incorporation, the Supreme Court eventually made most of the provisions of the Bill of Rights applicable to the states. Before we begin our examination of specific constitutional liberties, we must first consider a few other basic doctrines, or rules, that have an important effect on civil liberties more generally.

   A. The first of these is the *state action doctrine.*

   B. The second is the distinction between *positive* and *negative liberties.*

C. The state action doctrine is a principle that holds that the Constitution applies only to public action, or the actions of state actors, and does not apply to the actions of private individuals or organizations.

D. For example, there is no such thing as a constitutionally protected right of freedom of speech against private institutions or private individuals.

E. Consider the important case of *DeShaney v. Winnebago County* (1989). Here, the Court ruled that the due process clause of the Fourteenth Amendment protects due process rights only against state actors, not against the actions of private persons.

    1. We begin with the facts of the *DeShaney* case, which are exceptionally tragic.

        a. Randy DeShaney viciously beat his son, Joshua, time and time again; on at least two occasions, emergency room physicians, as they were required to do under Wisconsin state law, notified local child protection and police authorities of their suspicion that Randy DeShaney was abusing his son—who was later committed to an institution in a persistent, vegetative state.

        b. Melanie DeShaney, Joshua's mother, sued the state, Winnebago County, claiming that the Fourteenth Amendment's due process clause imposed upon the state an obligation to protect her child from the violence inflicted upon him by his father.

    2. We then take up the majority opinion for the Court by Chief Justice Rehnquist. In his opinion, Rehnquist explained that the due process clause of the Fourteenth Amendment guarantees our liberty against the state, as evidenced in part by the language "No State shall...." Consequently, in this case, the state could not be liable because the violence committed against Joshua was done by his father, not by the state.

    3. In addition, Chief Justice Rehnquist argued that no action by the state had left Joshua worse off than before the state's limited involvement in the case.

    4. Finally, the Chief Justice argued that Joshua's case did not fall into one of the rare exceptions to the general rule that the state is under no obligation to protect private persons.

II. Another basic premise of the constitutional order concerns the distinction between positive and negative liberties.

   A. What does it mean to say that a right is guaranteed? Does it mean only that the government may not interfere with the right, save on certain conditions? Or does it mean that the government must make efforts to help citizens realize and exercise those rights? The former, we shall see, are commonly called *negative rights*. The latter are so-called *positive rights*.

   B. *DeShaney* might also be treated as a positive-negative liberties case. Joshua DeShaney, one might argue, claimed a positive right to be free from violence—or to constitutionally protected liberty. The Court rejected this claim, noting that the due process clause protects only a negative version of the liberty.

   C. Writing for the Court, Chief Justice Rehnquist explained that a constitutional rule embracing positive liberty would expose the state to potentially disruptive and fiscally unsound liability.

III. Finally, *DeShaney* is important to us because it illustrates a third and vitally important constitutional principle.

   A. *DeShaney* should remind us that behind abstract constitutional rules and grand theoretical principles are real people. It is sometimes too easy to forget that behind these rules and principles are live human beings and unspeakable tragedies.

   B. Consider, though, a response: The Court does not necessarily have a roving license to go out and do "good." And even if it did, is it clear what "justice" demands in the *DeShaney* case?

Essential Reading:

Isiah Berlin, *Four Essays on Liberty*.

DeShaney v. Winnebago County (1989).

Kommers, Finn, and Jacobsohn, *American Constitutional Law*, pp. 306–311.

Supplementary Reading:

Sotirios A. Barber, *Welfare and the Constitution.*

Benjamin C. Zipursky, "*DeShaney* and the Jurisprudence of Compassion," 65 *New York University Law Review* 1101 (1990).

Questions to Consider:

1. In the abstract, it is not difficult to understand the distinction between state action and private action. But why should the protections of the Constitution apply only against the former?

2. Consider the distinction between positive and negative liberties. Is there anything in the actual language of the Bill of Rights that suggests that the state sometimes has an affirmative obligation to protect life, liberty, and property or any other constitutional liberty?

Lecture Three—Transcript
Two Types of Liberty—Positive and Negative

In our last lecture, we saw that, through the doctrine of selective incorporation, the Supreme Court eventually made most of the major provisions of the Bill of Rights applicable to the states. You might think that would be enough, finally, to launch us into a specific consideration of specific parts of the Bill of Rights, but there are still a few basic rules we need to consider. In this lecture, we're going to focus heavily on just one Supreme Court case. The case is called *DeShaney v. Winnebago County,* and it was decided in 1989. I'm going to tell you what happened in *DeShaney,* but *DeShaney* really isn't the point here. *DeShaney* teaches us about two other basic constitutional rules that we need to consider before we get into a specific discussion about specific cases.

Our first topic is called the state action doctrine. The state action doctrine is a principle that holds that the Constitution applies only to public action, not to private action. I'll elaborate on this in a bit. We'll also concern ourselves with a second principle. That principle is known as the distinction between positive liberties and negative liberties. *DeShaney* illustrates both of these.

Let's start with the state action doctrine. Before I go into a specific discussion about how that principle is illustrated in *DeShaney,* let me give you just a little bit more definition. The state action doctrine holds that the Constitution applies only to the action of public actors, or to public officials, or, if you prefer, to the actions of state actors. It does not apply to private individuals or organizations. So, for example, there is no such thing as a constitutionally protected freedom of speech against private institutions or actors. If you attended a private university, for example, your professor was not restricted by freedom of speech in terms of what he or she could cover in the classroom. Your professor could say all sorts of terrible, slanderous, horrible things about you as a student, and that professor could presumably do that in front of other students or other professors, and that professor would not necessarily have violated any of your constitutional rights. On the other hand, it's important to understand that the state action doctrine isn't a precise, clear rule that always admits an easy application.

One of the chief difficulties of the state action doctrine is knowing precisely when it is the state that's acting and when it is not a private individual that is acting. So, imagine you have a child in the public school system, and your teacher does or says something hurtful to that child—to your son or your daughter. There's a good chance that that teacher is a state actor, because that teacher is presumably hired in the employ of the state, and the state is paying that person's salary. If so, then what the teacher said to your child is probably covered by the state action doctrine. On the other hand, if you were to meet that teacher at a grocery store, outside of the work context, and the teacher were to say something unflattering about your child there, that might not be state action because that person then is not necessarily acting in the context of their state employment.

It will be very important to understand, as we go throughout the course, that the state action doctrine is a fundamental rule of the constitutional order. How many times have you heard somebody say, "I'm going to take that all the way to the Supreme Court!" or "You can't interfere with my freedom of speech!"? Most of the time, those statements are constitutionally illiterate, because most of the time, threats to our speech liberties or other kinds of liberties don't actually come from the state. They might come from our employer, if it's a private employer; they might come from our family members; they might come from friends, or acquaintances, or even enemies. That doesn't necessarily mean that the First Amendment is implicated. The First Amendment, or any provision of the Bill of Rights, is implicated only when the state is somehow responsible for or engaged in the action involved.

In a college context, the easiest example I can think of is the following: if you attend a private university, that university's administration may enter into your dorm room whenever it chooses to do so; it isn't restricted by the Fourth Amendment's provisions on search and seizure; it's not restricted in terms of speech or any other kind of constitutional provision.

That's the basis of the state action doctrine. It's an enormously and fantastically complicated doctrine in its actual application. Case after case after case involves a simple, yet complex question, "Is it the state that has acted to deprive you of your liberty, or is it a private actor that has acted to deprive you of your liberty?" That is the first issue, maybe the only issue, in *DeShaney v. Winnebago County*.

I'd like to spend a little bit of time telling you about *DeShaney*, in part because the state action doctrine requires us to look very carefully at the facts and circumstances of every case. But I have a larger reason for asking you to pay particular attention to *DeShaney*—because it illustrates a third constitutional rule, the one that I think is the most important part of this course.

Every constitutional case can be described in terms of a specific, doctrinal, narrow, legal issue, and we can teach *DeShaney* as just a state action case; or, as you will see, we can teach it as a positive liberty case; but that's to consider it in terms of its basic constitutional doctrine, and I suggested in our first lecture that that is what I did not want to do—that I did not want to concentrate just on constitutional doctrine.

I choose *DeShaney* because it illustrates a larger principle of the kind I hinted at in the first lecture. That larger principle is simply this: every constitutional case is about a person or persons; every constitutional case is a potential tragedy, a celebration, a potential story about the chaos and the majesty of human life. No case does a better job of showing us all how important the Bill of Rights is in personal, human terms than *DeShaney*. And I want to forewarn you, the story in *DeShaney* is difficult to hear. It is difficult for me to tell.

Joshua DeShaney was born to Melanie and Randy DeShaney. Not long after his birth, his parents divorced, and the father, Randy DeShaney, was awarded custody of the young boy. He moved, with his son, to another state. Thereafter, Randy DeShaney entered into a series of relationships with other individuals. Some he married, some he didn't; some moved in, some moved out. If there was a constant in Randy DeShaney's life, it was the presence of his son, Joshua. You might think that that would be an uplifting, rewarding thing, but apparently it wasn't an uplifting, rewarding thing for Randy DeShaney because the other constant in Randy DeShaney's life was that he viciously beat his son, Joshua, time and time again. He beat his son so often that, on at least two occasions, Joshua DeShaney was rushed to the emergency room, and on both of those occasions, attending physicians, as they were required to do under Wisconsin state law, notified local child protection and police authorities of their suspicion that Randy DeShaney was abusing his son, Joshua.

The state investigated each and every one of these claims. The state assigned a social worker to Joshua's case. That social worker, on at least one occasion, concluded that Joshua should be removed from his father's custody, and a special child protection team was put in place to assess Joshua's case. That team concluded that there was not enough evidence to permanently remove Joshua DeShaney from his father's custody. Joshua was returned to his father's custody, and the beatings continued.

One day, Randy DeShaney beat his son so badly that he was rushed to the emergency room yet again, where the doctors concluded that he would never regain full cognitive function. Joshua DeShaney was committed to an institution in a persistent, vegetative state, and he will remain in that institution with no hope of recovery for the remainder of his life. The social worker assigned to Joshua's case stated in a court proceeding, "I always knew one day I would get a phone call and Joshua would be dead."

How does this become a constitutional case? Melanie DeShaney, Joshua's mother, sued the state, Winnebago County, claiming that the Fourteenth Amendment's Due Process Clause imposed upon the state an obligation to protect her child from the violence imposed upon him by his father.

Now let's think about this in more specific constitutional terms. What constitutional rights are implicated, potentially, by the father's actions? When the mother goes to court, what constitutional vindication does she seek? Before we can answer that question, we run up against a fundamental objection. That fundamental objection, which now I hope takes on a distinct, human cast, is the constitutional rule of state action. The first thing a judge will ask in Joshua's case is simply this: Who harmed Joshua? And in order for this to become a public constitutional controversy, Melanie DeShaney and her attorneys are going to have to convince a court that it is the state that harmed Joshua. If they can't convince the court that it is the state that is responsible for Joshua's condition, then there's no state action and there's no constitutional violation.

This is a fundamental constitutional rule. We are at a point in the course where we are still trying to consider under what conditions does the Bill of Rights govern behavior at all. We're not interested yet in whether or not there's actually a Fourteenth Amendment violation, whether it is Joshua's liberty that has been violated or his privacy, because we're not clear; we can't be certain that the

Constitution is even relevant to his predicament. That is the state action doctrine in practice.

In this case, Chief Justice Rehnquist and a majority of the Court admitted that the state had been involved in that complex of actions that affected Joshua DeShaney. The state admitted that it had once taken Joshua from his father. The Court acknowledged that admission. Chief Justice Rehnquist expressed his utter horror at what had happened to Joshua, but went on to conclude that, in the end, the state had done nothing to put Joshua in a position that was worse than it would have been if the state had never acted at all. In other words, the majority, writing through Chief Justice Rehnquist, concluded that the state was not responsible for Joshua's condition. As Chief Justice Rehnquist noted, it was his father that deprived Joshua of his liberty, not the state.

Now, I think I suggested in an earlier lecture, that pretty much everything concerning the Bill of Rights is open to interpretation; that few points, if any, are uncontested. Certainly this is a contestable point. As two of the dissents noted, it's arguable that Joshua was in a much worse position after the state had acted and then returned him to his father's custody. So one argument would be simply this: If Randy DeShaney thought he could abuse his son with impunity before the state acted, what was he likely to think after the state returned his son to him?

Think about all the other people who might have had a legal obligation, or an ethical obligation, to do something on Joshua's behalf. Imagine you are one of the attending physicians when Joshua is reported or taken to the emergency room. Those physicians, under Wisconsin state law, are under an obligation to report suspicion of abuse. But what happens once they report their suspicion of abuse? What does a doctor do after he or she has told the state, "I think this child is being harmed"? Does that doctor retain any continuing responsibility for that child's welfare? Does a teacher retain any continuing responsibility for that child's welfare after the teacher has reported suspicion of abuse? The dissents argued that Joshua was foreclosed from other sources of help because those other sources of help relied on the state to protect Joshua; and in that sense, there clearly was state action.

I mentioned before, and I hope you can see now, the state action doctrine, when listed as a legal definition and printed on the bottom of the screen, is remarkably easy to understand. The difficulty is trying to give the meaning life, trying to understand what the doctrine means when it's applied to real living human beings. Whether there was state action in Joshua's case is a difficult question to answer, and it requires a certain amount of speculation, not simply on our part, but on the Court's part. We don't know and can't know with certainty whether Justice Rehnquist was correct that the state didn't leave Joshua any worse off, nor can we know whether the dissents were correct in arguing that the state had harmed his condition.

Before we leave the doctrine of state action and move to positive liberties, let me push just a little bit more broadly. Maybe Joshua's case should lead us to ask a more fundamental question: Why should we have a state action doctrine, if at all? What positive good is promoted by insisting that the Constitution only protects you against the state and not against other individuals?

There are powerful arguments for why there should be a state action doctrine. It limits the state's liability. It limits the application of the Constitution to a certain realm of our shared experience. Maybe we don't want to, as lawyers, say, "constitutionalize" every aspect of our lives; but we make trade-offs when we make that decision. Some of those trade-offs have names and faces. Joshua DeShaney is one of those names.

Now I've described *DeShaney* in terms of the state action doctrine. There are a lot of judges and a lot of scholars who think that Joshua DeShaney's case isn't about the state action doctrine at all; that it's about another fundamental constitutional principle applicable to the Bill of Rights, and that is the distinction between positive and negative liberties. This, too, is a basic fundamental premise of the American constitutional order, and we can't understand any part of the Bill of Rights without understanding this decision. And again, it is a distinction that is fairly easy to appreciate in the abstract, and difficult to apply in concrete cases.

In the abstract, this is the distinction: What does it mean to say that a right is guaranteed by the Bill of Rights? Does it mean only government may not interfere with the right save on certain conditions? Or does it mean something potentially much more expansive? Does it mean that the government must make efforts to help citizens actually realize and exercise those rights? The former position comprises "negative rights"; the latter position comprises so-called "positive rights."

Before I go into *DeShaney*, let me try to give you a smaller example of the distinction; and again, I return to freedom of speech because it is the best possible example here.

If the freedom to speak our minds is a negative freedom, that means that the government may not interfere with it, except in those certain conditions where the Constitution allows it to do so; that's the negative liberty. I'm free to speak my mind most of the time, save on certain conditions; so is the *New York Times*; so is the *Seattle Post-Intelligencer.*

But when the *Post-Intelligencer* speaks, when the *New York Times* speaks, when CNN speaks, I think it's fair to say that they speak with a louder volume than when I speak. One might say that there is a kind of equality involved in negative rights. Everybody has the right to speak, save certain limited times. But there is also a profound inequality involved there, because people with more money or with louder voices; people who are smarter, or more persuasive, or more clever than you, may be able to get more volume out of their speech than you can. Their speech may be more persuasive, or may have more of an impact in the public square than yours. You might argue, then, that the government has a duty not only to refrain from interference—that's the negative liberty position—but that it also has an obligation to help us realize our rights. Maybe the government ought to be under an obligation to make it possible for people to speak, or to ratch it up, people who have been traditionally silenced to a larger louder place in the public arena.

I'll give you another example before we go on to *DeShaney*. As you'll see later in the course, under certain conditions, a woman has a constitutionally guaranteed right to procure an abortion during a certain part of her pregnancy. That's the negative liberty. Government may not interfere, except on certain conditions. That means that wealthy women have the same right to an abortion that women more mired in poverty have. That's the negative liberty. If we adopted a positive liberty approach, we might say that the government not only has a right to refrain from keeping certain women from having an abortion, but it has to enable women to pursue an abortion, as well; in which case, we might say that there would be a constitutional obligation to make abortion services or other kinds of reproductive services available to poor women, so that they might actually achieve their right to an abortion. That's the distinction between a negative liberty and a positive liberty, and it's possible that that's what *DeShaney* is really all about. So let's consider *DeShaney* in those terms.

I mentioned before that we had to settle the state action doctrine before we considered what specific right was actually involved in DeShaney's case, but let's get to that question now. If you were the attorney representing Melanie DeShaney and Joshua DeShaney, you'd be required in court to say, "I don't think something bad has happened here. Instead, I think some specific provision of the Constitution has been specifically violated by the state's behavior."

In this case, DeShaney's attorneys argued that Joshua's right to liberty under the Fourteenth Amendment had been violated by the state. I think you can probably see, in fact, that his liberty had been infringed upon in some important sense. His basic liberty to choose which foods he will eat, to choose where he will live, to choose where he will go to school—all of those have been harmed by the action in this case. Things that you and I take for granted, basic liberties of everyday life, are foreclosed to Joshua and will be forever. So we shouldn't be surprised when Joshua's attorneys in court, in response to a specific question by Chief Justice Rehnquist, argue that it is Joshua's liberty interest that is implicated in this case.

Do we describe that liberty interest in negative terms or positive terms? If we describe it in negative terms, there's no constitutional violation here; or, at least, it's difficult to make the argument that there's a constitutional violation. If the state is required only to protect Joshua's negative liberty, then that means simply the state is simply required not to interfere with the liberty itself, and this takes us back to the state action doctrine. It's not clear that the state deprived Joshua of his liberty. That's the negative liberty aspect.

But consider a different kind of claim. Consider a claim that says the state isn't only interested in protecting Joshua's negative liberty, but it's under a positive obligation to protect his liberty—this is a very different kind of claim. Now it's a claim that says the state is responsible for making sure individuals—citizens—can exercise their liberty, and the state failed miserably in this case, because it didn't protect Joshua's claim to positive liberty. The distinction is as fundamental as any in any constitutional order. There isn't a constitutional order in the world that doesn't make some assumption about whether it is negative liberty that's protected only, or whether or not positive liberty is protected. And if we were to construct a constitutional system from scratch, one of the first things we would have to consider would be, do we mean to protect the negative version of liberty, or do we want also to protect the positive vision of liberty?

Chief Justice Rehnquist—again, writing for a majority—concluded that the American Constitution protects only negative liberty. He quotes the Fourteenth Amendment and notes that it begins with, "No state shall deny...." The reference to the phrase "No state" harkens us back again to the state action doctrine; but the phrase "deny" points to the positive/negative liberty distinction. According to a majority, the state was only under an obligation to protect Joshua's negative liberty, not his positive liberty. There are exceptions to this rule. If the state itself deprives you of your liberty—for example, the state incarcerates you for a crime—then Chief Justice Rehnquist acknowledged that the state would be under a corresponding obligation to protect you. It's important to think about why that is. According to Chief Justice Rehnquist, if the state deprives you of liberty by incarcerating you, then it has, in effect, deprived you of the opportunity for self-help. And because it's deprived you of the opportunity for self-help, it assumes an obligation to protect you. So, if the state incarcerates you, or somehow deprives you of your negative liberty, then there's a corresponding positive liberty.

The other situation that Chief Justice Rehnquist referred to makes an awful lot of sense in the abstract. If the state commits you to an asylum or an institution because you are of impaired mental health, then the state is under a corresponding obligation to protect you, again, because it has deprived you of the opportunity to protect yourself. Neither one of those exceptions, according to Chief Justice Rehnquist, applied to Joshua's case; in part, because Joshua was in his father's custody, not the state's custody; and in part, more generally, because there were still help options available to Joshua.

This looks like a complicated case, but there's one more complication that we have to add to it. Chief Justice Rehnquist also noted that if the state had deprived Joshua from his father, if he had removed him from custody on a permanent basis, then there was a good chance that Randy DeShaney would be in court, with his attorneys, arguing that the state had deprived him of his parental liberty to educate and bring up his child. The DeShaney case isn't simply a question of positive liberties versus negative liberties, or the state action doctrine; it's not simply a question about what rights does Joshua bring to this litigation; it's also a question about what rights does the state bring to this litigation? And that question is going to be addressed slightly differently, depending upon whether or not we conceptualize this case as a state action case or as a positive and negative liberty case.

Now, by way of summary here, just on the specific terms of *DeShaney, DeShaney* stands for two fantastically important propositions, at least in my mind: first, that there is a state action doctrine and it is a fundamental premise of the Bill of Rights; and second, that the American constitutional order—the Bill of Rights, in particular—protects only negative liberties, not positive liberties. We won't really see this distinction articulated again in any of the subsequent cases that we will consider.

On the other hand, it's always background information. There is always an implicit assumption in the cases we'll consider that certain kinds of harm to individuals, certain kinds of threats to liberty, simply don't rise to the level of constitutional violation—either because they can't satisfy the state action doctrine requirement, or because they would have to be articulated as a form of positive liberty as opposed to negative liberty.

There are a couple of other things we need to know about these basic doctrines; but more importantly, there are a couple of other things we need to know about *DeShaney*. There is another fundamental principle—one far more important than the state action doctrine or the negative liberty doctrine—that we need to reconcile ourselves to now. It's very easy to forget that Joshua DeShaney is a real person; very easy to forget that he will spend the rest of his life in an institution; very easy to forget that, behind all of the legal rules, behind all of the constitutional doctrines, there are lives at stake.

And you might think that's melodramatic, that, like so many other professors, I have some need to dramatize how important the issues are because, otherwise, nobody will care about them; and I might be guilty of that. But I might be guilty, too, of thinking that, when I leave today, and you turn off the tape, we can go back to our lives, and Joshua can't. And I might be guilty, too, of the most fundamental of constitutional violations myself; because, as Justice Scalia will note in another case, far down the road, and as Chief Justice Rehnquist at least hinted at in *DeShaney,* the Constitution isn't about doing all good things to all good people. The Court doesn't necessarily have a roving license to go out and create or fix every social ill that it confronts. In the end, it can only do what the Constitution authorizes it to do; and it's not clear that the Constitution authorizes anybody to fix Joshua DeShaney's case, much less authorizes the Supreme Court to do anything about Joshua's case. And before you think, "How heartless!"—maybe not—there is one other tiny little aspect of the case.

Imagine that DeShaney had won the case. As Chief Justice Rehnquist reminds us, imagine that the state was found liable for the harm that befell Joshua; then what will happen in every other case? Is it not possible that, in future cases, the state will choose not to protect anyone, because doing so proposes far too great a risk to the state's pocketbook? If Joshua had won, what would he have won? Money. Money's not an unimportant thing. Neither is Joshua DeShaney's life.

Lecture Four
The Court and Constitutional Interpretation

Scope:

In this lecture, we begin with a brief history of the Court's early years. We then take up important institutional issues: How are justices appointed to the Court? What are the nature and limits of judicial power, as derived from Article III of the Constitution? How does the Court actually decide cases? Finally, when, if ever, should the Court refrain from deciding a case? Our primary method in tackling such issues will be to read Supreme Court opinions. This lecture will instruct students in how to find those cases and give some practical advice about how to read and study them. The lecture also introduces students to the complexities of *constitutional interpretation*, which may be defined as the various ways by which judges and others seek to determine what the Constitution actually means. We begin with an obvious but vitally important question: Why is constitutional interpretation necessary? We will consider the various sources and methods of constitutional interpretation, such as *textualism*, *originalism*, *doctrinalism*, *precedent*, and *structuralism*. The definitions of these various terms, we shall see, are also open to dispute. We will also find that constitutional arguments may be drawn from a variety of possible sources.

Outline

I. Much of the Constitution, at least when applied to hard cases, is sufficiently vague to require some interpretation to get at its meaning. Consequently, what we call *constitutional law* is better thought of as *constitutional interpretation*. There are at least three reasons for this vagueness.

    A. First, language is always an imperfect and imprecise means of communication, and especially so when the underlying concepts, such as liberty, power, and authority, are themselves controversial and vague.

    B. Second, sometimes the Founders deliberately sought constitutional ambiguity, in part because vague constitutional provisions allow for compromise and cooperation.

C. Third, the Constitution is vague also because the Founders knew that the document would have to incorporate change over time.

II. There are various methods and sources of constitutional interpretation. In this lecture, we will explore a few of the more common methods, including the following:

A. *Textualism.*

    1. Textualism is a method of interpretation that suggests that we consult, first and, perhaps, last, the actual language of the Constitution.

    2. As a method, this has obvious appeal, but it also suffers from a profound flaw: In most cases, it is the language itself—its maddening ambiguity—that is the reason why we need to interpret in the first place.

B. *Founders' Intent/Originalism.*

    1. Some justices suggest that in interpreting the Constitution, we should look to the intentions of the Framers. This, too, has an intuitive appeal, but there are problems as well.

    2. Which of the Founders should we consult and why?

    3. Remember, too, that we have little evidence of what they intended—the documentary records are sparse and incomplete.

    4. There are also serious definitional difficulties: Who, exactly, is a Founder? And shouldn't we look to the ratifying conventions as well?

    5. Some justices, such as Scalia, have favored a slightly different approach, typically called *originalism*. Instead of seeking evidence about intentions, originalists ask us to consider and apply the "original" meanings of various provisions of the Constitution.

Balancing and Prudentialism

Two other methods of constitutional interpretation mentioned but not examined in this lecture are balancing and prudentialism.

In *balancing*, judges weigh one set of interests or rights against another set of interests or rights. This method is often found in First Amendment cases. So, for example, in such cases the Court often speaks about the need to reconcile—or to balance—our commitment to freedom of speech with other constitutional values, such as equality or the dignity of other persons. Critics of this approach, such as Justice Frankfurter, sometimes observe in response that the Constitution itself gives us no guidance about how to weigh or measure different interests, and thus no way to balance them.

Prudentialism counsels judges to avoid setting broad rules for future cases and offers a particular understanding of the limited role courts should play in a constitutional democracy. Justice Frankfurter often counseled such an approach, noting for example, in the two Flag Salute Cases that judges must always be alert to the ways in which exercises of judicial power may be fundamentally undemocratic.

C. *Doctrinalism.*
   1. Doctrinal methods of interpretation consider how various parts of the Constitution have been shaped by the Court's own jurisprudence.
   2. As we shall see, nearly every area in civil liberties has given rise to a doctrine of one sort or another, and some of our time in this course will be spent learning these doctrines and evaluating them.

D. *Precedent.*
   1. Closely related to the interpretive method of doctrinalism is the method of precedent.
   2. When a court uses precedent, it simply refers to an earlier case, finding in it a rule or principle that governs the current case as well.

E. *Structuralism.*
   1. Although it may seem more complex than other methods of interpretation, structuralism rests on a simple principle—that one can find the meaning of a particular

constitutional principle only by reading it against the larger constitutional document or context.

  2. There are, as we shall see, several variations of this method.

III. Because so much of our work will consist of reading Supreme Court decisions, we begin with an examination of the Supreme Court and its role in the constitutional order.

  A. Perhaps surprisingly, the Constitution proper actually has very little to say about the makeup of the federal court system in general and of the Supreme Court in particular. Article III of the Constitution provides some of the skeletal material, but much of the operation and functioning of the Court is a consequence of evolution and change.

  B. A study of the Bill of Rights, then, is at least partly an inquiry into the history of the Supreme Court as an evolving institution.

IV. If we are to understand the Court, there are three areas we will need to explore in greater detail.

  A. First, we need to understand the composition of the Court; in particular, we need to know how the Court is staffed and the process and controversies surrounding nominations to the Court.

  B. Second, we need to understand the nature and limits of judicial power, or what we shall call *jurisdiction*, especially as derived from Article III of the Constitution.

  C. Third, we need to know how the Court goes about the business of selecting which cases to hear and deciding them.

    1. You can see exactly what rules the Court uses to assess whether a case will be heard at: http://www.supremecourtus.gov/ctrules/ctrules.html

    2. Where there is conflict among lower courts over how to rule in a particular case, the Court may be more likely to take the case and to try to settle that conflict.

    3. Although there was an earlier point in the Court's history when the Court was theoretically obligated to hear certain kinds of federal cases, the Court has long since discarded that, and now its discretion is full. There

is no set of cases that the Court is genuinely obligated to hear.

4. According to the *political question doctrine*, some questions, in their nature, are fundamentally political and not legal; and if a question is fundamentally political and not legal, then the Court may refuse to hear that case.

5. The Court sometimes says that it will not hear a case because the case is not "ripe" (the underlying controversy isn't fully realized yet) or is "moot" (the case dies before it can be heard, e.g., because the parties have reached an agreement). More generally, the Court, indeed all federal courts, only decide concrete, "live" cases.

Essential Reading:

Kommers, Finn, and Jacobsohn, *American Constitutional Law*, chapters 1–2.

Keith Whittington, *Constitutional Interpretation: Textual Meaning, Original Intent, and Judicial Review*, chapters 1–2.

Herbert Weschler, "Toward Neutral Principles of Constitutional Law," 73 *Harvard Law Review* (1959).

Phillip J. Cooper and Howard Ball, *The United States Supreme Court: From the Inside Out*.

"Federalist No. 9" and "Federalist No. 10," *The Federalist Papers*.

Supplementary Reading:

William H. Rehnquist, *The Supreme Court: How It Was, How It Is*.

Susan Bloch Low and Thomas Krattenmaker, eds., *Supreme Court Politics: The Institution and Its Procedures*.

William Leuchtenberg, *The Supreme Court Reborn: The Constitutional Revolution in the Age of Roosevelt*.

Questions to Consider:

1. Why is constitutional interpretation necessary? Should the Founders have sought ways to minimize the need for interpretation?

2. Is there such a thing as a "right" answer to a difficult constitutional question? If so, how can a judge know whether

any particular answer is the right answer? If not, then is constitutional interpretation no more than an elaborate ruse for a system in which judges just make it up as they go along?

3. Why does the Constitution say so little about both the makeup of the Court and about how it works?

Lecture Four—Transcript
The Court and Constitutional Interpretation

Much of the Constitution—at least when it's applied to difficult cases—is really subject to interpretation. As *DeShaney* made clear, there is usually more than one way to understand a constitutional provision, usually more than one way to decide a case. Often there are several ways, and all of them might be constitutionally defensible in one form or another. In this lecture, we take up two aspects of that process.

The first process we take up is the Court itself. I talked about the Court in *DeShaney* as if everybody understands what the Supreme Court is—as if everybody understands how a justice gets to be a justice—as if everybody understands what the business of the Court is on a day-to-day basis. I hope to correct that oversight here.

Also, and perhaps more importantly, I want to talk about the process of constitutional interpretation itself. As you can tell from *DeShaney,* and from *Barron v. Baltimore,* and a few of the other cases we've briefly considered, constitutional interpretation is ultimately about making choices, and judges have at their disposal a variety of tools and mechanisms to help them make those choices. As a rule, a judge will think carefully about what method of constitutional interpretation he or she will employ in any particular case, and we'll want to consider what those different methods are.

More importantly, I think it's important to understand what constitutional interpretation is as an activity. Constitutional interpretation may be defined as the various ways by which judges—and others, but mostly judges for our purposes—seek to determine what "constitutionally" actually means in any particular case.

We begin with an obvious but vitally important question: Why is constitutional interpretation necessary at all? Under what conditions is constitutional interpretation necessary? Are there any conditions under which we shouldn't engage in the business of constitutional interpretation? We will consider the various sources and methods of constitutional interpretation. I'll run through a list. Briefly, they are textualism, originalism, balancing, prudentialism, and structuralism—and I will give definitions to all of these terms. Unfortunately, the definitions themselves are open to dispute. We shall see, too, that constitutional arguments may be drawn from a variety of possible sources. You may have heard, for example, of constitutional arguments that are drawn from Founders' intent or Framers' intent. Sometimes they are drawn from moral philosophy. Sometimes they're drawn from other documents such as the Declaration of Independence, or the Mayflower Compact, or even from foreign constitutions such as the German Basic Law, or the Irish Law, or the New South African Constitution.

I worry about conveying a misimpression. I don't want to mislead you into thinking that it is only the Supreme Court or other federal or state courts that are involved in constitutional interpretation. Legislatures are involved in the act of constitutional interpretation as well; so are presidents; so are chief executives in every state. Indeed, there are times when schoolteachers, police officials, nurses, doctors, and other public officials are engaged in the act of constitutional interpretation, as well. It isn't only the Court that makes constitutional meaning. Indeed, sometimes the Court's constitutional meaning is expressly rejected by other actors. It isn't necessarily clear, in other words, that the Court is the only constitutional actor entrusted with constitutional interpretation; and nor is it clear that the Court is the most important actor. But here we are, considering Supreme Court cases on the Bill of Rights; and for the most part, we will concern ourselves with judicial interpretation.

Why is constitutional interpretation necessary at all? As I've suggested, it's necessary primarily because the Constitution is a wonderfully elastic, vague document. It was made that way deliberately. There are at least three reasons why the Founders drafted a Constitution that has as its chief characteristic its vagueness and its ambiguity.

First, as you know well, language is always an imperfect and imprecise means of communication. This is especially so when the underlying concepts involved in our language—such as liberty, power, and authority—are themselves controversial and vague. Indeed, as Madison once noted, "If the Almighty Himself were to communicate in the English language, we would still not understand much of what he said."

Second, perhaps more important for our purposes, the Founders weren't afraid of constitutional ambiguity; they embraced it. Constitutional ambiguity is desirable from a Founder's point of view, from a Framers' point of view, because it allows for compromise and cooperation. It is much easier at a constitutional convention to agree that we are all committed to a freedom of speech than it is to think carefully about precisely what kinds of speech we're going to protect and what kinds of speech should not be protected. It is certainly an easier constitutional enterprise to agree on broad concepts than it is to agree about specific conceptions about what any particular right means. So, for example, if we were to construct a constitution from scratch, it is much easier to protect speech than to think carefully about whether or not our protection ought to extend to hate speech, or whether it ought to extend to obscenity and pornography, or what we should do about the Internet. Those are precise questions, and those precise questions, those precise meanings about speech—according to the Founders anyway—ought to have been left, and were left to subsequent generations to work out on their own from time to time. Constitutional ambiguity, in other words, isn't a constitutional defect; it's a constitutional advantage, especially in the drafting stage.

Then, related to that, the Founders were well aware that the constitution that they were proposing was a constitution for themselves, yes, but more importantly, a constitution for subsequent generations. I sometimes say that the most important words in the Constitution of the United States are not "We, the People," not "No state shall deny," not "No cruel and unusual punishment," not "Freedom of exercise." The most important words of the Constitution are found in the Preamble, near the end, and they are, "And to our posterity." The Constitution, on this generous understanding, is a gift from one generation to subsequent generations. I say that's a "generous understanding" but maybe it is not a gift; maybe it's a curse. That will be for you and us to decide as we proceed. But it is nevertheless a transmission to future generations.

The Founders knew, perhaps better than even we understand it, that constitutions must change over time if they are to endure. The most obvious mechanism for change is not the freedom to amend the Constitution, not the authority to engage in a new constitutional revolution, but to build play into the joints, to build ambiguity and flexibility into the very words of the Constitution, so that they might mean different things for different generations. Every constitution wrestles with this problem. How much is static? How much is change? How much is fixed? How much is flexible?

I don't mean to suggest that the Constitution never fixes anything in any level of particular detail. As you probably know, there are specific rules buried throughout the Constitution: you need this number of states to affect a constitutional amendment; you must be this age to run for public office, and a different age to run for a different public office. I don't mean to suggest that every case that comes up under the Constitution is a "hard case." There are easy cases; we just won't address them here. We'll address only the difficult cases. Because we'll address only the difficult cases, we are always engaged, fundamentally, in an act of constitutional interpretation, not so much an act of constitutional law.

As I suggested, there are several methods and sources of constitutional interpretation. Over the course of these 36 lectures, we will see all of the following methods of constitutional interpretation used at one time or another. Before I go into them, I simply want to give you a few words of introduction.

First, no judge is committed to any one single method of interpretation. Most judges will use all of them, or at least some combination of them, and the combinations are likely to change depending on the nature of the case involved. Judges tend to be more pragmatic than doctrinaire, and as a consequence, they will use whatever method of interpretation seems to them appropriate in a case. At times, we'll see a judge adopt a method of interpretation that he or she rejected as inappropriate or illegitimate in earlier cases, and then, seemingly without hesitation, pull it out of the hat and use it in the next case. Judges don't worry so much, necessarily, about interpretive consistency; they are more worried about getting the case right, and the methods are simply tools that they use. Also, my summary of these methods isn't comprehensive. It's fairly conventional in that almost all students of the Constitution would recognize these methods; but some might call them by different names. Some might delete one or two and add others. These cover the most common, ordinary methods.

The first method is textualism. Most people know this method better as the "plain words" approach to the Constitution or to the Bill of Rights. The argument here is simply this: if you want to know what the Constitution means, if you want to know what any particular provision in the Bill of Rights means, consult the text; consult the plain words of the document. And, in fairness, in the easy cases, this method works pretty well.

But it doesn't work very well in difficult or complicated questions. In fact, it can't work at all in the difficult or complicated questions we're going to be talking about for one simple reason: if the text were clear, we wouldn't need to interpret. I like to call this the "anti-interpretive" method. It denies that there is a problem of interpretation to be had, by insisting that we should simply look at the plain words of the text. Unfortunately, the plain words of the text are often not very plain.

Alternatively, many judges insist that, if we want to know what a particular provision means, we should consult the Founders. This is sometimes known as the doctrine of Founders' intent (Framers' intent) and the argument here is one that I think is intuitive to most of us. If you want to know what a provision means, ask the person who wrote it what it means; consult the author. It is misleadingly simple. First, who wrote the Constitution? Is it Madison's Constitution? Hamilton's? Gouverneur Morris's? Thomas Jefferson's? There are arguments to be had for all of these individuals, and more importantly, arguments against all of them: Jefferson wasn't even in the country; Hamilton walked out of the Convention in a fit, only to return later. Second, how do we know what the Founders intended? There are no official public records of the Constitutional Convention. We have Madison's notes. In Madison's notes, Madison looks like a pretty smart guy; some other people don't come off so well. Is anybody surprised by that? If I write an autobiography, it's going to be very flattering. I undoubtedly will be a better human being than I really am at home or at work.

The truth of the matter is that we don't have consistent, reliable records about what any of the Founders intended. We do have a patchwork of records and notes. One of those patchworks should be called *The Federalist Papers*. Remember what *The Federalist Papers* are: some insight into some of what the Founders intended— John Jay, Alexander Hamilton, James Madison—but only those three. And there are places where those three men seem to be engaged not in an act of persuasion for the people at large, but in a set of internal squabbles. If you have nothing else to do, go home, read *Federalist No. 9* and read *Federalist No. 10*. They are both addressed to solving the same underlying problem. They propose fairly different solutions to that problem. Which one is the correct constitutional solution? It's difficult to say.

Then there's another question: Who are the Founders? Is it really clear that you want to consult the persons who wrote the document, or should you consult the individuals who ratified it, who turned the Constitution from a piece of paper into an organic act of law? Maybe we should consult the state ratifying conventions, and determine what they thought the Constitution meant at any particular point; except that we don't have access to most of the state ratifying conventions.

Most individuals, I think, have concluded that, on most of the important questions, we do not have consistent, reliable evidence about what the Founders intended that provision to mean. That doesn't mean we should give up on Founders' intent.

Another position would be to adopt the doctrine of originalism. As promoted by some scholars and some judges—notably Justice Scalia—the doctrine of originalism asks what the original understanding of the particular provision was. What was its original meaning? We don't mean to search so much for specific evidence of intent, although it's great when we can find it. The important point is to put ourselves in the position of the Founders, and to ask what the original meaning of any particular provision would have been; and it is that meaning, that original meaning, that governs the meaning of any constitutional provision for our time.

Another method of interpreting the Constitution is doctrinalism. Doctrinalism suggests that every constitutional provision should be understood by the complex of legal rules and doctrinal rules that have grown up over time. We will see many of these rules over the course of these lectures. Here's one quick doctrinal rule: A woman may procure an abortion at any time during a pregnancy, unless the state has a legitimate interest in overcoming it and that state's interest does not constitute it an undue burden on the woman's right to choose. That's not in the Constitution; that's a doctrine that grew up around the constitutional liberty—privacy, in this instance. We'll see all sorts of doctrines that govern; for example, the Supreme Court's First Amendment jurisprudence, particularly as it regards speech and religion. The Court has fashioned an inordinate number of exceptionally complicated rules that govern under what conditions cities and municipalities may display nativity scenes during the Christmas holidays.

One method of constitutional interpretation is to take the rule and to fashion it to cover specific cases. Related to that would be the doctrine of precedent. One way to decide what the Constitution means in any particular case is to look at what previous decisions have said about that case. The Supreme Court is under a powerful and self-imposed obligation to follow precedent, to follow the decisions that it has reached before, in a way that is consistent with those decisions. The doctrine of precedent suggests that prior cases control current cases. This has a powerful constitutional resonance with all of us, because we don't want the Constitution to change its meaning from case to case. Doctrine is a way, precedent is a way, of contributing to consistency in the constitutional interpretation.

Then, finally, a method, perhaps the least familiar even in the legal academy: it's called structuralism. Structuralism is a way of interpreting the Constitution that says that no provision should be approached or interpreted on its own; that it must be understood in this larger complex of constitutional meaning; that if you want to know what any particular provision of the Constitution means, you must check it against the rest of the constitutional document. So, for example, if we want to know whether or not the "cruel and unusual" clause in the Eighth Amendment prohibits the death penalty, we need to acknowledge that there are other places in the Constitution that seem to speak to the legitimacy of capital punishment, and it would be a mistake to think about the Eight Amendment's "cruel and unusual" clause without consulting those other parts of the Constitution that might be relevant to it.

Somebody has to employ these interpretive methods, and for our purposes, that will be the Supreme Court of the United States. Almost all of our readings will involve decisions by the Supreme Court. I do not want to spend a lot of time describing the Supreme Court, in part because it will take up an inordinate amount of time, and in part because there are so many easily available sources (many of which you can find in the lecture materials that accompany this course) that will tell you how to find these materials, as well as give you information about the Court itself. But let me explain a couple of things that I think are very important to understand, and that I'm worried you might miss.

First, the Court is a unique institution in the American constitutional order. It's unique, in part, because the Constitution has surprisingly little to say about the makeup of the Supreme Court. Article Three of the Constitution provides that there will be a Supreme Court. It tells us that there should probably be a set of inferior federal courts, but pretty much everything we know about the way the Court really works, about how it is staffed, about how it reaches decisions, is a function of evolution, and not necessarily of constitutional prescription. One quick example: there is no constitutional requirement that there be nine justices. The number has been fixed at nine for well over a century; but it is fluctuating, and there have been times in the Court's history when there've been fewer than nine and times when there have been more than nine. We may yet see a time when that number changes. The Court is an evolving institution.

Secondly, the Supreme Court justices, as you probably know, are nominated by presidents and must be confirmed by the Senate. But that nomination and confirmation process is described hardly at all in the Constitution. And every Supreme Court nominee is judged on his or her merits, and judged also on a wide array of factors that may or may not be legitimate. Nearly every nomination to the Court comes with question about a candidate's judicial philosophy, questions about a judicial candidate's personal life. Some of you may remember when Judge Bork was nominated to the Court, some individuals went so far as to secretly steal the records of what videotapes he had been watching from the local video store. The Constitution tells us nothing about when it is legitimate to inquire into a judge's personal life, when it is illegitimate to inquire into a nominee's life, much less about any kinds of qualifications a judge must have. There is no requirement that a nominee to the Supreme Court have prior judicial experience. There is no constitutional requirement that a nominee even be an attorney. At different times in American history, there have been campaigns to put non-lawyers on the Court. One of the most famous constitutional law scholars of the 20th century, Edward Corwin, was not a lawyer. He was undoubtedly the greatest constitutional scholar of his era, and there was an active campaign to put him on the Court. It didn't work, but it might have worked; and there may yet be a time when a non-lawyer will be appointed.

The Constitution tells us nothing about how the Court is staffed. It doesn't say anything about whether a judge should have law clerks. It doesn't say anything about whether the Supreme Court must issue an opinion. It doesn't say anything about a majority opinion, a concurring opinion, a dissenting opinion, a *seriatim* opinion—all of these things that we take for granted about the Court, about how it decides cases, about who accepts responsibility for authoring the opinion, about what a dissent even is, about what a concurring opinion is; all of those are products of history and evolution. The Court is governed more by internally self-developed rules than it is by constitutional practice.

Another thing we should spend a little bit of time on is how the Court goes about selecting cases. Few things in life are as annoying to a constitutional law professor as hearing somebody on television say, "I'm going to take my case"—usually a traffic ticket—"to the Supreme Court of the United States!" You have a better chance of winning Powerball than you have of getting any case accepted by the United States Supreme Court. There are three avenues of appeal into the Court. I do not want to go into them in excessive detail, but I think you'll need to know the basic distinctions among them.

The first, and by all means, most important method of admission into the Court is by appeal from a lower court. There are two ways this could happen: a lower court might certify a case, stamp it, and send it up to the Supreme Court before deciding it, and ask for the Court's guidance. This is the process of certification. It is a rarely used method of getting a case to the Supreme Court. Theoretically, you might get to the Court through its original jurisdiction. The first method I've described is by appeal from a lower court. There are actually a number of kinds of cases in which you don't need to appeal from a lower court, where you can invoke the court's original jurisdiction; in other words, where you can go to the Supreme Court originally, where the case originates in the Supreme Court. The Constitution specifies in exceptional detail what kinds of cases are available to the Court through original jurisdiction. You can find them in Article Three. There are years when the Court hears no cases through original jurisdiction, years when it may hear as many as three or four; but in any case, original jurisdiction constitutes a remarkably small part of the Court's business, as does certification;

which means it is in the third category—simple appeal from a lower court, where the Court spends most of its time.

The Court is not required to hear any case. Lawyers sometimes formally describe their petitions to the Court to hear their cases as prayers—prayers for relief; and "prayer" is an appropriate term here, because that's really what it takes to get your case heard by the Supreme Court. If you want to, you can look at the Supreme Court rules that are available online (and there will be a citation to them in your course materials), where you can see exactly what rules the Court uses to tell it against whether a case is more likely to be heard. It helps, for example, if one lower court has decided the issue in your favor and a different lower court has decided the issue differently in somebody else's favor. Where there is that kind of conflict among lower courts, the Court may be more likely to take the case and to try to settle that conflict. But in any event, the Court's jurisdiction is discretionary; it doesn't have to hear your case. In the same way that the Court doesn't have to be nine justices, it doesn't have to hear any kind of case that it really doesn't want to hear. There was an earlier point of the Court's history when there were certain kinds of federal cases where the Court was theoretically obligated to hear them, where you had a so-called right to the Court's jurisdiction. But the Court has long since discarded that, and now its discretion is full. There is no set of cases where the Court is genuinely obligated to hear it.

We will see over time, in specific instances throughout the course, that the Court has developed a number of tools and mechanisms that it uses to decide which cases to hear, and just as importantly, that it uses to decide not to hear. One quick example: the Court has developed the doctrine called the "political question doctrine." The political question doctrine holds that some questions, in their nature, are fundamentally political and not legal; and if a question is fundamentally political and not legal, then the Court will refuse to hear that case. It will claim that it doesn't have jurisdiction, and it will leave that question to some other aspect of the political process to settle out.

One other quick set of doctrines: the Court sometimes says that it will not hear a case because the case is not ripe. What the Court means in that instance is that the underlying controversy isn't fully realized yet; all the dimensions to the controversy cannot be fully seen. For example, if you want to argue that a statute has interfered with some particular individual liberty, you must wait until the statute has been passed, enacted by Congress, signed by the President, and then actually enforced. It is not enough to say, there is legislation pending in front of Congress that I think would violate my right to this particular aspect. In that case, the case isn't ripe. Alternatively, some cases die before they can be heard. Some cases become, as lawyers say, "moot," they expire; and if a controversy has expired, perhaps because the parties have reached an agreement, then the Court will say, "We're not going to hear that."

These are all aspects of a larger principle, long held by the United States Supreme Court and all federal courts, that says that they only decide concrete, "live" cases. We don't issue advisory opinions, we don't sit as a consulting authority; we decide only concrete cases that involve the rights of concrete, identifiable individuals and governmental actors, and it is only in that situation that we will reach a constitutional decision. All of these mechanisms, in other words, are devices that the Court uses to constrain itself, to limit its involvement in the political process; more generally, to conserve its authority; or, if you prefer, to conserve its capital, its legitimacy, its moral authority as an actor. The Court can't be a force for social, legal, or political change in every case that might need it. The Court is fundamentally a reactive institution; you probably are familiar with the phrase that the Court has neither the "power of purse nor sword. It has only the power of persuasion;" and that persuasive authority must be exercised with great care, with great discretion, and with great attention to the tools the Court uses to decide the cases. In other words, it must pay particular and careful attention to the methods of constitutional interpretation that it employs.

Lecture Five
Marbury v. Madison and Judicial Review

Scope:

This lecture introduces students to the practice of *judicial review*, or the authority of the Supreme Court and other federal courts to declare some governmental action unconstitutional. On some accounts, the power of judicial review is the cornerstone of the American constitutional order. Whether this is true or not, this lecture will trace the early beginnings of the doctrine, beginning with Alexander Hamilton's defense of the doctrine in *Federalist* no. 78. As we shall see, many of Hamilton's arguments were echoed in Chief Justice John Marshall's opinion for the Court in the celebrated case of *Marbury v. Madison* (1803). In this lecture, we explore the logic of *Marbury* in greater detail. We will conclude with criticisms of *Marbury*, especially as developed by Thomas Jefferson. In particular, we consider exactly what kind of claim Marshall made. Did he claim that the Supreme Court is the final, ultimate interpreter of the Constitution? Or did he claim only that the Court must have at least an equal right to interpret? This is still an open, controversial question in constitutional law. Does the American system of judicial review establish judicial supremacy, or does it promote the latter understanding, sometimes called *departmentalism*? The lecture concludes by suggesting that there is probably not a single clear answer to the question, thus underscoring the complexity of the American constitutional order.

Outline

I. *Judicial review* is one of the cornerstones of the American constitutional order.

   A. Judicial review, defined in brief, is the authority of a court to nullify any law or policy that violates the Constitution.

   B. Judicial review is not synonymous with *constitutional review*; the authority to declare a law incompatible with the Constitution need not be vested in courts or judges.

      1. There is nothing in Article III, or any other part of the constitutional text, that clearly gives judges this authority.

2. The power of constitutional review exists in other constitutional democracies, such as France [via the *Conseil constitutionnel*], but it is not vested in judges.

II. Although there are colonial antecedents, the doctrine of judicial review in the United States is largely the result of Chief Justice John Marshall's opinion for the Court in the celebrated case of *Marbury v. Madison* (1803).

A. As is true of so many of the cases we will consider, it is important to understand the political context of *Marbury*. At stake in the case were different visions of America, as well as different understandings about such important concepts as separation of powers and checks and balances.

1. We begin with the presidential election of 1800 between John Adams and Thomas Jefferson and the so-called "midnight" judges appointed by Adams in the last moments of his presidency.

2. Once it was clear that the Federalists had lost control of the presidency and Congress to the Jeffersonians, they reacted, in part, by "retreating," in Jefferson's terms, to the judiciary. As a part of this strategy, the Federalists created several new positions of "justices of the peace" for the District of Columbia, awarded to Federalists.

3. One of those justices of the peace was William Marbury, who sued the new secretary of state, James Madison, to get his appointment.

4. The lawsuit invoked the Court's "original" jurisdiction and was of such consequence to lead the new Congress to cancel the Court's 1801–1802 term.

B. Chief Justice Marshall wrote the opinion for the Court. The opinion held for Madison insofar as Marshall ruled that the Court did not have jurisdiction to grant Marbury relief. But more broadly, Marshall claimed for the Court the extraordinary authority to declare an act of Congress unconstitutional.

C. Marshall's opinion for the Court was deceptively simple: He declared that under the Constitution, "it is emphatically the province and duty of the judicial department to say what the law is."

1. From this and other premises, Marshall reasoned that the Constitution's status as "supreme Law" must mean that it controls inferior acts and laws and that judges, by warrant of their oaths, their legal training, and their authority under Article III to hear cases and controversies, must have the power of judicial review.
2. Marshall offered several other justifications for judicial review, but none goes to the real issue in the case.

III. Marshall's opinion for the Court, although celebrated by some, met with serious criticism from President Jefferson, as well as from some other judges.

A. President Jefferson, for example, argued that Marshall's opinion elevated the Court from a branch separate but equal to a branch independent and superior. Jefferson even went so far as to call for the impeachment of federal judges who would dare to disallow acts of the coordinate and equal branches of the federal government.

B. In another criticism, Judge John Gibson of the Pennsylvania Supreme Court argued that the doctrine of checks and balances weighed against judicial review. Abuses of the Constitution, he argued, could be forestalled by that system and should be corrected, not by courts, but by the people themselves in their exercise of sovereign power.

IV. Chief Justice Marshall claimed in *Marbury* that the Supreme Court must have the power of judicial review. But what exactly does that power entail? Two centuries after *Marbury*, judges and scholars alike continue to disagree about both the breadth and the depth of that power.

A. One understanding of the power suggests a theory known as *judicial supremacy*, or the claim that in any conflict over the Constitution's meaning, judges' interpretations should prevail over the interpretations of other branches. Some passages and suggestions in *Marbury v. Madison* seem to support this account. Alexander Hamilton had first elaborated this position in "Federalist No. 78."

B. Another approach, however, suggests that the Court claimed only a co-equal right to interpret the Constitution for itself, not a broader, more final interpretive authority.

V. These two readings of *Marbury* give rise to two very different understandings about the power of judicial review and, indeed, of the proper role of the Supreme Court in the polity.

   A. *Judicial supremacy* underscores a constitutional order in which conflicts over constitutional meaning are settled largely by judges. In *Cooper v. Aaron* (1958), the Court said, in effect, "We are the final, ultimate interpreter of the Constitution."

   B. *Departmentalism*, on the other hand, assumes that all branches have an ongoing and equal responsibility for determining what the Constitution means. This is, the Jeffersonian understanding: in cases of genuine conflict, the branches must ultimately seek some kind of political resolution or political compromise amongst themselves, and if they cannot reach a resolution, ultimately, it will revert to the people to make these kinds of decisions

   C. American constitutional history and ongoing practice teach us that neither understanding of the power of judicial review is the "correct" one.

   1. On a day-to-day basis, most people assume and most constitutional authorities assume that the Court will have the final word.

   2. However, *every* president has asserted an independent authority to interpret the Constitution for himself.

   D. There is much at stake in choosing between these two approaches, and the choice is influenced as much by everyday politics as it is by the abstractions of constitutional theory.

Essential Reading:

Marbury v. Madison (1803).

Ralph Ketcham, ed., *The Federalist Papers*, No. 78.

Kommers, Finn, and Jacobsohn, *American Constitutional Law*, chapter 3.

Supplementary Reading:

Eakin v. Raub (1825).

Alexander M. Bickel, *The Least Dangerous Branch: The Supreme Court at the Bar of Politics*, chapter 1.

Cass Sunstein, *One Case at a Time: Judicial Minimalism on the Supreme Court*.

William Van Alstyne, "A Critical Guide to *Marbury v. Madison*," *Duke Law Journal* 1 (1969).

Mark Tushnet, *Taking the Constitution Away from the Courts*.

Cooper v. Aaron (1958).

Questions to Consider:

1. Marshall wrote that the question of "whether an act, repugnant to the Constitution, can become the law of the land, is a question deeply interesting to the United States; but, happily, not of an intricacy proportioned to its interest." Do you agree?

2. How would our system of government differ if the Supreme Court could not declare acts of Congress or the executive unconstitutional? Could individual freedom and limited government be preserved under such a system?

3. Does the constitutional text express any preference for a system of judicial supremacy or departmentalism? If so, what is the evidence for such a claim? Is a system of judicial supremacy compatible with a system of checks and balances?

Lecture Five—Transcript
Marbury v. Madison and Judicial Review

In our last lecture, we considered how various actors interpret the Constitution. We were primarily interested in the strategies or the methods of constitutional interpretation that any particular interpreter might use. You will recall that we discussed several different approaches, including textualism, originalism, Founders' intent, and structuralism. We move to a slightly different question in this lecture. Here, we're less interested in how the Constitution should be interpreted, and more interested in the question of who bears institutional responsibility for interpreting the Constitution. In my experience, almost everybody assumes that there is an easy, obvious answer to the question of who bears responsibility for interpreting the Constitution. Almost everybody assumes, naturally—because it has always been that way—that judges bear the final institutional responsibility for making sense of the Constitution's vague provisions. In this lecture, we will see that it was not always the case that judges would bear that responsibility. It was not inevitable that judges would come to have that responsibility. This is a product of constitutional evolution, and, in particular, it is the product of a series of important Supreme Court cases, one of which we will spend a great deal of time with here, the celebrated case of *Marbury v. Madison,* decided in 1803—or, in other words, decided very early on in the nation's constitutional history.

Before I get into the case itself, let me give you a couple of quick definitions. Judicial review itself refers to the practice or the authority of a court or of a judge to nullify any law or governmental policy that seems to violate the Constitution. That's a quick, easy, and accurate definition, but it hides a great deal of complexity. First, judicial review is not synonymous with constitutional review. More broadly, constitutional review refers to the authority of some actor in some constitutional place to declare something unconstitutional. Let me be a little bit clearer about this. It is not necessary, as a matter of constitutional theory, that the power to declare something unconstitutional should have to rest with judges. It might rest with the legislature itself, or with some agency in the executive branch. There is no necessary reason why judges or judges alone should have that authority. More importantly, there is nothing actually in the text of the Constitution, and nothing in particular in Article Three—

which constitutes the judiciary itself—which clearly or unequivocally gives to judges the authority to declare things unconstitutional. This is a power—as fantastic as it is, as important as it is—that the Court has taken unto itself over time. It was not obvious that it had to happen in this way, and there are several constitutional democracies—France springs immediately to mind—where the power to declare things unconstitutional does rest with some other institutional actor, and not necessarily with judges.

Now I've said that Article III of the Constitution doesn't actually include the power of judicial review, at least explicitly. Nevertheless, there are historical antecedents for the power, occurring particularly in colonial America, where some courts—at least we think—might be read as having said, "We have this power," although it clearly did not amount to the kind of great power we see now associated with judicial review. In truth, the doctrine of judicial review, notwithstanding these colonial antecedents really should be traced to John Marshall's opinion of the Court in *Marbury v. Madison*. As is true of so many of the cases we're going to consider over the course of these lectures, it's important to understand the political and the social context of *Marbury*. In order to understand that context, we need to review a little bit of history.

We should start our history lesson with the great presidential election of 1800 between John Adams and Thomas Jefferson. I think it's fair to say that this election was one of the most controversial, one of the dirtiest, and one of the most important in American history. At stake were two great different visions of what the new country would look like.

John Adams was a Federalist, a member of the Federalist Party. We don't have time, unfortunately, to go into an extended history of what the Federalists believed, but the Federalists were largely responsible for the new Constitution; and in their vision, this new Constitution would constitute a great national society—a society that transcended the historical prejudices, the historical idiosyncrasies, of the state governments. They imagined, in other words, a united states.

Jefferson was always associated with the Republican Party, not our Republican Party, but a much earlier version of Republicans sometimes known as "anti-Federalists." It pains me to simplify it in these terms, and please don't take me too literally—but broadly speaking, unlike the Federalist Party, the anti-Federalists were states' rights activists. They believed importantly in the power of local attachments and the power of state and local governance, and they were very much fearful that the new constitutional order would destroy historical attachments to historical state governance.

At contest, then, between these two presidential candidates were two visions of America: the Federalist vision and the anti-Federalist vision; and the rhetoric that these two men used to conduct their campaign was truly extraordinary. After Adams lost the presidency to Jefferson, he complained viciously that the country had been taken over—and I use this word deliberately—"by terrorists," by which he meant the Jeffersonian Party.

I assume that many of you will have heard of the following phrase: "a lame duck presidency." A lame duck presidency refers to a president who has lost an election or cannot run for re-election, presumably in November, but sits in office, nevertheless, until the new president is inaugurated. In our time, that "lame duck" period rests or runs from about November to about January. It was not always so. In the 1800 presidential election, the "lame duck" period lasted from November to sometime in March. That's an enormous length of time, and it provides a great opportunity, not for malfeasance, not for bad things, generally, but let's just say it provides a great opportunity for mischief; and there was much mischief about in the 1800 election.

Once it was clear that Jefferson had won the presidency once it was clear that the Federalists no longer controlled the presidency, panic set in in the Federalist Party. That panic was exacerbated by the fact that the Federalists also lost control of Congress. What to do? We've lost control of two branches of the government. The Federalists hit upon a brilliant plan: staff the judiciary with good, loyal, patriotic Federalists; and that's what they did. First, they persuaded the ailing chief justice, Oliver Ellsworth, to resign his position as chief justice, so that a new, younger man—a loyal, patriotic Federalist—could be appointed to the position. That man was John Marshall, who, perchance, was also secretary of state for John Adams, and did not feel it was necessary to resign that position in order to assume chief justiceship of the United States. It wasn't enough simply to stock the existing courts with Federalists. The Federalists went so far as to create a number of new judicial positions, justices of the peace—19,

I believe—for the District of Columbia. And I think that it is fair to say that, as large as the District of Columbia is now, it doesn't need nineteen justices of the peace now, and it certainly didn't need 19 justices of the peace—all of whom were good Federalists—in the year 1800.

It was a madhouse at the end of the presidential election. Imagine yourself—you're Adams; there are so many things you need to do before you leave office. Imagine that you're Secretary of State John Marshall—you have a lot of things you need to do before you leave office as well, one of which is, learn how to be chief justice. One of those persons who would have been a justice of the peace, his name was William Marbury, did not actually get the piece of paper, the presidential commission that would have made him a justice of the peace. He didn't get it because John Marshall didn't give it to him; or I should say, John Marshall failed to make sure he received that commission. Marshall gave it to his younger brother, his assistant, James Marshall; and James Marshall refused, or forgot, or was neglectful, or simply didn't bother to give the commission. The new president, Thomas Jefferson, was sworn in. He has a new secretary of state, James Madison, and Marbury politely requests of Madison, "May I have my commission that would make me a good Federalist judge?"

Now you can imagine, of course, that Jefferson wanted nothing to do with this. This is a straightforward, political contest. And of course, James Madison refuses to give that piece of paper, that commission, to William Marbury, who does what any good American would do under the circumstances—he sues. Imagine the gall involved here! He sues James Madison, the father of the Constitution, and complains that Madison has acted unconstitutionally. Of course, by suing Madison, who is really only a figurehead in this controversy, he's really suing Thomas Jefferson. The first thing the Federalists do about losing power, in other words, is set out to embarrass the new Jeffersonian administration by accusing them of acting in ways that are contrary to the Constitution.

This case is all the more extraordinary because Marbury doesn't go to some little federal court, doesn't go to some state court or District of Columbia court; he has the nerve to walk directly, without an appeal from anywhere else, into the United States Supreme Court. And guess who is heading the court? His fellow patriot, his fellow

Federalist, John Marshall, who, you might think, has a small conflict of interest here, because it is his office and his brother who is, in part, responsible for this lawsuit, by having failed to deliver the commission in the first instance. That small inconsistency doesn't trouble John Marshall at all, and he has no difficultly going ahead to rule on the case.

Imagine the stakes here: one political party suing another political party; one branch of government, the Supreme Court, in direct conflict with another branch of government, controlled by a different political party, the presidency. All of Washington was abuzz with the potential conflict. I can't stress enough how profound and important this conflict was to the political scene in Washington. Here's one small example of how important it was.

The new Congress, controlled by the Jeffersonians, instructed the Supreme Court to take the 1801–1802 term off by refusing to budget the Court that year. This was a broadside across the bow, a straightforward warning to Marshall and to the Supreme Court that they had better be careful about how they decide this case. Everybody understood that if Marshall reached the wrong opinion— in other words, ruled against Jefferson and Madison—that there would be terrible consequences to follow. What were those consequences exactly? The Supreme Court might be abolished. If not that, there was at least the distinct possibility that John Marshall, and perhaps some other sitting Supreme Court justices, would be impeached. And to make sure that Marshall understood that threat, in the meantime, the Jeffersonians had started impeachment proceedings against a lower court federal judge. Nobody misunderstood what the stakes were; and imagine if, today, if in a contest, say, over abortion, Congress told the Supreme Court, "We are really concerned about how you might rule on this case. Why don't you just take the next year off to think about it and then come back and give us an appropriate decision?" That's essentially what happened in this great conflict between 1800 and 1803.

Marbury, as I said, didn't start with a lower court. He invoked something called the Court's original jurisdiction, and we spoke about this briefly in an earlier lecture. The original jurisdiction of the Court refers to that class of cases clearly articulated in Article Three itself, where the Court may actually hear a case without it having gone anywhere else first. So, if you represent William Marbury, you knock on the courthouse door; the first question John Marshall will ask you is, "Why are you here? Under what authority are you here? Are you here, for example, because you have lost in a lower federal court and you are invoking our appellate authority?" To which Marbury, through counsel, will have to say, "No. That's not it." "Then why are you here?" And presumably Marbury will say, "Mr. Chief Justice, we are here because we are invoking your original jurisdiction." To which John Marshall, or any other competent judge, will say, "Please show me that provision in Article III of the Constitution that specifically applies to your case."

That's the one question William Marbury doesn't actually want to hear, because he is going to put his hands behind his back and hem and haw, and he's going to have to say, "Actually, your honor, there isn't any provision in Article III, Section 2 that specifically authorizes us to be here." "Then why are you here?" "Because an earlier Congress, controlled, coincidentally, by the Federalists, had passed a statute, and the statute said that, in addition to those cases in which the Court has original jurisdiction by virtue of the Constitution itself, there is an additional class of cases, that we will describe for you in the statute, where we think the Court should also have original jurisdiction." And one of those involves (please pardon my jargon) when we want something that we call a writ of *mandamus*.

A writ of *mandamus* is a letter, an order, from a judge to an official, directing that official to do something. You see how it applies to Marbury's case. Marbury wants a letter from John Marshall or from the Supreme Court (let's not personalize it so much) directing James Madison to give the commission to William Marbury. That's all a writ of mandamus is involved in this case. It's not any more complicated than that.

We could end the case here if John Marshall had said, "Yes, you may have your writ of mandamus." Or we could end this case here if he said, "No, you may not have your writ of mandamus." I think Jefferson would have preferred the latter option; but strangely enough, I think he also would have preferred the former option to the one he got, because Marshall took neither approach. Marshall, instead, said that there are two classes of jurisdiction that the Court possesses, original and appellate, and the Constitution tells us in tedious detail what kinds of original jurisdiction we have.

As you recall in the last lecture, I said one method of constitutional interpretation is structuralism. Look at a provision of the Constitution against the backdrop of the entire Constitution; and that's precisely what Marshall does. He says, if you look at how Article III is written, you'll see that our original jurisdiction is, in fact, laid out in excruciating detail.

What does the Constitution have to say about our appellate jurisdiction? And two important factors emerge from looking at this contrast. The Constitution says almost nothing at all about the Court's appellate jurisdiction. It simply announces that, in all other cases, the Court shall have appellate jurisdiction; but then, importantly, also goes on to say that Congress may alter the appellate jurisdiction of the Court whenever it wants to do so. That provision that authorizes Congress to change the appellate jurisdiction does not appear with regard to original jurisdiction. Marshall says, if Congress had the authority to alter our original jurisdiction, as this congressional statute purports to do, then the Constitution would clearly have said so; and we know that because the Constitution clearly did say so with respect to our appellate jurisdiction. And I hope you can see where this was leading. Marshall concludes, in other words, that that congressional statute, which purported to enlarge the original jurisdiction of the Court, violated the Constitution itself.

Now before I go into any more sort of detail about this, once he reached that conclusion, we need to understand that, as a matter of law, Jefferson had won the case. Marbury had no right to be in the Supreme Court; he couldn't claim the Court's jurisdiction, in other words; and because he couldn't claim the Court's jurisdiction, there was not any possibility that the Court would instruct Madison and Jefferson to make him a judge.

At this point in the case, Jefferson, as a matter of legal doctrine, is the clear victor, and yet Jefferson went to his grave insisting that what happened in *Marbury v. Madison* was a constitutional travesty. We need to understand exactly why he was so upset, but here's the short version: in the declaring of that congressional statute unconstitutional, the Court assumed to itself a power which does not clearly exist in the text—the power to declare things unconstitutional. As it turns out, in exercising that power, Jefferson was the beneficiary; but we must always distinguish between who is the immediate beneficiary and who are the long-term beneficiaries. And Jefferson understood, as clearly as anyone ever could, that a Supreme Court possessed of the power to declare things unconstitutional—and, coincidentally, controlled by Federalist—was a threat to the Jefferson administration for as long as there would be a Jefferson administration; because that power of judicial review, the power to declare things unconstitutional, now could be—turns out it wasn't, but might have been—a sword hanging over the heads of the Jeffersonians. And who would control the sword? The vanquished Federalists.

It's an extraordinary political case, as important as any case, politically, ever decided by the Court; but it's also important, theoretically, because it is the first time the Court has claimed for itself the authority to declare things unconstitutional.

How did Marshall justify that decision? To be honest, we could spend several lectures—I would be happy to spend the entire remainder of the course talking about the logic that Marshall used in this case; but I'm going to try to summarize it in much quicker terms.

First, Marshall announced (and I will quote him directly) that, "It is emphatically the province and the duty of the judicial department to say what the law is." It is difficult to argue with that, but there is an assumption built into it. The first assumption built into it is that we should understand the Constitution primarily as an act of law, and not as an act, say, of political identity, as we talked about in an earlier lecture. But follow the logic here—if the Constitution is law, then who is best entrusted with making sense of what the law means or requires in any particular case? Alexander Hamilton had first elaborated this position in *Federalist No. 78*, arguing that judges, by virtue of their legal training, would necessarily bear, or might necessarily bear, the primary responsibility for giving the Constitution meaning, for applying it on a day-to-day basis; because, in the end, of course, it was judges that possessed that great expertise in the study of law. So when Marshall says, "it is emphatically the province" of the judiciary to determine what the law is, he's making a set of assumptions that is, in fact, law we're dealing with, and that judges, of course, would possess the kind of expertise that would be necessary to give the law meaning.

He goes on to refer to several other justifications. He goes on to say, for example, that judges take an oath to support the Constitution, and that it would be outrageous for judges to take an oath to support the Constitution and then not have the authority to determine what the Constitution actually requires or forbids in any particular case. He also suggests that our Article Three has a provision in it, which says that judicial authority shall extend to all cases and controversies. Of course, there is no definition of what cases and controversies mean, but it's some oblique support for the position that there might be a power of judicial review.

These are all very interesting arguments. They're all persuasive to some extent, although any good scholar and any good judge could point out what the flaws are with all of them as well. My biggest complaint about the reasoning in this case, at least to this point, is that, while it's a very interesting set of arguments, it's a set of arguments that beg the real question. All Marshall has done so far is argue that, because there is a Constitution, and it is law, some things must therefore be unconstitutional—what everybody agreed to; that if there's going to be a Constitution, it must control acts of Congress, or acts of the presidency, or acts of states. All he's done, in other words, is make the theoretical argument that it is possible that some things will be unconstitutional. Fair enough. That's not the question in *Marbury*. The question isn't, "Can we imagine that something will be unconstitutional?" The question in *Marbury* is, "Why should judges get to say that things are unconstitutional?"

Remember, at the beginning of the lecture, I suggested there was a difference between constitutional review and judicial review. Judicial review is just a more specific form of constitutional review. Judicial review, in other words, is an assumption that judges should possess that authority. Marshall never really addresses that, except perhaps through the argument about legal expertise; but it's not a very persuasive, and certainly not a very far-reaching, argument. In other words, too much of *Marbury v. Madison* is directed to the question of whether something can be unconstitutional, and not enough of *Marbury* is directed to the fantastically critical question about who gets to say so. And there's nothing in *Marbury,* of course, that hints that the question of who gets to say so is deeply complicated by the fact that, in most cases, it's easy to come up with arguments that say that something is unconstitutional, and just as easy for a well-trained attorney or judge to make the counter-argument as well. That's what lawyers and judges do. This is not a criticism. This is a celebration of their activity. They are trained in the art of being able to argue different sides of an issue. Marshall's opinion was celebrated and castigated at the same time, and still is today.

There are scholars, for example, who argue that no course on civil liberties and the Bill of Rights should even bother with *Marbury v. Madison,* either because it's unimportant or because it's so badly reasoned that we shouldn't expose students to such faulty logic. There are others of us (and I won't say which camp I'm in) who think that we could spend a couple of years on *Marbury* and not lose interest in it. (Well, okay I am in that camp!)

Contemporaneous criticisms came from two primary places. The first, you'll not be surprised to hear, was from President Jefferson. Jefferson argued that Marshall's opinion that the doctrine of judicial review elevated the Supreme Court from a branch "separate but equal" to a branch independent and superior. Behind his claim, here, is an interesting problem: what do you make of the system of checks and balances when, at least theoretically, one branch has the final say? That might not be a very effective system of checks and balances. That might be a system where there are checks and balances to a point; but at some point, we get tired of the game and we give final authority to one branch—in this case, the one branch that isn't elected, that isn't accountable to the people, to have the final word.

Jefferson even went so far as to call for the impeachment of any federal judge that would dare to follow up Marbury by actually declaring something unconstitutional. He once wrote a letter to the prosecutor in the Aaron Burr case in which he said, "Under no circumstances will you even cite *Marbury versus Madison* at any point during the proceedings, because the case is entirely illegitimate."

Another criticism came from John Gibson, who was a judge on the Pennsylvania Supreme Court. He argued that checks and balances, as I suggested before, mitigated against judicial review. He acknowledged part of what *Marbury* had established—that there must, in fact, be the possibility of unconstitutional action, or there wouldn't be a need for a Constitution in the first instance; but he went on to argue that, just because there might be abuses of the constitutional system, that did not mean, necessarily, that it fell to judges to correct those abuses. Instead, he argued that if a legislature, for example, or if a governor or a president had acted unconstitutionally, the correction for that abuse ought to be with the people themselves in the exercise of their sovereign power, presumably through elections or amendments, and not with courts.

Let me move back again from the details of the case to a larger perspective. Chief Justice John Marshall claimed in *Marbury* that the Supreme Court must have the power of judicial review. What exactly does that power entail? Two centuries after *Marbury,* judges and scholars alike continued to disagree and to fight about what that power means—about its breadth, how far it extends, and its depth.

One understanding of *Marbury* and of judicial review is known as judicial supremacy. I strongly suspect that this is the theory of judicial review that most of you are familiar with. It certainly is the theory that is routinely taught in high school civics courses. The theory of judicial supremacy holds simply this: when there is conflict over what the Constitution means among the various branches of government (in particular, among the various branches of the national government), that there must be a final resolution somewhere—an interesting assumption, that constitutional conflict is inherently a negative thing, and that ultimately there must be some way, some authority to resolve it. And the theory of judicial supremacy, you'll not be surprised to hear, assumes that when there are these kinds of conflicts, ultimately, it is the judicial authority that is responsible for determining what the Constitution means.

There is one Supreme Court case not directly relevant to our understanding, but nevertheless, it does have a beautiful quote in it; it's called *Cooper v. Aaron,* and in *Cooper v. Aaron*, the Court said, "We are the final, ultimate interpreter of the Constitution." In the end, we decide what the Constitution means.

The other understanding, which is really a Jeffersonian understanding, is known as departmentalism. The departmentalism understanding of judicial review makes a much more modest claim. It claims that, when there are conflicts between the branches, each branch has a co-equal right to interpret the Constitution for itself. This could be very unsettling to most students.

The idea that each branch might decide for itself what the Constitution means seems to run counter to what many of us assume that a constitutional democracy is really all about; but it was the

Jeffersonian understanding. The Jeffersonian understanding is that, in cases of genuine conflict, the branches must ultimately seek some kind of political resolution or political compromise amongst themselves, and if they can't, ultimately, it will revert to the people to make these kinds of decisions.

Which one of these two positions accurately describes the American constitutional order as we speak? Both. On a day-to-day basis, most people assume and most constitutional authorities assume that the Court will have the final word. But every president—and I do mean every president—has asserted an independent authority to teach, to interpret, and to understand the Constitution for himself. And when presidents make these kinds of assertions, or when courts make these kinds of assertions, it is well to remember that behind them are two very different visions of what it means to live in a constitutional democracy, and who bears responsibility for the Constitution.

Lecture Six
Private Property and the Founding

Scope:

One of the Constitution's central purposes, according to the Preamble, is to secure the "Blessings of Liberty." There is little doubt, as we shall see in this lecture, that chief among those liberties was the right to own private property. Indeed, the original text of the Constitution, before there was a Bill of Rights, was riddled through with protections for property. In this lecture, we ask why the Founders, Federalists and anti-Federalists alike, were so intent on protecting property, and we begin to consider the mechanisms they devised for doing so. What did the Founders mean by *property*? As we review their work and the Court's earliest cases, we will see that the Founders' conceptions of liberty and property were wonderfully rich and complex. We shall see, too, that behind those conceptions were important understandings about what it means to be free, what it means to be a citizen, and what constitutes good government and civic virtue. Among the cases we will explore are *Calder v. Bull* (1798), *Fletcher v. Peck* (1810), and *Charles River Bridge v. Warren Bridge* (1837).

Outline

I. Before we take up our examination of particular cases, this may be an appropriate time to say a few words about Supreme Court opinions and how to read them.

   A. A judicial opinion is both an act of explanation and of persuasion.

   B. Most opinions purport to explain how the judge or judges arrived at a decision, usually by tracing a series of questions, answers, and arguments from a set beginning to a seemingly inevitable end. In this sense, a judicial opinion helps to ensure the accountability of power—a fundamental constitutional imperative—by declaring in public the reasons why a case has been decided in a particular way.

   C. Every judicial opinion is an exercise in persuasion. Difficult cases, at least, often admit of more than one solution.

1. A judge who fails to say why his or her solution is preferable to another, no less obvious, solution is a judge who has failed to understand the difference between judicial power, or the capacity to reach a decision, and judicial authority—that is, the circumstances under which it is constitutionally appropriate to reach a decision.

2. Judicial authority requires an understanding of the proper nature and limits of judicial power in a constitutional democracy as well as an understanding of the reasons that a judge has a constitutional obligation to tell us why, to persuade us, that his or her solution is superior.

D. There are other purposes to opinions, as well. [Note: Opinions also have more than one audience—sometimes the litigants alone, sometimes legal scholars, and sometimes the entire polity.] In every case, then, students should read for the following information:

1. *Legal doctrine*: What question of law does the case raise? How do the judges or justices answer that question? What doctrines of law do they utilize or formulate? Does their answer conform to existing legal doctrine or does it change it?

2. *Institutional role*: Almost every constitutional case decided by the Supreme Court involves some question about the proper role of the Court in the political process. What understanding of judicial power does the majority embrace? Does the opinion envision a broad or a narrow role for the power of judges? Does that vision rest on a particular understanding of democratic theory and of the authority of the community to govern itself through the means of majoritarian politics? Does it rest on a particular view about when judges should protect individual liberty from regulation by a majority?

3. *Methods and strategies of constitutional interpretation*: Translating the "majestic generalities" of the Constitution into a practical instrument of governance requires interpretation. What methods and strategies of interpretation do the judges employ? Do they explicitly acknowledge their choices? Do they justify them? What

sorts of justifications and evidence does the opinion marshal to support its argument?

   4. *Commentary on the American polity*: As I said earlier, a course on constitutional law should be a commentary on the meaning of America. Judicial opinions can be a rich source for such commentary. As you read them, consider what an opinion says about American history, about contemporary politics, about political theory, and about the success or failure of the American experiment.

II. The Preamble to the Constitution includes among its purposes to "secure the Blessings of Liberty." Chief among those blessings and, hence, foundational to the new constitutional order was the protection of private property.

   A. When the Founders spoke of property, they meant not a single right but, rather, an expansive collection of liberties. These included the right to own property, as well as the right of propertied men to participate in governance.

   1. Indeed, the protection of property was so important that the Founders included several provisions in the original text, including Article I, Section 10, which prohibits *ex post facto* laws and laws impairing the obligation of contracts.

   2. Nor can we fully appreciate the significance of property without understanding how expansive the definition of *property* was. Madison, for example, wrote: "A man has a property in his opinions and the free communication of those opinions, and he also has a property in his religious opinions."

   B. For the Founders, as we shall see, the protection of liberty itself meant protection for property, and, indeed, property was sometimes said to be the first object of liberty.

III. Why were the Founders so intent on protecting property?

   A. Most of the Founders believed that property was at risk under the Articles of Confederation, in part because the Articles had left property under the control of state governments, each of which set its own trade and tariff policies, as well as coined its own money.

B. Just as important, the Founders believed, albeit for different reasons, that ownership of property was the key to human autonomy and dignity—Jefferson even drafted a constitutional provision for the Virginia state Constitution, which would have given property to every white male who didn't already possess it.

IV. The Court's early cases on property illustrate both its importance and the complexity of the Founders' views about the definition of property and its role in civic society.

A. In the case of *Calder v. Bull* (1798), the Court considered the origins of property and the extent of the state's authority to regulate it. In this case, the Court proffered a somewhat narrow view of the *ex post facto* clause, limiting it to criminal matters and, thus, making it somewhat less useful as a mechanism for protecting property.

    1. In the Court's judgment, the *ex post facto* guarantee applies only to matters of criminal law and procedure.

    2. Elsewhere in the opinions, various justices wax eloquently about the importance and priority of property, with one justice going so far as to suggest that under no conditions may the state take property from A and give it to B.

B. In *Fletcher v. Peck* (1810), on the other hand, the Court advanced a definition of property that made it nearly immune from regulation. In the Court's view, property was so important that it was protected from governmental regulation either by the Constitution or by "the very nature of things."

    1. The significance of this language should not be underestimated. Chief Justice Marshall seems to argue that property must be a protected value even absent a specific constitutional provision saying so.

    2. In a separate concurring opinion, Justice William Johnson went even further, claiming that not even God ["the Deity"] can violate the right to property.

C. Just over a quarter century later, however, the Court, writing in *Charles River Bridge v. Warren Bridge Company* (1837), advanced a very different understanding of property. Here, the Court stressed that the community has an interest in private property and that private rights must sometimes give way to communal interests.

1. There are important differences between *Fletcher v. Peck* and *Charles River Bridge*. First, Marshall no longer led the Court. He had been replaced by Chief Justice Roger Taney, in his own right a towering figure in American constitutional history. Unlike Marshall, Taney was less inclined to favor national interests over state interests and less inclined to elevate individual liberties over the public welfare.

2. In this case, Taney found for the owners of the second bridge—or against the property interest—writing: "The object and end of all government is to promote the happiness and prosperity of the community. While the rights of private property are sacredly guarded, we must not forget that the community also have rights."

3. Taney's opinion rested explicitly on how a particular definition of property would either inhibit or promote economic growth and expansion in the new country.

4. Justice Joseph Story also wrote an important dissent in this case. An intellectual compatriot of John Marshall, Story held closer to *Fletcher v. Peck* on the relative balance between the community interest and the liberty interest.

5. At issue in the two opinions were different understandings about the nature and importance of property and how those different understandings could lead to different Americas.

V. The cases we will read throughout this course are available in many places and formats.

    A. Full copies of the cases are available at most public libraries and there are several sites on the Internet, including the official site of the U.S. Supreme Court, which has most of the cases.

    B. However, the cases are often extremely long and include information not directly relevant to our inquiry. For this reason, I advise students to purchase a casebook, or a collection of edited cases. Many such collections are available. The readings and cases I have recommended are from Kommers, Finn, and Jacobsohn, *American Constitutional Law*, 2nd edition, volume 2 (2004), but any casebook will have most of the cases.

Essential Reading:

Calder v. Bull (1798).

Fletcher v. Peck (1810).

Charles River Bridge v. Warren Bridge (1837).

Kommers, Finn, and Jacobsohn, *American Constitutional Law*, chapter 5, pp. 181–187.

Supplementary Reading:

Bruce Ackerman, *Private Property and the Constitution*.

Charles Beard, *An Economic Interpretation of the Constitution*.

Richard Ely, *The Guardian of Every Other Right: The Constitutional History of Property Rights*.

Morton Horwitz, *The Transformation of American Law, 1780–1860*.

Ellen Frankel Paul and Howard Dickman, eds., *Liberty, Property, and the Foundations of the American Constitution*.

C. Peter McGrath, *Yazoo: The Case of Fletcher v. Peck*.

Questions to Consider:

1. There are several places in the Constitution that offer protection for property, but few if any that give us a definition of the term. What does *property* actually mean? And why did the Founders fail to offer a comprehensive definition?

2. It is difficult to resolve the Court's treatment of property in *Yazoo* and *Charles River*. Assuming that there are important differences between the two cases, which opinion best reflects the constitutional text? Consider as well: How do these different opinions understand the relationship between individual property rights and the public good?

Lecture Six—Transcript
Private Property and the Founding

In our first five lectures, we've been largely concerned with fundamental principles, the kinds of principles that are necessary to understand the Bill of Rights as an abstraction. In this lecture, and throughout the remainder of the course, we're going to be more concerned with specific provisions of the Bill of Rights, or, alternatively, with more specific individual liberties. For the next three lectures, we'll be concerning ourselves with the right to property. Before I get there, however, I want to suggest something about how you should approach the materials.

Unlike our first five lectures, throughout this lecture and the remaining lectures, we'll be covering a whole series of cases; until now, we've concentrated on one case at a time. As you read these cases, I'd like you to think about some basic principles and some basic strategies that will help you. Remember, if you haven't read legal materials before, these materials will be very difficult to understand. This would be the appropriate place to insert a joke about how lawyers write or can't write; but instead, I'll point out that much of the language they use is archaic because the opinions are often old, or detailed and institutionally intricate; because, in fact, legal concepts are often very difficult to understand, and lawyers try to use precise language to describe them.

As you read the opinions, try to remember that every opinion has at least two primary purposes. The first purpose is simply to explain the issue and the Court's resolution of the issue. So the first purpose is that of explanation. The second purpose, which is no less significant, is simply this: every judicial opinion is meant to be an act of persuasion as well. It is critically important that we understand this.

There are usually several different appropriate resolutions to a constitutional issue. A judge is constitutionally obligated to tell you why his or her resolution is the appropriate or the most persuasive resolution. One thing you should think about as you read these cases, then, is, "Does the explanation itself make sense?" and then, secondly, "Am I persuaded by the explanation?" One little piece of advice here: please do not be alarmed if you read a majority opinion and it seems to you to be very persuasive; and then, if you read a concurring opinion, or perhaps even more dramatically, a dissent, and that seems to you to be equally persuasive. That is not a lack of comprehension on your part; that's a sign of extreme intelligence.

There are other purposes to opinions as well. Let me just run through two or three of them very quickly. Every opinion attempts to explain the appropriate legal doctrine; so, as you read the opinion, try to think about what the legal doctrine involved in that case is.

Second, every opinion, whether explicitly or implicitly, has in it some set of assumptions about what the proper role of the judiciary is in trying to decide cases. Sometimes, we'll read cases where the judges are as explicit as one could possibly imagine about that issue. In other cases, it will be hidden.

Third, every judge will usually adopt, as we've seen before, a particular method or methods of constitutional interpretation, and it may help you to understand these cases if you think about the methods of interpretation that the judge is using. So try to identify— is this judge using Founders' intent? Is this judge using structuralism? Is this judge trying to balance different kinds of provisions?

Then, finally, in many cases, you'll see the judges express opinions about what it means to live in a constitutional democracy; or, even more broadly, what it means to be an American, and it's worth reading these opinions to find out what that commentary is on the state of the American polity.

All of these purposes, all of these readings, all of these strategies, appear in our property cases. There is a simple good reason for that. At the founding, there is no question that the Founders were most intent, of all civil liberties, on the right to protecting property. There is lots of evidence for this assumption.

First, before there was a Bill of Rights, when the original Constitution was reported out of Philadelphia, there were two civil liberties that that Constitution meant to protect. The first need not concern us, it was the writ of habeas corpus, and there were property provisions riddled throughout the text. One quick example, which we'll spend some time with today, Article I, Section 10 of the Constitution includes at least two different provisions: the No Impairment of Contracts clause and the *ex post facto* clause, both of which we'll discuss in greater detail. Both of those provisions were intent on protecting property well before there was a Bill of Rights, with its additional protections for property.

Indeed, property was so important that I'm not sure we can do it justice without a quick understanding about what they meant by property; because in some ways, their understandings about what property meant was wonderfully expansive—much more expansive than our own.

Here is a quote from James Madison, which I hope will give you some sense of what property meant for Madison: "A man has a property in his opinions and the free communication of those opinions, and he also has a property in his religious opinions." He has a property, in other words—I'm not doing this quote justice—in himself. What do you make of such a provision? Now, he meant, literally, that you have a property in your arm, that you have a property in your leg, that you have a property in your physical self, as well as a property in your emotional, spiritual, and intellectual self. There are some remnants of that conception of property even today; so you will probably have heard, for example, of notions of intellectual property. That's how expansive a concept property was for the Founders, and there should be no surprise that they were concerned with protecting it.

As I mentioned before, there are several provisions in the original text that are designed to protect property. Those provisions are slightly misleading. They are misleading in this way—the language used to protect property in the Constitution is highly individualistic, by which I mean only this simple claim: there is no space in the wording of the Constitution, there is no hint in the text itself, that there would ever be a time when it would be appropriate for the community or for the state to impose regulations on property. When I say the Founders had an individualistic conception of property, or alternatively, that they at least wrote in individualistic terms, I mean that they started from an assumption, and the assumption was that individual property rights would always trump any contrary community interest.

Now why is that misleading? It's misleading because there has never, in fact, been a time in American constitutional history when property has been so important that it always trumps a countervailing community interest. There have been times, particularly early on, as we shall see, when property was so important that it almost always trumped any countervailing social interest; but there have been other times when the Court has developed a conception of property that leaves it extremely vulnerable to community regulation. In other words, the trajectory of property hasn't been linear; it has been dynamic and fluid. There has never been a time, in other words, when the right to property, understood as a fundamental constitutional liberty, hasn't waxed and waned in terms of its importance.

One other primary, foundational position: why were the Founders so intent upon protecting property? This is complicated question. There are several different explanations, some fundamentally historical, some perhaps conspiratorial. A brief version of that: the Founders were intent on protecting property because they were wealthy; and when they meant to protect property, they didn't mean property in the abstract; they meant their own property. And if you look at the recommended readings for this course, they will direct you to different versions of that argument.

But I think that there is another argument that we must take at least as seriously as that one. All of the Founders, notwithstanding their political persuasion, believed, albeit for somewhat different reasons, that ownership of property, or at least the capacity for ownership of property, was the key to human autonomy and human dignity; that human beings couldn't flourish, that civic virtue could not flourish, unless people had the capacity to acquire property.

Some people think this Jeffersonian position is apocryphal, but it's not. Jefferson genuinely believed that every citizen of Virginia ought to possess property, and even drafted a constitutional provision for the Virginia state constitution, which would have given property to every white male who didn't already possess it. That's how critical property was to the development of the human being, and perhaps, just as importantly, to the development of good citizenship.

The Court's earliest cases on property illustrate both its importance to the Founders and its complexity in their intellectual lexicon. Indeed, a case decided even before *Marbury v. Madison* is a good clue to this. In the case of *Calder v. Bull,* decided in 1798, the Court considered explicitly where property comes from, why human beings are entitled to possess it, and under what conditions the state might choose to regulate it. In particular, the case was concerned with the *ex post facto* clause in Article I, Section 10.

The *ex post facto* clause is not difficult to understand. It simply refers to an understanding in the law that criminal behavior must be defined as criminal at the time it occurred. It would be fundamentally unjust, according to this maxim, for somebody to be able to commit behavior on day one, thinking it is legal, and then on some subsequent day—let's say day three—to have the legislators say, "We didn't know it at the time, but now we think your earlier behavior should have been illegal, so you will be prosecuted for it." The *ex post facto* clause is a fancy way of saying, "You can't criminalize behavior after the fact."

This was originally designed as a protection for private property, the fear being that state legislatures would redefine property—most importantly, redefine debts—in ways that would advantage their own state's citizens—sometimes creditors, sometimes debtors—after the fact. If there were not *ex post facto* provision, for example, one might imagine that the state of Virginia might say, at some point in time, "If you owe money to New York creditors, we are hereby going to wipe out that debt." Or, alternatively, "We'll make the debt payable in Virginia money as opposed to New York money." Remember, before the Constitution itself, each state had its own monetary and tax system. The *ex post facto* clause, in a sense, might be a very important protection for certain kinds of property interest. As it turns out, however, in *Calder v. Bull*, the Supreme Court decided that the *ex post facto* clause did not extend so far as to cover property, but instead, only applied to criminal behavior; that is the current understanding as well.

There is one wonderful quote, however, in *Calder v. Bull* that underscores the importance of property for the founding generation. In it, Justice Chase says, "The general principles of law and reason forbid taking property from 'A' and giving it to 'B.'" He didn't say, "This specific provision, 'XYZ,' in the Constitution, prohibits it"; he says, "general principles of law and reason." The very nature of human society protects property to such a fundamental extent that it must be protected, even in the absence of any particular constitutional provision that would do so. That is an extraordinary degree of protection for property. It's not quite as extraordinary, however, as the Court's position in the next case I'd like to talk about *Fletcher v. Peck*, decided in 1810.

We run the risk, as we did in *Marbury,* that I will spend the remaining 30 or so lectures talking about *Fletcher v. Peck. Fletcher v. Peck* refers to an extraordinary time in American politics, and, perhaps, to the first great political scandal in the United States history. It involved something called the "Yazoo land frauds."

Those of you who are familiar with popular lexicon will probably have heard the phrase "up the wazoo." That is a derivation from the original phrase, which was "up the Yazoo," which is both a description of a particular river in the American South and a description—although nobody seems to remember it anymore—of the first great political scandal in American politics: the Yazoo land frauds.

Briefly described, it's as simple as this: Northern investors—that's a generous term—went to the South, and for a penny and a half an acre—through bribes—managed to persuade the Georgia legislature to sell them over a million and a half acres of undeveloped land to the west of Georgia. Even in 1800, a penny and a half an acre is a pretty good price and, in part, because every single member save one of the Georgia legislature accepted bribes for the sale.

And you can guess what happens next. The whole point of a land fraud scheme is to buy cheap and to sell it off; and all these million and a half acres were sold from the original investors to second, third, fourth, fifth parties down the line. This would all be fine, except the good citizens of Georgia chose to vote out every member of the Georgia legislature, even the one who hadn't accepted a bribe. Some explanations for that person's behavior were that he was holding out for more money. I don't know if that is true or not—it's simply a legend—but he was voted out as well.

The new legislature assumes office and says, "We hereby rescind the original sale, because it is fraudulent." There is a wonderful story associated with this case. The Georgia legislature went so far as to say, "We want to burn, in a public ceremony in a capital square, every piece of paper that pertains to this original sale," as if to obliterate the very memory of this whole dirty episode. Legend has it, as they were starting the bonfire, an old man rode up in a horse, and said, "I'm here to see an act of justice done. But the fire should not be set by the hand of man, it should be set by God!" He pulled out a spyglass, started the fire, then rode away and was never seen again. Beautiful story. It doesn't matter if it's true. It should be true.

What happens next? Well, imagine you are the fifth, sixth, or seventh party who purports to have bought this land. Now Georgia is telling you, you don't own this land. You know what you have to do—you're a good citizen. The law requires that you sue somebody when you're harmed. So you sue the person who sold you the land; and that person, in turn, sues the person who sold him the land; and back up the chain we go—it's a beautiful thing to imagine—until we ultimately get to the first sale.

How in the world is this a constitutional controversy? Every person who bought the land from somebody else bought the land with a warranty, a guarantee, that the owner had the legal authority to sell it to you. If you buy a house, you're going to spend a lot of money on insurance that guarantees that warranty, which guarantees the authority of the seller to sell it to you. The claim here must be, then, this: that my warranty to sell it to you is invalid because the person who sold it to me had an invalid warranty; and the reason all of these are invalid is because the state of Georgia has impaired the original contract.

Remember Article I, Section 10? We saw in *Calder v. Bull* that it includes the *ex post facto* clause. That same constitutional provision states that there shall be no impairment of contracts. Perhaps what the second Georgian legislature has done is to impair that contract; and that's what the Supreme Court said. Again, writing through John Marshall, the Court concluded that the private interest in property, the importance of property as a liberty, a constitutionally protected interest, was superior to, and hence trumped, the interest of the state of Georgia in reclaiming the fraudulent sale of a million and a half acres.

Now, in the abstract, if we didn't have to run this through a constitutional calculus, we could argue about that. It doesn't seem to me to be implausible that somebody might say, "No, the public interest in reclaiming a million and a half acres is superior to anybody's individual interest in owning two, three, or perhaps even a thousand acres of fraudulently acquired property."

Marshall handled that, in part, by coming up with a doctrinal rule. Remember, we're considering different methods of interpretation. Here is a doctrinal method. Marshall said that an innocent third party purchaser—innocent, meaning that this person spent money for the property and had no knowledge of the underlying fraud—should be protected, even against the state's overwhelming interest in reclaiming the land. That is a powerful degree of protection for the property interest.

But that's not really why I'm interested in *Fletcher v. Peck;* because, as if we didn't know enough about how important the property was, Marshall says something that is genuinely extraordinary. He says that either basic constitutional principles or principles general in nature to the very nature of things would restrain the Georgia legislature from reclaiming the property.

Let me put that in a more succinct language. He says that either the Constitution prohibits Georgia from doing it, or more basic principles would, in the absence of any constitutional provision. Imagine a judge today saying, "I think the following is unconstitutional, perhaps because the Constitution actually prohibits it. But even if it doesn't, it should have prohibited it." What an extraordinary thing for a judge to say.

But Marshall said it, and even that's not the best part of *Fletcher v. Peck,* because the concurring justice isn't happy with that. The concurring justice says, "Not even God can violate the right to property." And that's not a paraphrase—well, it is a paraphrase—but it's not a misleading paraphrase. He says, "I would declare that Georgia action unconstitutional, not necessarily because the Constitution says so, but because there is a general principle in the nature of things—a principle that would bind even the Deity."

I'm not sure how to reconcile this in theological terms. If God can create property, then presumably, God can take it back; but not according to Justice Johnson. Property is so fundamental to the human order that not even God can violate the right to property; and, of course, if God can't violate the right to property, then there's no chance that Georgia can violate the right to property.

We are at the high water mark for the protection of private property in American constitutional history. It's difficult to imagine how you could have a more expansive protection for property than that described in *Fletcher v. Peck;* but that is the John Marshall Court, and twenty years later, John Marshall would no longer sit on the Court; he would be replaced by Chief Justice Roger Taney.

In his own way, Taney is also a commanding, towering figure in constitutional history; perhaps not quite as towering as Madison, perhaps not quite as towering as John Marshall, but then who would be? Taney's first important property case was one known as *Charles River Bridge v. Warren Bridge,* decided 27 years after *Fletcher,* in 1837.

In *Charles River Bridge*, the Court advanced a very, very different understanding of property. Let me briefly describe the facts to you. Those of you familiar with New England know that the Charles River cuts right through the middle of Cambridge and Boston, and on the Cambridge side is an august university known as Harvard. There has always been a Harvard, or, at least, almost always been a Harvard. In the early days, students got from Boston to Cambridge to attend John Harvard's Theological Seminary by ferryboat; but eventually, Boston and Cambridge agreed to build a bridge. That's bridge number one. It was a toll bridge. Some years later, perhaps because of increased traffic, Boston and Cambridge agreed to build a second bridge right next to the first bridge. It, too, would be a toll bridge, but only until cost to them recoup, and then it would be free.

Imagine you own the first bridge. It shouldn't be too difficult to understand that, at some point in the very near future, your bridge is not going to be a very productive economic asset, because the state has undermined it by agreeing to build this second bridge. So what do you do? It helps to recall that we are in the property section of the course. You sue the state or the other bridge company, claiming that your right to property, your right to profit from the first bridge, has been impaired by the state, in the same way that the state of Georgia impaired the ownership of lands by withdrawing title. I hope you can see that, in fact, notwithstanding different fact patterns, the issue in *Charles River Bridge* is not different at all from the issue in *Fletcher v. Peck*; indeed, not different from the issue in *Calder v. Bull.*

If you represented the first bridge company as an attorney, presumably, you would go scour the law books; you would find a particular method of constitutional interpretation—precedent—that you think will help you; and you'll turn up *Fletcher v. Peck, Calder v. Bull,* a number of other cases; and I think you'll advise your client that, on the strength of *Fletcher v. Peck,* in particular, you have a very good chance of winning this case.

Most attorneys know that if you advise a client that if you have a very good chance of winning a case, you have misspoken. You never speak in such absolutist terms. And, in point of fact, *Fletcher v. Peck* doesn't provide the appropriate precedent in this case. Or, I should say, to be more precise, the Court doesn't feel compelled in *Charles River Bridge* to follow the precedent in *Fletcher v. Peck.* Remember, the language in *Fletcher v. Peck* was about this sacred right to property. The language in this case, in *Charles River Bridge,* is stunningly different.

I quote now Chief Justice Taney, who rules in favor of the state; who rules that the state's interest in commerce trumps the private interest in property. Here is the quote:

> The object and end of all government is to promote the happiness and the prosperity of the community. While the rights of private property are sacredly guarded, we must not forget that the community also have rights.

Imagine the significance of what he's just said. Yes, there is a sacred right to private property; but the community, the state, the society, also has an interest; and sometimes, those interests (what would it be in this case? Presumably increased economic prosperity? Increased commerce between Boston and Cambridge?) sometimes trump the property interest.

And I can't help but think, is Massachusetts's interest in facilitating commerce between Cambridge and Boston more significant than Georgia's interest in reclaiming a million and a half acres of land? I don't mean to belittle the Massachusetts interest, but if the Georgia interest isn't sufficiently strong to overwhelm private property, I'm not sure I see why the Massachusetts interest should be that strong; but it is.

And it is important to understand that this is Chief Justice Taney's Court. Chief Justice Marshall has left the Court. It's a different point in American history. It is important to understand how dramatic a change occurred in the infrastructure of the United States between 1810 and 1837. We're talking about a period of remarkable economic expansion.

Taney's position is that that expansion will be retarded, might be completely forestalled, if every time an improvement to public facilities is made, somebody will have to be paid off because their earlier interest has now been harmed economically. Taney goes so far as to say that all public improvements will be halted. The old turnpike corporations, he suggests, will awaken from their slumbers and demand to be compensated every time a new road or a new bridge is constructed.

This introduces us to two important points. First, property waxes and wanes. Sometimes, it's protected more fervently by the Court; other times, the Court seems to assert its power on behalf of communal interest. Second, we have introduced now a method of constitutional interpretation that we haven't yet seen. Here we have a method of constitutional interpretation that suggests that the Court should account for different conceptions of what constitutes good public policy. That will be an important method of constitutional interpretation as we continue our surveys.

There's also an important dissent in *Charles River Bridge*. That dissent is by Joseph Story. I don't believe we've encountered Joseph Story yet. Joseph Story is among the greatest of American constitutional law scholars. Story's multivolume commentaries on the Constitution, produced in the 1800s, is still used by teachers and still consulted by judges. I continue to look for a first edition, but I don't look too hard, because I know I won't be able to afford it. It is a fantastically significant book because it is erudite, learned, and opinionated. One other thing you need to know about Joseph Story— he was John Marshall's closest confidante on the Court; I mean closest confidante in the sense of being a personal friend to John Marshall, but more importantly, an intellectual colleague. And I think we can say with a fair amount of certainty that, when Story wrote an opinion, it accurately reflected what John Marshall would have written, had he had the opportunity.

Joseph Story dissents. He would have preferred to uphold the original *Fletcher v. Peck* rule; and in direct response to Chief Justice Taney's insistence that we need this new conception of property to promote economic development, Story says "For my own part, I can conceive of no surer plan to arrest all public improvements than to make the outlay of capital uncertain." He's suggesting, in other words, that nobody will pony up the money if the state can undercut that investment at any point in the future.

I am not an economics professor. I know nothing about economics, to be honest; and I don't know whether Story's position is superior as a matter of economic theory or Taney's position is superior as a matter of economic theory. I do find it peculiar that judges are not arguing about a constitutional provision, so much as they are arguing about which understanding of that constitutional provision best promotes the economic prosperity and health of the Union—a fascinating claim. And behind that discussion, which might seem technical, is a more fundamental discussion about what kind of America, America will be.

Lecture Seven
Lochner v. New York and Economic Due Process

Scope:

As we saw in the last lecture, the Court's protection for private property has waxed and waned. In this lecture, we trace property through the 20th century, from the great case of *Munn v. Illinois* (1877) and the rise of economic due process in the infamous case of *Lochner v. New York* (1905) to the fall of that doctrine in *West Coast Hotel v. Parrish* (1937). We shall see that at its height, economic due process envisioned a Supreme Court aggressively committed to the protection of property. This commitment was premised on a particular understanding of property and of the proper role of the Court in a constitutional democracy. When the Court turned away from *Lochner*, it turned away from these larger understandings as well. The rejection of economic due process thus signaled the end of aggressive judicial scrutiny of state and federal economic activity in favor of an approach that reduces the role of courts in overseeing the regulation of property and, instead, entrusts such matters to legislatures.

Outline

I. *Charles River Bridge* initiated an era in which the Court was less protective of property rights and, instead, focused on the communal interest in regulating those rights.

   A. This doctrine was ratified in *Munn v. Illinois* (1877), which involved a lawsuit concerning the Grangers and the owners of grain silos in the state of Illinois. The state had passed a law regulating how much the silo owners could charge for storage of grain in elevators.

   1. The Court ruled that the public interest in this case overrode the property interest and that the property, to the extent that it was dedicated to a public purpose, was consequently subject to public regulation.

   2. In response, the owners argued that the determination of a "reasonable rate" for storage should be settled by judges. The Court ruled that for "abuses" in the regulation of private property, the aggrieved parties must

seek resolution in the legislature, not in the courts. Further, "For protection against abuses by legislatures, the people must resort to the polls."

3. Elaborating on the public use claim, Chief Justice Waite wrote: "Property becomes clothed with a public interest when it is used in a manner to make it of public consequence."

4. Justice Field wrote an important, sharply worded dissent: "This decision is subversive of private property."

B. *Munn* galvanized commercial interests to organize in opposition to state regulation of private property and to promote, instead, the doctrine of laissez-faire economics.

1. *Laissez-faire economics*, as we shall see, refers to a conception of the marketplace that leaves it free from most state regulation.

2. The American Bar Association was formed with the purpose of getting the Court to overrule *Munn*.

II. In the infamous case *Lochner v. New York* (1905), the Court embraced laissez-faire, ruling, under a doctrine known now as *economic due process*, that courts must protect property against "mere meddlesome interferences" by the state.

A. *Lochner* is infamous, at least in part, because the majority claimed that it could find "no reasonable ground" for the state law in question.

1. The law in question, based on *the police power*, limited the number of hours bakers could work in commercial bakeries. The Court found that this law interfered with the employer's and the employees' right to contract.

2. Justice Peckham's opinion for the majority invoked a type of argument lawyers like to call "the parade of horribles": If we permit the state to regulate the working conditions of bakers, then it will be allowed to regulate the working condition of almost every occupation.

3. The majority further claimed that the law could not be justified on any "reasonable" ground.

4. To most critics, the Court appears simply to substitute its judgment about sound public policy for the legislature's assessment.

B. In this sense, *Lochner* seems the opposite of *Munn*: Here, we have a Court determined to correct "abuses," instead of counseling the aggrieved interests to resort to the polls.

C. In a well-known dissent, Justice Holmes argued that the Court had no business deciding the case on an economic theory that was not in the Constitution proper. Holmes also announced that the Constitution "is made for people of fundamentally differing views...."

D. *Lochner* is infamous, in other words, because it appears that the Court acted, not on the basis of an identifiable constitutional principle, but, instead, on its own opinion about the utility, desirability, or wisdom of the law.

    1. This claim is based partly on the assumption that the Constitution does not privilege laissez-faire economics over any other economic theory.

    2. Consequently, the state legislature was well within its constitutional authority to regulate the workplace. A majority of the Court simply disagreed, as a matter of sound public policy, with the legislature's choice.

E. *Lochner* is also important because it stakes out a vision of the relationship between the individual and the community, a vision that reminds us of the Court's position in such cases as *Fletcher v. Peck*.

F. *Lochner* provided much of the ammunition down the road for the Supreme Court to declare key parts of President Roosevelt's New Deal program unconstitutional. In response to two Supreme Court decisions, President Roosevelt replied that he and the Congress were entitled constitutionally to act on their own understandings about the nature of their constitutional authority.

    1. This recalls, of course, our discussion earlier about the differences between departmentalism and judicial supremacy.

    2. In addition, the crisis gave rise to Roosevelt's ill-fated Court-packing plan, of which we shall hear more shortly.

III. Eventually, in the case of *West Coast Hotel v. Parrish* (1937), the Court rejected *Lochner* and the doctrine of economic due process, or the doctrine that judges must take special care to protect property rights.

    A. Chief Justice Hughes, writing for the majority, specifically noted that the liberty protected by the due process clause is a "liberty in a social organization which requires the protection of laws against the evils that menace the health, safety, morals, and welfare of the people."

    B. In addition, the Court noted, "Even if the wisdom of the policy … is debatable … still the legislature is entitled to its judgment."

IV. How do we explain the difference between *Lochner* and *West Coast Hotel*? Between the two cases is the Great Depression, and the Court took up *West Coast Hotel* in the midst of the controversy of President Roosevelt's Court-packing plan.

    A. The Court-packing plan was a reaction to several decisions following the logic of *Lochner*, in which the Court had declared unconstitutional key parts of President Roosevelt's New Deal.

    B. The Court reversed course after Roosevelt announced the plan, but there is evidence that the decision was made before the plan was announced.

    [**Correction to lecture**: Newspaper reports of the 1930s referring to the Supreme Court's reversal as "the switch in time that saved nine" played off, but did not predate, the much older, more familiar saying, "a stitch in time saves nine."]

    C. Perhaps the better explanation lies in the changing nature of society and changing beliefs about the proper relationship between the state and the market.

Essential Reading:

Munn v. Illinois (1877).

Lochner v. New York (1905).

West Coast Hotel v. Parrish (1937).

Kommers, Finn, and Jacobsohn, *American Constitutional Law*, chapter 5, pp. 188–192.

Supplementary Reading:

Howard Gillman, *The Constitution Besieged.*

Bernard Siegan, *Economic Liberties and the Constitution.*

Cass R. Sunstein, "*Lochner*'s Legacy," 87 *Columbia Law Review* 873 (1987).

Questions to Consider:

1. Does the Constitution give us any clear guidance about when the Court should defer to legislative choices or where to draw the line between private property and the public good? Why did Chief Justice Waite conclude in *Munn* that the Court should defer to the legislature? Why did the Court not defer to the legislature in *Lochner*?

2. Few decisions have been as sharply criticized as Peckham's majority opinion in *Lochner*. But what, precisely, was wrong with *Lochner*? Was the Court wrong to protect property against the powers of the state? Was it wrong because the Court substituted its judgment about sound public policy for the legislature's?

Lecture Seven—Transcript
Lochner v. New York and Economic Due Process

As we saw in the last lecture, the Court's protection for private property as a particular liberty interest has waxed and waned over time. In this lecture, we trace property through the 20th century, from the great case of *Munn v. Illinois*, decided in 1877, and the rise of economic due process in the infamous case of, and I use the word "infamous" deliberately, *Lochner v. New York*, decided in 1905; and to the fall of *Lochner* in *West Coast Hotel v. Parrish* in 1937. As we saw last time, *Charles River Bridge,* initiated an era in which the Court was less protective of property rights, and intended, instead, to focus on the communal interest in regulating those rights. The highlight of that particular approach to property, or the high point to that particular approach to property, was probably the case of *Munn v. Illinois*, decided in 1877.

Munn was a particularly interesting case in terms of its political dynamic. It involved a revolution, or a near-revolution, in any event, in the state of Illinois, where Grangers, a political party devoted to the protection of farmers' interest, had managed to overtake the state government. The Grangers were committed to economic justice for farmers; and once they assumed power, they changed Illinois's state law in various ways designed to protect the economic interest of farmers, as opposed to the economic interest of their creditors. One thing they did, in particular, was to determine that regulation for the price of storage in grain silo elevators—where vast hordes of grain would be stored communally—would be set by the state legislature instead of by the grain silo owners. This represented a dramatic change in the economic structure of the farming economy in Illinois and other Midwestern states.

Imagine for a minute, however, that you own one of those grain silos. Instead of charging what you want for the storage of grain, the state of Illinois is now telling you what an appropriate fee will be. Naturally, under such conditions, you will consult legal advice, and the legal counselors at your disposal will undoubtedly recommend that you sue. You will sue the state of Illinois, and you will claim that the state of Illinois, by regulating your degree of profit, has interfered with your constitutionally protected right to property.

At the highest level of abstraction, there is nothing different in *Munn v. Illinois* than any other case we have considered. Every case we have considered, *Munn* included, represents a tension, a conflict, between the rights of property owners and the rights of the community more generally. This is an interesting case because the Court built on, or reaffirmed, its position in *Charles River Bridge*. Here, the Court ruled that if there are, in fact, abuses in the regulation of private property, the aggrieved party (in this case, the elevator owners) should not turn to the Court for their redress of their civil liberty, but should, instead, go to the state legislature.

I want to quote the Chief Justice in *Munn*: "For protection against abuses by legislatures, the people must resort to the polls." What an extraordinary claim that is! If the legislative process has abused your civil liberty, your liberty interest, your property interest, don't turn to judges and ask to have that behavior or that action declared unconstitutional; but instead, use the political process to seek redress. Hiding here is a particular vision about under what conditions and when the Court should step in to protect civil liberties. Presumably, although the Court does not say this, one seeks the redress that is available from the courts only once one has failed to seek redress in the political process. And actually, I don't think that's quite right, because surely the Court doesn't want to say, "You must first go to the political process, lose, and then come to us." Losing is a natural, but not inevitable, consequence of some political conflict. Presumably, the Court wants to make a slightly different claim that "Even if you lose in the political process, you're not entitled to our help. You're entitled to our help only if there is something fundamentally flawed in the political process that would keep you from having a fair chance."

There is another aspect of *Munn* that I think is really quite interesting. The Chief Justice writes the following: "Property becomes clothed with a public interest when it is used in a manner to make it of public consequence." What he says is the following: "If you use your property in a way that causes it to have a significant impact on a public interest, then to that degree, and to that extent, your property is no longer private—or at least, purely private—but is instead subject to public regulation." There is an interesting sense in which the more private your property is, the less authority the state has to regulate it; but the more public it is, the greater the extent of the state to regulate it.

Following is a fascinating opinion made more fascinating, I believe, by an important dissent by Justice Field. This is a short, easy to understand dissent. It may be summarized in one quote from Justice Field's opinion: "This decision is subversive of private property." He might be right about that. It's a judgment call—they are all judgment calls—but I hope you can understand his extent to which you use your property is also the degree to which the state may regulate it; then, perhaps, you don't really own the property in any meaningful sense at all. What kinds of property could you possibly own that wouldn't have some public consequence? If you have a house, and you fail to mow your lawn, that, arguably, has a public consequence. If you own a house, and you paint it garishly, that might have a public consequence.

Almost any form of property you might own is likely to have an impact in some way, in some fashion, in some form, on some larger public interest. For me, this suggests that there is something inherently peculiar about the very phrase "private property." Under what conditions is property ever genuinely private? So, when Chief Justice Field says, "Property becomes clothed with a public interest when it is used in a manner to make it of public consequence," my initial thought is, when is property ever not clothed with a public interest on that term?

Nevertheless, I think we can see that the decision is fairly consistent with *Charles River Bridge*. It is a decision, in other words, that weighs a balance between private interest and public interest squarely on the side of the public's interest.

Munn, however, is important for yet another reason. *Munn* galvanized commercial interests in the United States to organize in opposition to the state regulation of private property. Those commercial interests wish to promote a different understanding of economic regulation. We now know that understanding as the doctrine of laissez-faire economics. And at the risk of butchering this definition, I will define it simply as, laissez-faire economics believes that the regulating hand of the state ought to be kept off the marketplace altogether, or at least most of the time.

Parenthetically, I said *Munn* galvanized certain kinds of economic interests or commercial interests to organize. One of those interests was the American Bar Association. The American Bar Association was founded with one single purpose: to get the courts to overrule *Munn v. Illinois.* Eventually, that purpose was realized. In the infamous case of *Lochner v. New York* (decided in 1905), the Court embraced the doctrine of laissez-faire economics. It developed a doctrine, or at least contributed to the development of a doctrine that we now call "economic due process," a fancy phrase for a simple concept.

The simple concept is this: under economic due process, courts are entrusted with the authority to oversee, or to supervise, a state's regulation of the marketplace, and to set aside any state regulation that it thinks is a violation of property rights or property interest.

In other words, economic due process describes a philosophy and a period in American history in which American courts, or at least the federal courts, believed that they had the ultimate authority to oversee any state regulation of the marketplace and to disqualify or to rule unconstitutional any state regulation that it thought violated the premises of laissez-faire. And that's perhaps too theoretical, so let's bring it down to ground and discuss precisely what happened in *Lochner v. New York.*

Lochner involved a law, passed by the New York state legislature, designed to protect bakers who work in commercial baking establishments. It limited the number of hours a baker could work in any particular week, as well as regulated certain aspects of wages and other terms of employment. Such laws are ubiquitous now. There is hardly an occupation now that isn't subject to some similar state regulation. But in 1905, these regulations were novel.

In *Lochner v. New York,* a bakery owner sued the state, or challenged the constitutionality of this law, claiming that it interfered with his "right to contract"—we would call that a right to property—his right to engage in particular contractual formations with his employees, and the owner also claimed that it interfered with his employees' rights to enter into terms of employment, to enter into contracts with him, as well. The Court called this, at one point, a "right to liberty," at other points, "a right to contract;" but in contemporary understandings, it would be the "right to property," because what's involved here is monetary compensation for employment—the classic form of property.

Now, on what ground could this possibly be unconstitutional? There are always two questions we ought to consider when we decide these kinds of cases, or when we begin to assess these kinds of cases. First, what is the interest involved? What is the constitutional liberty claimed? And, as we have seen, it's a straightforward property claim. The other thing we always need to consider—and this is hinted at by *Fletcher,* hinted at by *Calder,* hinted at by *Munn*—that we must always consider what interest the state proffers for its regulation.

Every state has something called the "police power." The police power refers to the constitutional authority of government—of a state, in this instance—"To regulate the health, safety, welfare, and morals of the community." And New York claimed to exercise its police power to protect the health of individual bakers; as well as the quality of the bread supply; as well as the quality of public welfare, more generally. This is a classic conflict. The interest of the state in protecting the health of certain kinds of employees and protecting the public health, more generally, as opposed to the private interest in property.

Following *Munn,* this ought to be a fairly easy case. Surely, bakery owners have "clothed their property with a public interest." We all have an interest in the quality of bread. We all have an interest in making sure that employees don't suffer. Under the *Munn* test, it seems reasonably clear, I would propose, that the New York legislature's law regulating the marketplace ought to stand. It doesn't seem to raise any particular constitutional objection. And precisely because it seems like an easy case (remember many lectures ago I did say that there are some things called "easy cases") the court ruled the other way.

I suggested that *Lochner* is infamous. I use "infamous" in the same sense that we might call other Supreme Court cases "infamous," such as *Dred Scott v. Sanford,* or *Plessy v. Ferguson,* or *Korematsu v. United States*—all cases we will address at some point. And, in that sense, "infamous" simply means, "We look back, and perhaps we are embarrassed or mortified or, at least, ashamed of a court's decision; or at least we would question its wisdom." I don't think it's unreasonable to put *Lochner* in the same category, but perhaps for different reasons. Let me go into Justice Peckham's opinion for the court, and then I'll tell you why it might be a problem.

In his opinion for the court, Justice Peckham ruled that laws such as the New York state's statute are, "mere meddlesome interferences with the right to property," which is just about as profound a discounting of the state's interest as one could possibly imagine.

Peckham continued, "There is no contention [by the state, he means] that bakers, as a class of individuals, are stupider than other human beings, or need the protecting arm of the state to a greater degree than any other class of workers."

He goes on to say, "If we can protect bakers, then sure, the state will have the constitutional authority to protect tinsmiths, lawyers, doctors, nurses, and just about every other capacity or form of human occupation." Lawyers like to call these kinds of arguments, "the parade of horribles." If we permit this, then the following parade of horrible things will happen. "We can't allow the state to regulate the working conditions of bakers, because then it will be allowed to regulate the working condition of almost every occupation."

Now why would that be infamous? Most scholars and most judges think that the profound difficulty in Peckham's opinion is simply this: he wrote into the Constitution a particular economic theory, that economic theory being laissez-faire economics; and, indeed, on a theory of laissez-faire economics, the opinion makes a certain amount of sense. Remember, laissez-faire economics stands for the proposition that the state ought not to regulate the marketplace, particularly if there is no obviously good reason for doing so. And Peckham's view—a majority of the Court's view—found that there was obviously no good reason for regulating this particular aspect of the marketplace. Peckham went on to say that the majority "could find no reasonable ground" for the legislation.

Think about that for a minute: "No reasonable ground"? Could it really be the case that the New York state legislature had no reasonable ground at all for the passage of this statute? But that is precisely what the Court concluded.

I hope now you can begin to see what the difficulty is, and why *Lochner* is infamous. It's infamous for this simple reason: it appears to most observers that Peckham, writing for a majority of the Court, simply substituted his judgment about what good economic theory required for that of the New York state legislature. I want to be very clear about this. If there were a provision in the Constitution that clearly articulated a laissez-faire understanding of the marketplace, then Peckham could say, "I have no opinion about which theory of economics is the best one. I know only that the Constitution commands me to use this one."

That isn't what he said. He didn't say it for one simple reason: there is no theory of laissez-faire economics in the Constitution! There's arguably no economic theory at all, and for him to choose one is to commit the most awful of constitutional sins. That sin is simply this: he substituted his own judgment for the judgment of the legislature. To put it in somewhat more sophisticated terms, he just made it up.

No judge is ever permitted to simply substitute his or her theory about what justice requires or what economic theory requires to that of the legislature if the Constitution doesn't clearly command that judge to do so.

The great sin that makes *Lochner* infamous is this: it represents judges bending, mangling, ignoring the Constitution, and replacing their judgment about sound public policy for that of the legislature. It is an affront to the basic premises of constitutional and democratic theory, more generally. We live in a political system where the following must be an uncontested truth: judges may only act when there is a clear, constitutional authority, a clear constitutional warrant for their opinions.

Lochner is infamous because it represents a great failure of constitutional interpretation, perhaps the greatest failure there can be—failure to be faithful to the actual terms of the Constitution itself; failure to understand that a judge traces his or her authority to what can be found in the text; to what can be found in the Constitution, more broadly; and to nowhere else.

Justice Holmes wrote a blistering dissent. First, Justice Holmes argued that the Court had absolutely no business deciding the case upon an economic theory that could not be found in the Constitution proper. Holmes argued that if it were simply a question of which economic theory was the best one, that he'd like to take his time and study it. But he did not understand that it was his job, as a judge interpreting the Constitution, to engage in those kinds of questions.

That field of study was opened to him as a private individual, not open as a legitimate constitutional inquiry to a judge.

Holmes went on to scold the majority in the following way. Holmes announced that, "The Constitution is made for people of fundamentally differing views...." And, of course, what he is suggesting is that we all might have very different views about what the proper relationship is between the state and the marketplace. And unless the Constitution clearly articulates that one understanding is superior to another, then it is no business of judges to simply impose their view on the rest of us.

Lochner is so infamous that it's no longer just a name for a badly decided case. *Lochner* has long since transcended that triviality. *Lochner* has assumed a position as a verb, as an insult. As you read cases later for this lecture and for subsequent lectures, you'll occasionally see one judge accuse another judge of "Lochnerizing." To "Lochnerize" is to commit the cardinal sin: to substitute your own opinion for what the Constitution requires. And I hope it's obvious that, when one judge accuses another judge of Lochnerizing, it's not a compliment; it's perhaps the most fundamental insult one constitutional judge can level at the door of another constitutional judge. Because it is such a powerful claim, shorthand for the gravest of constitutional errors, we will read more cases than we will be able to recall where the majority opinion starts off by saying, "We are not Lochnerizing!"—which ought to be a clue that it is at least possible that they really are Lochnerizing. What's at stake over, "I'm not Lochnerizing!" "Yes, you are Lochnerizing!" is a fundamental understanding about what the proper role of the judges is in a constitutional democracy.

That's at the level of high-constitutional theory. Let's bring it down to the level of everyday politics. *Lochner* provided the ammunition, 20, 30 years down the road, for the Supreme Court to declare much of President Roosevelt's New Deal reconstruction program unconstitutional. Remember what the premise is behind *Lochner*— that judges can strike down economic statutes based on their disagreement with the underlying economic theory; and if laissez-faire economics is fundamentally about "hands-off" by the state, the New Deal reconstruction assumes the state has a grave, perhaps primary responsibility for overseeing the marketplace. You might call this Keynesian economics or social welfare economics.

Whatever label you attach to it, the New Deal economic program understood the relationship of the state to the economy in ways that were fundamentally incompatible with laissez-faire economics—the kind of economics embraced by the Court in *Lochner*. And in a series of important cases, the Supreme Court did declare key parts of Roosevelt's reconstruction program unconstitutional. This provoked a constitutional crisis of the highest order.

Now, you'll recall in an earlier lecture, when we were talking about judicial review in *Marbury,* that there is an understanding of constitutional interpretation and judicial review called "departmentalism." This theory of departmentalism holds that every branch, at least of the federal government, is co-equal in its authority as a constitutional interpreter.

Think about that application to Roosevelt. Roosevelt responds to the Supreme Court in a variety of different ways. One is to send the exact same legislation that the Court declared unconstitutional back to the same congressional committee that reported it, with a note. And the note says, "I do hope you won't let considerations of constitutionality influence your judgment about whether this legislation ought to be passed." What a polite, elegant, refined way of saying, "Ignore the Court. I want this legislation. I don't care if it's unconstitutional. You go ahead and pass it anyway." I say it's polite, refined, and elegant, but it's not unusual. Many presidents will have encouraged Congresses to act in the same way.

Roosevelt has another plan, and I suppose it's fair to call this plan "infamous" in the same way we called *Lochner* infamous; it's the infamous Court Packing Plan. We don't need to know the details. As a matter of general description, the Court Packing Plan was an effort by Roosevelt to persuade some of the members of the Supreme Court to resign their positions. Once they had reached a particular age, according to the plan, they would either resign and they couldn't be replaced; or the president would have the opportunity to appoint another justice. And it's difficult to calculate how this plan would have worked, in particular, but some scholars have suggested that, if nobody retired under his plan, that Roosevelt might have had as many as six new appointments, and the Court would have risen from nine justices to fifteen. Presumably, the new justices would be more sympathetic, and the Court would change its mind.

The Court did change its mind, but not because of the Court Packing Plan. As it turns out, the plan failed, and it's difficult to know precisely why the plan failed. I think one argument is simply that Roosevelt oversold it. He went to the nation and, in a fireside address, argued that it was necessary to save the country from the Court, that it was necessary to save us all from hardened judicial arteries. I am inclined to think that he simply oversold the rhetoric, and that in some ways, the rhetoric might have struck many Americans as being deeply offensive.

But there's another, perhaps, more important reason why the plan failed. That is because the Supreme Court did, in fact, change its mind. In the important case of *West Coast Hotel v. Parrish* (decided in 1937), the Court rejected *Lochner,* and rejected the doctrine of economic due process more generally. In other words, it rejected the understanding in *Lochner,* and in some of the earlier cases we saw, that judges must take special care to protect property rights. Chief Justice Hughes, writing for the majority, specifically noted that the liberty protected by the Due Process Clause is "liberty in a social organization, which requires the protection of laws against the evils that menace the health, safety, morals, and welfare of the people." In addition, Chief Justice Hughes said the following: "Even if the wisdom of the policy…is debatable…still the legislature is entitled to its judgment."

Now let me sort of backtrack here for a second. I want you to see the change. We start with *Munn;* and in *Munn,* the language is very similar to the language used by Chief Justice Hughes in *West Coast Hotel v. Parrish.* Remember the Court in *Munn* said, "For abuses of property, the people must turn to the polls." What does Chief Justice Hughes say? "Even if the wisdom of the policy…is debatable…still the legislature is entitled to its judgment."

If we could draw a straight line between *Munn* and *West Coast Hotel v. Parrish,* we'd have cases that are fundamentally consistent with each other, that rest on a fundamental understanding about the limited role of judges in a constitutional democracy. What disrupts our straight line is *Lochner,* and the line of *Lochner* cases, where the Court entrusts to itself special authority to displace those legislated choices, because they think those choices are not sufficiently protected of the right of private property. So, in *West Coast Hotel v. Parrish*, the Court upheld the Washington state minimum wage law that, in most respects, was indistinguishable from the law that the Court had struck down in *Lochner*.

One final historical oddity; many of you will have heard of the phrase "a stitch in time saves nine," or some such? That phrase originally originated around the Supreme Court's change. It was said that a switch in time saves nine. The theory here is that the Court's change of position in *West Coast Hotel* took all the energy, deflated all the air from the balloon from the Court Packing Plan; that the Court Packing Plan was no longer necessary, because the Court caved to presidential or to public pressure. We now know that that's not literally true. The Court had actually changed its mind internally before the Court Packing Plan was proposed; but it does suggest, in a larger sense, that the Court always does have it's eyes, or at least one eye, on public perceptions at large.

Lecture Eight
The Takings Clause of the Fifth Amendment

Scope:

The Court's rejection of economic due process has meant that the right to property, arguably the most important of rights at the founding, is substantially less important than it once was. As we shall see in this lecture, however, a few cases arising under the Fifth Amendment's takings clause suggest that the right to property may be more robust. In such cases as *Nollan v. California Coastal Commission* (1987), *Lucas v. South Carolina Coastal Council* (1992), and *Tahoe-Sierra Preservation Council v. Tahoe Regional Planning Agency* (2002), the Court hinted that it may begin to scrutinize takings more closely, though it has yet to agree about exactly what standard it should employ or why. In contrast, in *Kelo v. New London* (2005), a sharply divided Court upheld a decision by a municipal government to use its power of eminent domain to take private property and to transfer it to private developers, based on the assumption that the economic benefits of such development would accrue to all residents.

Outline

I. The Court's position of deference to legislative choices has remained largely unchanged since *West Coast Hotel*. As a consequence, many critics contend that property, once the most prominent of rights, is of little constitutional weight.

    A. The rejection of economic due process, like the Court's earlier contraction of the contracts clause, is grounded partly in a particular understanding of the relationship between the individual and the community.

        1. The current doctrinal rules tell us that in property cases, the Court asks but one question: Is the regulation at issue rational?

        2. This test is about as relaxed as one can imagine. The test is not whether the legislature had a rational purpose in mind when it passed the legislation but whether any sane adult can provide a rational reason for the policy or rule.

B. As we have seen, this test is grounded on a particular and limited understanding about the authority of judges in a constitutional democracy.

II. In a few cases, however, the Court has seemed to suggest that some elements of private property warrant greater judicial protection.

   A. Three cases in particular seem to show a Court intent upon giving weight to another provision in the Constitution, the takings clause, designed to protect private property.

      1. The clause states: "Private property may not be taken for public use without just compensation."

      2. What does it mean to "take" property?

      3. What constitutes a public use as opposed to a private use?

      4. Is there any constitutionally derived standard that would allow us to distinguish between just compensations and unjust compensations?

   B. These are difficult questions. But there is another issue, at least as important, that we must also consider: Who gets to decide?

   C. In *Nollan v. California Coastal Commission* (1987), the Supreme Court concluded that there was not a substantial "nexus" between a condition imposed on a homeowner seeking to expand his beachfront cottage and the end this condition was meant to promote, in this case, greater beachfront access for the community.

      1. The commission had imposed an easement as a condition for a permit to improve a beachfront property. The easement was intended to preserve public access to the beachfront.

      2. As I said, the Court struck down the easement. In doing so, it seemed to use a somewhat more stringent version of the rationality test.

   D. In *Lucas v. South Carolina Coastal Council* (1992), the Court again seemed to give more teeth to the takings clause, this time holding that it would require local officials to "do more than proffer the legislature's declaration" as a reason for regulation.

1. *Lucas* involved a property owner who sought to develop a coastal lot in South Carolina. The state, however, had put a moratorium on development, ostensibly to protect the dune environment and to prevent beach erosion.
2. Lucas claimed that the moratorium in effect had "taken" his property—even though Lucas still owned it, and the state did not physically take his property, e.g., through the power of eminent domain.
3. The Court, writing through Justice Scalia, agreed. The Court announced that such "temporary takings," if they deprived an owner of 100 percent of the value of his land, would run afoul of the takings clause.

E. In *Tahoe-Sierra Preservation Council v. Tahoe Regional Planning Agency* (2002), the Court concluded that a moratorium on housing development was not necessarily a "temporary" taking under *Lucas*.

III. The divisions evidenced in these cases continue to fracture the Court, as witnessed in *Kelo v. New London* (2005).

A. In this case, a sharply divided Court ruled, 5–4, that a city may take private property and transfer it to a private corporation for development and, in so doing, satisfy the "public use" requirement of the Fifth Amendment.

B. Writing for the majority, Justice Stevens concluded: "The city has carefully formulated an economic development that it believes will provide appreciable benefits to the community, including—but by no means limited to—new jobs and increased tax revenue."

C. The Court also noted: "For more than a century, our public use jurisprudence has wisely eschewed rigid formulas and intrusive scrutiny in favor of affording legislatures broad latitude in determining what public needs justify the use of the takings power."

D. In a sharply worded dissent, Justice O'Connor, joined by Rehnquist, Scalia, and Thomas, wrote: "Any property may now be taken for the benefit of another private party, but the fallout from this decision will not be random." There are two important claims here.

1. First, it might now be the case that you can, in fact, take property from A and give it to B, but I suspect that is a gross overstatement. In this case, the city did appear to have a plan for economic development.
2. Second, *Kelo* appears to have started up the process of constitutional dialogue, thus reminding us that it is not courts alone that give the Constitution meaning. Following *Kelo*, several states have begun to consider legislation that would limit the authority of public officials to take property to facilitate economic development.

IV. This concludes our examination of the right to property. Here, then, we should ask: What is the status of property as a constitutional liberty? We can say with reasonable accuracy, I think, that property is no longer the "great fence to liberty" that it was at the founding. If it is no longer the lynchpin to the constitutional order, then what, if anything, is?

Essential Reading:

Nollan v. California Coastal Commission (1987).

Lucas v. South Carolina Coastal Council (1992).

Tahoe-Sierra Preservation Council v. Tahoe Regional Planning Agency (2002).

Kelo v. New London (2005).

Kommers, Finn, and Jacobsohn, *American Constitutional Law*, chapter 5, pp. 192–193.

Supplementary Reading:

Richard Epstein, *Takings: Private Property and the Power of Eminent Domain*.

Questions to Consider:

1. All property cases involve disputes about the limits of individual liberty and the demands of community. How does the Court weigh the balance in these three takings cases? Should the balance differ depending on whether the case arises under the takings clause or the due process clause of the Fourteenth Amendment?

2. Consider the majority opinion and the dissent by Chief Justice Rehnquist in the *Tahoe* case: Which opinion best advances sound public policy? Should the Court consider such issues?

Lecture Eight—Transcript
The Takings Clause of the Fifth Amendment

The Court's rejection of economic due process, whatever its wisdom, has meant that the right to property, arguably the most important of the rights of the Founding, is substantially less important than it once was. I want to give you just a little bit of doctrine to underscore the change. Under the current doctrinal rules, a state's regulation of private property will be constitutionally permissible, as long as the state's action is rational. And it might not be a bad idea to go back to some of the earlier cases we considered, such as *Calder v. Bull, Fletcher*, or *Lochner*, and ask ourselves this simple question: Was the state's action in any of those cases rational? Now, before you actually try to apply that test, let me give you just a little bit of background on this so-called rationality test.

First, this is the test that this Court in 2005 actually applies. When any kind of property case comes to the Court, the Court will go through this doctrinal evolution. It will ask itself, what is the nature of the interest? Is it a property interest? What is the nature of the state's interest? And then, is the regulation designed to protect that interest rational?

Secondly, the Court's definition of rational is truly expansive. There are few things, if any, that the Court will be prepared to call irrational. The test isn't whether you think it's rational. The test isn't whether I think it's rational. The test is whether any sane adult located at any place might think that this is a rational regulation. I hope you can see how far we have come from the Founding. It is, of course, an exaggeration, but for purposes of illustration, let me exaggerate: Property is no longer a significant constitutional liberty. You might as well write it out of the Bill of Rights. Now remember, that's an exaggeration; but only a slight exaggeration, and one that I think is warranted by theatrical license.

All of that said, there have been hints in a series of cases, starting in the late 1980s through now, through 2005, in which the Court has suggested that it might resuscitate property. I don't want to overstate this case; the Court's position of deference to legislative choices has remained largely unchanged since *West Coast Hotel v. Parrish*. In a few cases, however, involving a different constitutional provision, the Court has seemed a little uncertain. That constitutional provision is one we have not yet spoken of, the Takings Clause. Let me quote for you what the Takings Clause says: "Private property may not be taken for public use without just compensation."

There are a number of interesting questions that immediately suggest themselves. What does it mean to "take" property? We'll see that the Court has struggled with this. Second, assuming the Court allows a taking, the next issue would be, what constitutes a public use, as opposed, perhaps, to a private use? And then there's a third obvious question: If private property may not be taken for public use without just compensation, obviously we will want to know who decides whether the compensation is just, and is there any standard, constitutionally derived, that would allow us to distinguish between just compensations and unjust compensations?

These are all difficult constitutional questions, all difficult questions of constitutional interpretation. Behind them all is one that puts those questions to shame. The overarching question, the one question that we have been fundamentally concerned with over the past three lectures is simply this: Who gets to decide? What we have seen is a contest between two different answers to that question. Sometimes the answer is that, fundamentally, it is the legislature that gets to decide. Sometimes—as suggested by *Lochner*—it is the courts that get to decide these questions. What is involved here, then, in every case—although it may not seem immediately obvious—is a dispute—perhaps a better word would be dialogue—between different branches of government about who bears final institutional responsibility for regulating the relationship between this individual liberty of property and the public interest more generally.

Let me suggest a couple of these cases to you, but I would like to do them quickly. Perhaps the first important case that suggested a reworking in the Court's philosophy of property came in 1987, in a well-known case called *Nollan v. California Coastal Commission*. We don't need to spend a lot of time with the facts here. Briefly put, a homeowner desired to expand dramatically his beachfront cottage in California. It went to a zoning commission and to something called a coastal commission in California. The Coastal Commission decided that this homeowner would be free to erect a substantial addition to his cottage, but only if the homeowner satisfied a particular condition. This particular condition was to grant the community an easement (an easement is simply a right-of-way) behind, past his house, to the publicly owned beach.

Now, there was a reason that the California Coastal Commission imposed this requirement. If we read their records, we will find that the commission was concerned that the continued expansion of private homes on the coast would ultimately hide the coast from public view, and might, inadvertently, at least, tell citizens, or lead citizens, into thinking that they didn't have a right of access. So, by guaranteeing this easement, this right-of-way, the California Coastal Commission was hoping to preserve public access to the beaches.

I am fairly confident that, under the traditional rationality test, this is a rational stated interest; and I am reasonably confident that, using the Court's loose rationality test, that this is a rational way—imposing an easement—of achieving that interest.

Nevertheless, the Court struck down the easement. Arguing that there was not "a substantial nexus" between the condition imposed on the homeowner and the greater end, i.e., preserving greater beachfront access for the community. In the abstract, we could probably have an interesting dispute about whether this is really a rational state goal, and whether it is a rational state means for achieving that goal; but I think it is reasonably clear that, under the old rationality test, that there was very little room for doubt.

Remember, the whole point of the rationality test, as developed after *West Coast Hotel,* was for the Court to disabuse itself of constantly overseeing state regulations of property. The point of the rationality test was to conserve judicial power for those rare cases when there would be an abuse and that abuse could not be corrected—to hearken back all the way to *Charles River Bridge* or to *Munn v. Illinois*— when that abuse could not be corrected through normal legislative channels, or through the normal political process.

It is, I think, very difficult to reconcile the heart and the soul of *Nollan v. California Coastal Commission* with some of the Court's earlier property cases. Still, it was only one case, and it did involve a different provision of the Constitution.

The Court continued this course in a subsequent case called *Lucas v. South Carolina Coastal Council,* decided in 1992. *Lucas* is a very interesting case. Loosely speaking, the facts were these: in *Lucas,* an individual purchased a parcel of land located directly on the South

Carolina coast. This individual desired to subdivide the land, and to then develop the land into private housing. After he purchased the land, he submitted his development plans to the appropriate authorities. The Coastal Council rejected his plan, largely because it was concerned about the effects of overdevelopment on the dune coast of South Carolina.

I want to be careful here; these are Takings Clause cases. Where was the taking in *Nollan*? They didn't literally take the property away; they influenced how the homeowner could use the property. And they are not literally taking away Lucas' ocean front property; they are simply imposing a set of conditions about how he can utilize that property.

Now, Lucas went to court arguing that what had happened in *Nollan* was similar to what had happened in his case. He described these as "temporary takings." Presumably, at some point in the future, South Carolina might change its mind; indeed, it had only put a temporary moratorium on development. At some point in the future, presumably, Lucas would be permitted to develop the land. We are not sure precisely when that would be, but the state didn't physically take his property through the power of eminent domain, for example. Lucas still owns the property.

Lucas makes another claim that is attached to the temporary taking claim. Now his claim is this: the temporary taking has deprived me of the entire economic value of my property. I purchased it for one reason only—to develop it. I can't develop it; it is worthless. The Court was very sympathetic to the claims proffered by Lucas. Indeed, the Court went on to say that, under the Takings Clause, there could be such a thing as a temporary taking, which is a fascinating idea. The Court was even more sympathetic to Lucas by concluding that, in those cases where temporary taking had occurred, if the state had, in fact, deprived the property owner of the complete economic value of the property in question, that that owner—in this case Lucas—would be entitled to just compensation by the state.

Now plug in the doctrinal language that we have used a few times now. Was the South Carolina decision rational? Almost certainly it was. It seems reasonably clear, on the strength of these two cases, that the Court, without having entirely developed a constitutional theory for how it was acting, was intent on resuscitating some protections for property.

If there is one clear rule that we can take out of *Lucas,* it is this: When the state temporarily takes property, it must deprive you of 100 percent of the value of the property. The Court stressed this point in *Lucas,* and in subsequent cases. At the risk of hitting this point too hard and too often, I want to stress that a state regulatory decision that deprives you of 90 percent of your property will not get you compensation. Ninety-five percent is not good enough. It has to be 100 percent. You can imagine the criticisms that have since been leveled at this kind of rule. When, if ever, is property completely valueless?

It is easy to feel sympathetic for Lucas. He bought property, presumably paid a premium for it, with an understanding that he would be able to develop it and sell it for more money. Now he is being told he can't do anything with it.

But if Lucas were here, I would like to ask him, "Will you give me your property? I don't want to pay you for it; I just want you to give it to me, because it is valueless after all. It is worth no more to you than a hair that fell out of your head."

Or I'd like to be hired as an economic advisor to Lucas. I'd say, "I'm sorry. Life has dealt you a tough blow, but why don't we put up a fence. At the fence we'll put a gate; and by the gate we'll put a little tollbooth; and the tollbooth will have a sign on the top; and the sign will say 'Picnic here for the day. Watch the birds. Five dollars an hour.'" I know birders who will happily pay five dollars an hour for an unobstructed viewing on an undeveloped coast. Or maybe it will say, "Come see the last unspoiled part of South Carolina. Get it while it lasts. Buy your bottle of Dasani here, but please make sure you cart it out when you leave to preserve the unspoiled beauty of this last patch of virgin land." Is the land truly 100 percent valueless? Perhaps I'm carping.

It's reasonably clear, however, what the next case will involve, isn't it? Because, if the rule is going to be 100 percent constitutes a violation, how long will it take for some enterprising attorney to say, "Is there really a significant constitutional difference between 100 percent and 98 percent? Or 96 percent? Or 82 percent? Maybe, if it's only 82 percent, I should not get 100 percent compensation, but maybe I should at least get 82 percent compensation. Maybe it ought to be a sliding scale." Of course it's inevitable that these are the kinds of cases that will occur.

The Court addressed the issue again in 2002, in a case with the impossibly long name of *The Tahoe-Sierra Preservation Council v. The Tahoe Regional Planning Agency.* You can imagine what this case involved; somebody wanted to develop property near Lake Tahoe, and the Tahoe Preservation Council had decided that development was threatening the pristine integrity of the Lake Tahoe region, and imposed a moratorium on development—not a permanent ban on development, a moratorium. And the word, "moratorium" tells us that we are again dealing with a temporary taking under the terms of the Takings Clause.

The Court argued amongst itself; issued a lot of different opinions; and concluded, without a clear constitutional rule, that this was not actually a temporary taking. Why? We can't be sure. These cases appear to be driven by facts, by the unique complex of facts in every case, and not so much by general constitutional rules. Those constitutional rules, if they are going to be developed, are in their earliest stages.

These rules, if they exist at all, were applied by the Court again in the controversial case *Kelo v. New London,* decided in 2005. *Kelo* is a remarkably complicated case. It shows a Court deeply fractured over the most basic issues involving private property and the limits of judicial power.

In *Kelo,* a sharply divided Court, 5–4, ruled that a city—in this case, New London, Connecticut—may take private property—in this case, houses, homes—and transfer it to a private corporation. Why? The city council had a theory. The theory was this: If we take these properties through the power of eminent domain, and give them to a private corporation, the private corporation may develop that property commercially; thus increasing the tax space for the town at large, and thus benefiting the citizenry at large.

Remember, I asked you earlier to think about the three questions that are critical to any taking inquiry. What does it mean to take? Fortunately, that's not much of an issue in *Kelo.* It was in *Nollan* and *Lucas,* where we addressed the concept of temporary taking. So here we have a permanent taking.

And we have a different issue. The second question we must always ask with taking cases is: What is a public use? And, throughout most of American constitutional history, the underlying assumption (but it has only been an assumption) is that a public use means that a public authority takes the land. That's not quite what happened here. Public authority did take the land, but immediately transferred it to a private corporation.

And now we reach all the way back to *Calder v. Bull*, the first property case we decided, and you'll recall that Justice Chase said that if there was one thing that was unequivocally clear, it's that the state may never take property from A and give it to B. But arguably, that is precisely what happened in *Kelo*. The state's defense, of course is, "Well, we didn't take it just to take it. We're not trying to benefit B so much as we're trying to benefit the community at large."

And you can see, I hope, too, that the underlying question in *Kelo,* as it is in all takings cases, is, who ultimately is going to be responsible for adjudicating the constitutionality of this decision by this small city? Writing for the majority, Justice Stevens wrote the following: "The city has carefully formulated an economic development plan that it believes will provide appreciable benefits to the community, including—but by no means limited to—new jobs and increased tax revenue." Surely that would satisfy almost any version of the rationality test.

That is not the key part of *Kelo*. The key part is what the majority said next: "For more than a century, our public use jurisprudence has wisely eschewed rigid formulas and intrusive scrutiny in favor of affording legislatures broad latitude in determining what public needs justify the use of the takings power." I hope it's clear what he's saying. For more than a century, judges have ruled that they should not closely supervise, should not closely scrutinize, legislative decisions about when to regulate property in the public interest.

Now, of course, what he doesn't mention in that quote (in fairness, it is somewhere else in the opinion) is that it's hardly an unbroken century of judicial precedent. We have seen that precedent sometimes comes, sometimes goes, sometimes seems to favor public use authorities, sometimes seems to favor private owners; but I think he's correct in saying that the general trend over the past century has been to afford legislators great discretion. That leaves us with a question: What are we to make of *Nollan* and *Lucas,* which seemed partially to buck that trend? And perhaps the message is that *Nollan* and *Lucas* do not represent a significant change of the Court's overall jurisprudence.

Let me put that into slightly different terms. Perhaps individuals, judges, scholars, and citizens who thought that the Court might be trying to resuscitate property, at least partially through *Nollan* and *Lucas,* were wrong. Or perhaps it simply didn't come to pass, because *Kelo* does seem at odds with the *Nollan/Lucas* line of cases. Or perhaps it signals something else? Because it is, after all, a 5–4 decision, perhaps it signals that this is a Court that does not know yet when, if, or how it wants to or should resuscitate property. Maybe what these three diverse cases tell us—all of them decided by close majorities and close margins—is that the Court is uncertain about what the world of property should be in our society.

It's worth considering some of the dissents in *Kelo* as well. Justice O'Connor wrote a very sharply worded dissent, joined by Rehnquist, Scalia, and Thomas. She wrote: "Any property may now be taken for the benefit of another private party, but the fallout from this decision will not be random."

There are two very important claims here. The first is that you can always take property from A and give it to B now. I wonder if that's accurate. In this case, the city of New London did have an economic development plan, which at least provided a plausible justification for why the property should be taken for a plausible, public use; but surely not any plan would suffice. I'm inclined to call this a hypothetical, but in an important sense, it's a real case. What if, for example, a citizen activist in the great state of New Hampshire would seek to have Justice Souter's home taken from Justice Souter and turned into a hotel, without the benefit of any plan. Would that pass constitutional muster under *Kelo*?

Or consider another possibility. What if the city's plan is self-evidently (and I'm trying to be delicate about this) stupid? What if the plan is, let's take these homeowners, this entire block, which generates, say, ten thousand dollars a year in property taxes, and give it over to a private development corporation, who will turn the land into a public pedestrian lot, which is designed, ultimately, to allow the public to have access to street hot dog vendors. And we think the economic benefit will be that we might get a few hundred dollars a year in property taxes.

Is that rational? Under the old test, I'm sad to say, it probably is, because some wag somewhere would argue that rationality couldn't be measured by money alone. And the city might, in fact, be better off with an open-air pedestrian mall that serves gourmet hot dogs. The quality of life for all of us will be superior. That really would have passed muster under the old rationality test. Will it pass muster under *Kelo*? I don't know.

I hope you can see where I'm trying to push you toward here. Does the Court really want to put itself in the business, again, of assessing the economic wisdom of different development plans? That's precisely the role it took upon itself in *Lochner,* and for which the Court paid a very heavy price.

On the other hand, if the Court doesn't take to itself some supervisory role over the process, then where really will be the possibility of a correction for legislative abuses? And we saw earlier that the answer advanced in *Munn*—that the people should go to the polls—might be facile in some important respects.

Where does that leave us? I think it's instructive to think about what the reactions were to *Kelo* in 2005. *Kelo* generated a firestorm of public controversy. Indeed, several state legislatures, as well as the United States Congress, began to consider legislation that would overrule *Kelo*; or would at least try to modify *Kelo* by suggesting that, in this state, at least, it's not enough to simply proffer an economic development plan and then to transfer private property to another private owner. Different states adopted different versions of that legislation. Congress had considered it, as I suggested. What are we to make of these responses?

Imagine a congressional statute that says the following: "The Court got it wrong in *Kelo.*" Presumably, this statute, like most statutes, would have a preamble; and the preamble will wax eloquently about the importance of property to the Founding. Presumably, they'll give the same quote about Madison, "a man is a property in himself," that we used. You can imagine the rhetoric, can't you? It's not America without private property. Without private property, we're the Soviet Union, or Communist China, or some other infidel country that doesn't understand that private property isn't simply important because of its economic benefit to the person who owns it, but because, as Jefferson insisted so many years ago, "private property is the key to human autonomy and to human dignity." And because private property was so significant at the Founding, because property is so critical to what it means to be a citizen in a democracy, the Court must restore the right to private property. And part of that restoration means saying, "Sorry. We got it wrong in *Kelo*."

How would the Court react to a congressional statute that purported to tell the Court it had made a fundamental mistake in its application of the Bill of Rights? One might imagine that the Court genuinely takes up the process of rethinking its opinion. One could imagine a Court saying the power of judicial review entitles us to tell the community at large what we think through the power of deciding cases. But we share that power of making the Constitution have real meaning with the other branches. If the Court did that, we would call that—looking from the outside in—an example of departmentalism, where constitutional meaning is a shared enterprise; where the best way to understand constitutional interpretation is not through the mechanism of judicial review, but instead to understand it as an ongoing dialogue between the branches. And presumably, somewhere, Jefferson smiles.

Or perhaps we'd see something else. Perhaps we'd see the Supreme Court say, "There's a fundamental problem here, and the fundamental problem is, we decide what the Constitution means. And we're delighted to know you think we were wrong—we're always open to criticism—but we don't care, because we got it right; and in the end, it is our judgment that is final!" What is to be done then? There is really only one option left to the community at large, is there not? Presumably it is to pass a constitutional amendment; and the constitutional amendment will presumably seek to restore private property to the glorious position it once had.

One final point to consider: Where are we now with property? No one can say with complete certainty; but with reasonable accuracy, we can say that we've come a long way from the Founding, and that property is no longer the "great fence to liberty" that it was, to use Madison's language, at the time of the Founding. And it's worth asking ourselves, if property no longer serves as the fence to liberty, if it is no longer the linchpin under the constitutional order, then what is?

Lecture Nine
Fundamental Rights—Privacy and Personhood

Scope:

In this lecture, we continue to examine the relationship between liberty and community, but our focus broadens to a study of the development of the constitutional right to privacy. For the Founders, and throughout much of American history, the tension between these two values manifests itself most clearly in the Supreme Court's property cases. As we shall see in the next few lectures, these issues are not limited to questions of property but, instead, extend to the most fundamental questions of what it means to be an individual and what it means to be a member of a larger community. Should the community have a say in determining what rights, if any, a woman has toward the fetus she carries? Is the moral sense of the community reason enough to prohibit certain sexual practices? Implicit in these questions, and in the many others surrounding "privacy," are fundamental notions about what it means to be a person and what rights are, as well as questions about the nature and limits of judicial power in finding or creating constitutional rights.

Outline

I. In this lecture, we begin our study of the Court's complicated privacy jurisprudence.

    A. We begin with the Court's earliest privacy cases, almost all of which concern rights to privacy in the marriage relationship.

    B. We will then turn to the abortion and reproductive rights cases, followed in turn, by a series of cases involving family rights.

    C. Thereafter, we take up cases involving sexual privacy and same-sex marriages.

    D. We will conclude with the so-called "right-to-die" cases, which also address privacy issues.

II. Although we say these cases involve the right to privacy, in some ways, this statement is misleading. The Court's privacy cases cover a wide variety of different kinds of issues and interests.

A. It might be more accurate to say that these cases are about autonomy, or human personality, or self-determination.

B. Before we address specific cases, however, we should understand some of the broader concepts associated with the right to privacy more generally.

C. The first of these issues is simply this: Why should we turn from the property cases to the privacy cases?

    1. This transition is unconventional, but there are at least two good reasons for approaching the material in this fashion.

        a. First is a reason grounded in historical convenience. The Court's earliest privacy cases almost always involved a property interest as well.

        b. Second, property and privacy are similar in that both ultimately refer to larger questions about the nature of what it means to be a person and what it means to seek the good life in community with others.

    2. Like the right to property, cases involving the constitutional right to privacy and related interests raise important and complex issues concerning the boundaries between liberty and community.

III. Finally, there is yet another connection between the right to property and the right to privacy.

A. Recall our discussion of *Lochner*. We saw that a critical issue in *Lochner* was concerned with the limits of judicial authority and the rise of economic due process.

B. There were always two strands of substantive due process—the strand we saw in *Lochner*, concerned with matters of property, and a second strand concerned with liberties that might be described as *noneconomic*.

C. Although the first strand has long since been discarded, the second continues to exist in the privacy cases.

    1. This does not mean that the doctrine of substantive due process in noneconomic cases is not profoundly controversial.

2. Indeed, as we shall see, the same kinds of concerns that led the Court to reject *Lochner* as unsound continue to haunt the Court's work in the area of privacy.

D. Thus, at a certain level of abstraction, the kinds of issues we confronted in the property line of cases will occupy us with the privacy cases.

E. There is, however, also an important difference between the two lines of case law.
1. Unlike property, which is clearly tethered to the constitutional text, the right to privacy is perhaps less obviously grounded in the Constitution.
2. There is room for disagreement here—much depends on how narrowly or broadly we read the text or even what we choose to "include" in the definition of the Constitution.

IV. There is another issue we should address before we move to specific cases. Earlier in the course, in Lecture 2, we considered the case of *Palko v. Connecticut* (1937).

A. In *Palko*, the Court adopted the doctrine of selective incorporation, through which some parts of the Bill of Rights became applicable to the states.
1. In particular, those parts of the Bill of Rights that are "implicit in the concept of ordered liberty" apply to the state governments.
2. At bottom, *Palko* stands for the claim that some parts of the Bill of Rights are more important than others. Some rights, to use more contemporary language, are "fundamental," and others are not.
3. It is easy to criticize such claims, but we need to fully understand them to appreciate the Court's work in the field of privacy.

B. When the Court repudiated *Lochner*, it decided that the test to use in assessing the constitutionality of "economic" legislation, or policies that touch property, is the rationality test. And as we saw, the definition of *rationality* is extremely elastic.

C. Now connect this test with the decision in *Palko*. *Palko* tells us that there are two classes of constitutional rights—the fundamental and the nonfundamental. Property is nonfundamental and, hence, warrants the rationality test.

D. Fundamental rights, however, receive more aggressive judicial scrutiny. When a right is fundamental, such as privacy, as we shall see, the Court asks: Is the state's interest "compelling"?

   1. Note how different—how much more searching—this test, the *compelling state interest test*, is than the simple rationality test.

   2. Consider, for example, a state that wants to prohibit abortions in all instances. It will not be enough for the state to advance a rational set of reasons for its decision. Instead, the Court will require the state to produce a compelling reason.

E. What kinds of reasons are compelling?

   1. Can the state advance a compelling interest in regulating the sexual activities of same-sex partners? To answer this, we must be able to articulate the state's interests in a fair amount of detail.

   2. Would a state interest grounded in expressions of religious faith be enough?

   3. Would an interest grounded in concern for public health fare better?

   4. It is important to remember that states possess the police power, traditionally defined as the power to protect the "health, safety, welfare, and morals of society."

F. Consequently, it is often perfectly legitimate for the state to regulate individual conduct on the basis of some larger communal interest, and sometimes, that interest extends to the moral sensibilities of the community.

G. But to say that an interest is legitimate is not to say that it is, necessarily, compelling. As we read the cases on privacy, then, try to identify precisely what interest the state seeks to advance and what gravity we should attach to that interest.

Essential Reading:

Kommers, Finn, and Jacobsohn, *American Constitutional Law*, chapter 6, pp. 233–234.

Jed Rubenfeld, "The Right of Privacy," 102 *Harvard Law Review* 737 (1989).

Palko v. State of Connecticut (1937).

Supplementary Reading:

Alinda Brill, *Nobody's Businesses: Paradoxes of Privacy.*

Ronald Dworkin, *Life's Dominion.*

John Mill, *On Liberty.*

Rogers Smith, "The Constitution and Autonomy," 60 *Texas Law Review* 175 (1982).

Samuel D. Warren and Louis D. Brandeis, "The Right to Privacy," 4 *Harvard Law Review* 193 (1890).

Questions to Consider:

1. What, if anything, is the relationship between the right to property and the right to privacy? Why did the Founders fail to include a general right to privacy in the Bill of Rights?

2. In modern states, the many interests that might fall under the rubric of "privacy," such as protecting information about oneself or making decisions for oneself, must be strongly influenced by technology and society. Is the Supreme Court the appropriate forum for resolving such issues?

Lecture Nine—Transcript
Fundamental Rights—Privacy and Personhood

In this session, we begin a series of eight lectures, all of which will be devoted to the constitutional topic of the right to privacy. We will consider a number of different issues, and I'd like to run through them very briefly, just to give you a sense of what kinds of issues and topics we'll be covering over these eight lectures. We'll begin with the early privacy cases, almost all of which involve the notion of marital privacy. We'll then move quickly to the abortion and reproductive rights cases; those will take two lectures. We will then spend some time on a collection of diverse family interests, or "family rights" cases, also subsumed under the topic of privacy. And we'll move to topics about sexual privacy and same-sex marriage. Finally, we'll conclude with some "right-to-die" cases, which also implicate the constitutional right to privacy.

Now, as you can see, this covers a wide array of diverse kinds of issues and cases. All of these coexist under a broad umbrella called "privacy," but that's profoundly misleading. We call them "privacy cases" simply for purposes of convenience. In truth, these cases might together be called "autonomy cases," or maybe even "human personality cases," or, as I would prefer, cases about the right of self-determination. But all, in the end, are simply called "privacy cases," and all of them, I'm afraid to say, will involve a diverse set of interests that I cannot completely reconcile. We're simply going to use the phrase "privacy" as a convenience, as shorthand.

Before we actually get into these cases, though, however, and because it is sometimes too easy in a course on the Bill of Rights to get lost in a welter of specific cases, I think it's important that we understand some broad concepts involved with the right to privacy more generally. And the first important topic that we really need to address today is simply this: Why should we suddenly move from a line of cases involving the right to property, as we have done in the last few lectures, to privacy? That is not a conventional move in a civil liberties course; and I think I owe you an explanation about why we're going to take such an unconventional tack.

Generally speaking, I think it's important, or at least appropriate, to move from property to privacy cases for two basic reasons, perhaps three. The first is, again, simply a question of historical convenience.

As it turns out, the Court's earliest privacy cases usually also involved property interest; so, as a matter of historical record, the connection between property and privacy finds itself in the Court's own case law. Let me give you a quick example of that.

As it turns out, almost any definition of "property" that you'll encounter if you were, say, to go to law school, would be the following: "Property," your property professor would say, "should be understood as a bundle of sticks." There isn't any single property right. Property, like privacy, is a collection of diverse interests. That's what we mean when we say, "property as a right is a bundle of sticks."

As it turns out, one of those sticks, perhaps the most important of those sticks, is the right to exclude other people from your property; hence, the phrase, "private property." I hope this brief example shows that there are profound, not only historical connections, but theoretical connections between the right to property and the right to privacy.

Indeed, the whole concept of "trespass," which I am sure you have heard in other contexts, is predicated on the idea that when you are on your "private property," you do have a certain kind of privacy interest that you are entitled to enforce through the legal system. So there is that second connection between property and privacy, as well.

More importantly, however, as we saw when we dealt with the property cases, both property and privacy ultimately refer to larger notions about what it means to be an individual, what it means to seek the good life, what it means to flourish as a human being; but not simply on your own terms, but rather in a larger community of other individuals. None of us are islands alone. We all exist in this larger community. Property, as we saw with Madison's famous quote, is a "fence to liberty," by which he meant, property was the boundary mark between an individual and society.

Unfortunately—or perhaps, inevitably, as the case may be—property no longer serves that function. That was one of the major purposes of our treatment of the property cases—to see how that "fence to liberty" has somehow eroded or collapsed over time. What, if anything, has replaced it? My tentative argument, one that I'd like you to consider, and to reject if you feel free to do so, is that that fence to liberty is no longer property, but is instead that collection of diverse interests that we now call, for purposes of shorthand, privacy.

And then, finally, there is one other connection between the right to property and the right to privacy. You'll recall the *Lochner* case that we spent so much time with in an earlier lecture. One of the critical points of our discussion of *Lochner* was the issue of judicial power, and you'll recall Justice Holmes's insistence, in his blistering dissent in *Lochner*, that the Court had simply made up an economic theory, had read that economic theory into the Constitution, and then imposed it upon the majority in ways that were fundamentally illegitimate, at least as regards constitutional theory. That doctrine was known as "economic due process," and just by way of reminder, economic due process simply stands for the proposition that, at a certain point in the Court's history, it used the Due Process Clause to enforce a really aggressive, expansive notion of property rights against the community's interest.

There were always two strands of due process. There was the economic strand, as we saw rejected when *Lochner* itself was rejected. There was always this second strand of due process that the Court has sometimes used to protect a collection of interests not directly found in the Constitution itself, such as privacy, including the abortion right, for example, or rights to determine familial autonomy. That line of due process, although it was completely rejected in *Lochner*, continues to exist with a certain amount of vitality in the privacy cases. I say "a certain amount of vitality"— which is, of course, an imprecise phrase—because the continued use of substantive due process is among the most controversial of the Court's current doctrines. I say, "It's of some vitality," because there are some justices who think the use of due process to protect these privacy rights is perfectly legitimate, and another group of justices and scholars who think it is indistinguishable from what the Court did in *Lochner;* and as a consequence, those cases— for example, *Roe* or *Griswold*, both of which we'll consider later—are also illegitimate in the same way *Lochner* was illegitimate. So we move from property to privacy because, in my mind, at least, there are important ways in which the two lines of cases are indistinguishable.

Please don't take that too literally. Of course there are differences between the two, and we'll encounter those differences as we go on. All I need to say is that, at a certain level of abstraction, the issues involved with property, the issues involved with the repudiation of *Lochner* and economic due process, are issues we will encounter again as we begin to consider our privacy cases.

There is another basic, important factor that we need to consider as we move from property to privacy. Unlike property, which is clearly tethered in several different places in the constitutional text—as we saw, for example, it's tethered in Article I, Section 10. It's also tethered in the Fifth Amendment's Due Process Clause. It is clearly implicated by the Takings Clause, which we discussed in the last lecture. Unlike property, which clearly has those constitutional footholds in the text, privacy is an entirely different matter.

I need to be especially careful with my language here. Depending on one's point of view, those rights that we call "privacy rights" are entirely a function of judicial imagination. I say "imagination" because it is the least pejorative word I can think of to use in this context. I might have said that these privacy rights are a function of judicial creation. I didn't use that word for one simple reason: to call them an act of judicial creation is to suggest that these rights don't actually exist in the Constitution, and there are certainly justices and certainly scholars who would adopt that approach.

That prejudges the question, however, about whether or not, in fact, there is a constitutional right to privacy that might be implicit in the text or which might be fairly inferred from the constitutional document. So I try to avoid using the word "creation," because it suggests an answer to our most fundamental problem.

The fundamental problem in the privacy case is simply this: Didn't the Court Lochnerize in all of these cases? Hasn't the Court simply made up the constitutional right to privacy? And if I say the Court created those privacy rights, then I think I have sort of suggested that the Court did, in fact, make them up. I don't want to say that.

Alternatively, I might have said that the Court, in fact, inferred a privacy right from the Constitution. That, too, prejudges this most basic of questions. It suggests that somewhere, hidden in the constitutional text, perhaps in one provision, or in some collection of provisions, there really is some kind of a right to privacy. That prejudges the question as well, by suggesting that there is a fundamental legitimacy to the privacy right. I don't want to prejudge that question, either; hence, my phrase, "judicial imagination." It's probably not much of an improvement, but I hope that you can appreciate the problem. It is difficult to talk about the constitutional right to privacy without somehow expressing an opinion about whether the Court's work in this area is fundamentally legitimate, because it represents a fair, plausible interpretation, or perhaps, interpolation, from the text; or, alternatively, it simply represents judges making things up as they go along. And, as we saw, that is the most fundamental of constitutional errors.

Another issue before we actually go into a series of more particular fundamental issues involving the right to privacy. Reaching far back into the course, you will recall that we discussed the doctrine of selective incorporation. Selective incorporation, you'll recall, was that process through which the Supreme Court made certain parts of the Bill of Rights applicable to state governments through the Due Process Clause of the Fourteenth Amendment.

In the case of *Palko v. Connecticut*, the Supreme Court concluded that those provisions that should be made applicable to the states were those provisions that were, "implicit in the concept of ordered liberty." Which parts of the Bill of Rights are implicit in the concept of ordered liberty? Those which are central to American conceptions of justice, central to those conceptions of what it means to be an American who lives under a system of the rule of law. Those are fancy phrases. What do they mean, in fact?

Without trying to be too cynical about it, I think *Palko* boils down to the following proposition. Some parts of the Bill of Rights are more important that other parts of the Bill of Rights. The ones that are more important are applicable to state governance, and hence, protect us all against every level of government; and those that are less important may not necessarily apply against the state governance.

Let me put it in slightly different terms: *Palko* stands for the proposition that some parts of the Bill of Rights are really, really important; and the really, really important ones protect you against state governance. Let me put it in another way: *Palko* stands for the proposition that some parts of the Bill of Rights are really, really important and should be applied against the states. Which ones are those? The ones that are really, really, important.

In short, *Palko* might be thought of as a simple tautology. Whatever its flaws, however, *Palko* is critical for understanding the Court's work in the field of privacy; critical in at least this one sense: as we saw when the Court repudiated *Lochner*, when the Court decided it would no longer aggressively protect the right to property, it settled upon a particular doctrinal test for assessing property rights cases. And you'll recall that the test is fairly straightforward. The test is the one the Court continues to use to this day. When something concerns an economic regulation, when the state action involved in our case touches the right to property, the Court assumes that the legislation in question will be constitutionally permissible so long as the statutory regulation is—and you'll recall this word—rational.

One additional elaboration: The Court's definition of rationality is perhaps not the one most of us would use in ordinary conversation. The Court's definition of rationality is: Could some person, somewhere, have advanced a rational explanation for the state action in question?

Let me go a little bit further than that. That's not really, I think, a completely accurate definition of the Court's rationality test. Here would be a more accurate question: A state action will be considered rational, not simply if somebody might have advanced a rational explanation, because even if nobody does advance a rational explanation, the Court will go on to ask this additional question. Assuming no legislator actually could advance a rational regulation or a rational reason for this statute, the Court will ask the following question: If they have thought about it, could somewhere, someone, after the fact, somehow, have advanced a rational explanation?

Think of how minimal this test is. The question isn't, did this legislature, or did this particular legislator, have a rational explanation for the statute in question? That's not the question. The question of the test is simply this: Could someone, somewhere have possibly have thought of a rational explanation, even if nobody truly did? That test, the rationality test, is called by some wags "the insanity test;" not the insanity test that is used in a criminal defense in a criminal trial, but an insanity test in the following sense: Is this legislation insane? And if it's not, then it's rational; and if it's rational, it's constitutionally acceptable. That is the current state of the law, the doctrine, surrounding property cases.

Now let me draw this complex story to a close. *Palko* suggests that some rights are really, really important; or, to use the jargon, *Palko* suggests that some rights are fundamental; which means, of course, that some rights are non-fundamental. That distinction between fundamental rights and non-fundamental rights is the bedrock of all contemporary civil liberties' jurisprudence, and it is critical for understanding the Court's work in the area of privacy. Some rights are fundamental. Some rights are non-fundamental. Property, obviously, is non-fundamental.

Privacy however, falls into the category of a fundamental right; and because it falls into the category of a fundamental right, the Court's doctrinal tests vary dramatically from the rationality test. And please excuse the jargon, but I want you to be able to recognize it when you read it in the cases. When a case, when a constitutional controversy, involves a fundamental right, such as privacy, the Court will use the following test: The legislation, or the state action in question will be constitutionally permissible if the state has "a compelling state interest," and provided the state uses the least restrictive means available to restrict, or to impinge upon that right. We call this the "compelling state interest test."

Please note how profoundly different this test is from the rationality test. At the risk of being reductionist, every time the state acts to regulate property, the presumption is in favor of the statute's constitutionality, because everything is rational. The presumption is quite the opposite in fundamental rights cases, such as privacy cases. Now the state must meet the highest burden that we can imagine. Its interests must not simply be rational; its interests must not simply be important or substantial; its interests must be compelling, and the state must find a way to impose that interest on the privacy right in a way that does the least possible damage to the underlying right.

Perhaps this will be a little clearer if I use a specific example. Reaching ahead to a case that we will spend a fair amount of time with, imagine that the state, your state, wishes to outlaw abortions in all cases, with no exceptions. We know, following *Roe*—which we will spend a fair amount of time with—that that privacy right, the right to terminate a pregnancy, is a fundamental right. If the state wants to regulate that right following this logic, following this set of doctrines, it will not be enough for the state simply to claim that it has a rational set of reasons for regulating the abortion right. Instead, the state will be required to articulate in court why its interests are compelling; and that, of course, will first require the state to actually articulate what specific interests it possesses in trying to regulate the abortion right.

Or consider a similar statute that regulates access to birth control devices, or to contraceptives, more generally. It's the same fundamental issue—if there is a fundamental right to privacy, which covers your decision to engage in some kind of birth control; if such a right exists, and if that right is fundamental, then the state will be required to articulate a compelling reason why it ought to be allowed to regulate the use of birth control or to prohibit birth control altogether.

I realize how much jargon and legalese is involved here, but at some point, we need to understand this language in order to understand the fundamental controversies that surround the privacy right more generally. Please note that when I gave you the birth control example, or the *Roe* example, I didn't actually tell you what the state interests might be. And this takes us back away from the specifics of particular cases to the larger, grander issues.

If we use the rationality test to judge when the state may act, then, for all practical purposes, the state may act on the basis of almost any imaginable reason to regulate your property right. The state may find that your use of property is aesthetically offensive. Perhaps you have painted your house pink; perhaps you have erected a fence that is twelve feet high as opposed to eight feet high. The state is entirely within its rights, entirely within its authority, to regulate or to prohibit those uses based on any set of imaginable reasons. It might conclude it simply doesn't like the way your property looks, which is perhaps not entirely accurate. Perhaps what we should say in such cases is that the community has decided that it doesn't like the way you are utilizing your property.

What interests count as fundamental or as compelling state interests? Consider the following kinds of hypothetical problems. Is it a compelling interest for the state to regulate the sexual activities of same-sex partners? We can't possibly answer that question, either in the abstract or in constitutional terms, unless we can first articulate precisely what the state interest would be in such cases. Before we can weigh the gravity of the state's interests, we need to articulate precisely what that interest is.

Now what might it be in the case I have described? One might imagine a state legislator standing on the front steps of the state house, arguing that same-sex sexual activity ought to be prohibited because it violates some underlying notion of his or her religious faith. So, perhaps Legislator Finn says, "I am a Roman Catholic, and homosexual activity offends my sense of what the Bible and Jesus Christ teach." Would that be a legitimate source of governmental action? Consider another possibility; imagine this case goes to the Supreme Court, and one justice decides to say, "Well, of course the state may regulate sexual activity. There are long-standing prohibitions against homosexual activity in Western legal systems." Indeed, this judge would go on to say, "These proscriptions against homosexual conduct reach as far back, at least, as Leviticus." Would it be appropriate for a judge to say that?

Would you feel differently about the state's interest if, instead, Legislator Finn stands up and says on the steps of the state house, "This has nothing to do with my sense of ethics, morality, or religious conviction. I'm not entitled as a legislator to act on that basis. Instead, it has to do entirely with my sense of preserving the public health, and I am worried about the transmission of the HIV virus and of other sexually transmitted diseases"?

Note now the reason doesn't appear superficially to be grounded in some notion of faith or morality or ethics; now it appears to be grounded in some notion of the public health. And we might disagree with this legislator, but the kind of reason the legislator has advanced might be qualitatively different than the first set of reasons. Does an appeal to the public health constitute a compelling state interest?

Alternatively, the legislator in question might advance a third set of reasons, perhaps a third set of reasons that combines the first two. Maybe what the legislator wants to say is, "We are engaged"—you'll recognize the language from an earlier lecture—"in a process that will take us down a slippery slope. We have a potential parade of horribles. If we authorize or legalize this particular kind of behavior, then it is a short step, perhaps an inevitable step, to legalizing bestiality, or crimes of incest, or to almost any kind of sexual behavior that one might imagine."

This would then push us back and force us to ask the most difficult of questions: When, if ever, is the state entitled to restrict your liberty? When, if ever, is the state entitled to restrict your constitutional right to privacy because it defends the community at large? Obviously, this issue will come up when we take up the First Amendment, but it clearly appears in the privacy cases, as well. It might be that Legislator Finn stands on the steps of the state house and says, as I suggested before, that this is partly a question of the public health, but it is also a question about the community's moral sensibilities. And these are moral sensibilities that do not directly trace themselves to a particular religious faith; these are moral sensibilities that transcend the questions of religious faith or of specific religious faith.

Before we assume, as I think some of you will want to do, that there is never a time when the state may act to protect the moral sensibilities of the community, please remember the police power doctrine that we spoke about in *Lochner*. By way of reminder, every state is constitutionally entrusted with the so-called police power. That police power is, "the power to protect the health, safety, welfare, and morals of the community."

There is little, if any, room for argument under the Bill of Rights that the state may never act to protect the moral welfare of the community. That is not an open question. We are not a system that is committed to a million propositions that one can do whatever one wants so long as one does not bring harm to another human being. That might be a nice constitutional rule if we were to choose to enact a new Constitution. Whether we would do that or not should not influence our understanding of the way in which the system actually works now. We don't have that nil-principle of harm embedded in our Bill of Rights. For better or for worse, it is unequivocally the case that the state may sometimes act simply to protect the moral sensibilities of the community. And, of course, the state may always act to protect the physical health of the community, or of children, or of specific aspects of the community—all of which doesn't actually answer the question I started with.

The question I started with was this: Is it a compelling state interest to act on a basis of a shared, moral sensibility? It's clearly a legitimate interest in some cases. I want to make sure we understand this. The state may rationally act to advance a moral agenda. That would satisfy the rationality test. Is it enough to satisfy the compelling state interest test? This is one of the questions we'll have to consider as we begin to consider the privacy cases in more detail. So, again, as we read these cases, as we take up the next seven lectures on privacy, I want you to think, as you read through these materials, about these larger constitutional issues, so we'll remain centered on what's really important, and so we can throw away what is less significant.

And what is really important is simply this: Under what conditions may the state act? What reasons might the state legitimately advance for regulating this wide array of interests, which we have, for purposes of convenience, chosen to call "privacy"? That means that you should spend a fair amount of your time, in reading these cases, trying to identify precisely what interest the state has advanced; and then, secondarily, trying to figure out what kind of weight, what kind of gravity, we should attach to that interest.

Lecture Ten
Privacy—The Early Cases

Scope:

There is no explicit provision in the Constitution that protects a comprehensive right to privacy. Nevertheless, some concern for privacy does seem to appear in several places, including the Fourth Amendment, which protects against unreasonable searches and seizures, and the Fifth Amendment, which protects against self-incrimination. Other aspects of privacy intersect with the First Amendment's freedom of association. As we shall see in this lecture, the Court's earliest decisions on privacy tended to emphasize privacy as a right to exclude others from one's property, as in *Olmstead v. United States* (1928). In his dissent in that case, Justice Brandeis argued for a more expansive conception of privacy, untethered from notions of private property. The Court's first significant move toward this larger understanding began in the famous case of *Griswold v. Connecticut* (1965) and was further developed in *Eisenstadt v. Baird* (1972) and other cases.

Outline

I. As we saw in the last lecture, there is no explicit provision in the Constitution that protects a comprehensive right to privacy.

    A. Nevertheless, some concern for privacy does seem to appear in several places, including the Fourth Amendment, which protects against unreasonable searches and seizures, and the Fifth Amendment, which protects against self-incrimination. Other aspects of privacy intersect with the First Amendment's freedom of association.

    B. The Court's early decisions concerning privacy tended to emphasize privacy as a right to exclude others from one's property, thus underscoring the connection between property and privacy.

II. Thus, in the seminal case of *Olmstead v. United States* (1928), the Court ruled that the Fourth Amendment did not prevent the use of wiretaps on private telephone conversations, although the defendant had argued that they constituted a trespass.

A. In his dissent, Justice Brandeis argued for a more expansive conception of privacy, one largely free of property.

B. Justice Brandeis also wrote, "The Founders conferred, as against the government, the right to be let alone—the most comprehensive of rights and the right most valued by civilized men."

C. In 1890, Brandeis had written, with his law partner (Samuel D. Warren) in Boston, a famous article in the *Harvard Law Review* proposing that there should be a right to privacy.

III. The Court did not act on Brandeis's suggestion until the 1960s. In the landmark case of *Griswold v. Connecticut* (1965), the Court, speaking through Justice Douglas, concluded that there is a right to privacy of one sort or another.

A. I say "one sort or another" because the actual holding in *Griswold* is a matter of some uncertainty. Part of this uncertainty is a consequence of the Court's reasoning.

B. Before we take up the various opinions in Griswold, it might be a good idea to consider the different kinds of opinions that justices can write in any case.

   1. A *majority opinion* represents the collective judgment of a majority of the sitting justices. It represents a binding precedent, or a statement of what the law is and what it requires.

   2. A *per curiam opinion* also typically has the force of law, but in these opinions, no single justice is identified as the author.

   3. A *plurality opinion*, an opinion in which a plurality of justices joins but does not amount to a majority of the Court, does not constitute a precedent, though it does resolve that particular case.

   4. A *concurring opinion* is an opinion by one or more justices that expresses agreement with the result in the case, but some disagreement with the method or reasoning used to reach that result.

   5. Finally, a *dissenting opinion* is an opinion by one or more justices that disagrees with the result reached by the majority.

IV. Now, returning to *Griswold*, we see a fair amount of disagreement within the Court and a wide variety of concurring and dissenting opinions.

    A. In this case, Justice Douglas, writing for the majority, concluded that the Constitution does protect a privacy right of one kind or another. Again, I say of "one kind or another" because the opinion is unclear about the precise location of the right and, indeed, unclear about the nature of the right.

        1. In particular, Douglas declined to find privacy in the Fourth Amendment alone or in any single constitutional provision. Instead, he found it in the "penumbras and emanations" of several different constitutional provisions.

        2. The right to privacy, in other words, results from the confluence of a number of more specific constitutional provisions.

        3. In addition, Douglas wrote: "We deal with a right of privacy older than the Bill of Rights. To allow the state to regulate the sacred precincts of the marital bedroom would be repulsive to the notions of privacy surrounding the marital relationship."

    B. Another uncertainty concerns the actual dimension, or breadth, of the right in *Griswold*. In some places, the Court speaks about a broad right to privacy, but in others, it seems to focus on the narrower category of "marital" privacy.

    C. The issue was settled in the subsequent case of *Eisenstadt v. Baird* (1972), in which the Court concluded that the right to privacy "must be the same for married and unmarried alike."

V. In an interesting concurring opinion, Justice Goldberg sought help in establishing the privacy right from the Ninth Amendment.

    A. The Ninth, he argues, tells us that there must be implicit constitutional rights beyond those specifically articulated in the Bill of Rights.

    B. In response, Justice Black accused Goldberg of Lochnerizing—of using the Ninth as a way of simply reading into the Constitution protection of those rights that are important to judges or society, even though there is no secure constitutional warrant for doing so.

VI. There are important dissents in *Griswold*. As the dissents observed, the Court seemed to create the right of privacy from the scarcest of constitutional materials.

    A. As Justice Black wrote, "I like my privacy as well as the next one, but I am nevertheless compelled to admit that the government has a right to invade it unless prohibited by some specific constitutional provision."

    B. Justice Stewart voiced another important criticism: Absent any clear constitutional directive, the Court's "creation of the right to privacy represents an unwarranted judicial intrusion into the powers of state legislatures."

VII. One final point about *Griswold*: If the right to privacy is fundamental, we must then ask whether the state had, in this case, a compelling reason that would save the legislation. In this case, the majority was unable to find such a reason.

Essential Reading:

Olmstead v. United States (1928).

Griswold v. Connecticut (1965).

Eisenstadt v. Baird (1972).

Kommers, Finn, and Jacobsohn, *American Constitutional Law*, chapter 5, pp. 239–242.

Supplementary Reading:

Robert Bork, "Neutral Principles and Some First Amendment Problems," 47 *Indiana Law Journal* 1 (1971).

Thomas Kauper, "Penumbras, Peripheries, Things Fundamental and Things Forgotten," 64 *Michigan Law Review* 235 (1965).

Questions to Consider:

1. How persuasive is the majority's claim that the right to privacy is actually a part of the Constitution and not simply a creation of judicial imagination? Where in the Constitution does the Court find the right to privacy? Would the opinion be more or less persuasive if the majority had simply said that privacy is an "implied right"?

2. What is the significance of Justice Douglas's emphasis on the sanctity of marriage and "the intimate relation between husband and wife"?

3. In his strongly worded dissent, Justice Stewart argued that the majority had simply written its personal preferences, preferences he shared, into the Constitution. "But we are not asked to say whether we think this law is unwise, or even asinine. We are asked to hold that it violates … the Constitution. And that I cannot do." Why not? Is this position based on an understanding of judicial power?

Lecture Ten—Transcript
Privacy—The Early Cases

There is no explicit provision in the Constitution that protects a comprehensive right to privacy. We saw that in the last lecture. Nevertheless, some concern for privacy does seem to appear, at least, in several different places in the Bill of Rights, including the Fourth Amendment, which protects against unreasonable searches and seizures; and the Fifth Amendment, which protects against self-incrimination; and, perhaps, even with the First Amendment's freedom of association. As we shall see in this lecture, the Court's earliest decisions on privacy tended to emphasize privacy as a right to exclude one from property (You'll recall the "bundle of sticks" that we spoke about). We'll begin with perhaps the most important of these earliest cases. The case is known as *Olmstead v. United States,* and it was decided in 1928.

It's not immediately obvious that *Olmstead* would be a privacy case. In this case, the Court ruled that the Fourth Amendment did not prevent the use of wiretaps on private telephone conversations. How could this possibly be a Fourth Amendment, or even a privacy issue? The defendant in that case had come up with a novel argument that the actual wiretap itself constituted a physical trespass onto his property. Hence, *Olmstead* might be understood as a property case. In an important, fantastically important dissent, Justice Brandeis argued for a much more expansive conception of privacy, one that tried to distinguish privacy from property more generally.

I want to give you a quote, which indicates the kind of right that Brandeis was trying to articulate. The Founders, he said, "…conferred, as against the government, the right to be let alone— the most comprehensive of rights and the right most valued by civilized men." Now, as it turns out, that's a fairly comprehensive right. It may well be the most important right, as Brandeis suggested. But let's be clear; it's not a right that you can find in the constitutional text; at least, not articulated in that way.

It's important to understand some of the context for Brandeis's dissent. In 1898, when he was a law partner in Boston, Brandeis, with his partner, Warren, had written a famous article in the *Harvard Law Review* articulating, or proposing, that there should be a right to privacy; and 30 years later, now sitting as a justice, he began to campaign for that right. It was not a very successful campaign. The court didn't take up Brandeis's suggestion until the 1960s.

Speaking in the landmark case of *Griswold v. Connecticut,* decided in 1965, Justice Douglas, writing for a majority, concluded that there is a privacy right of one sort or another. Before I go into his opinion, this would be an appropriate place to point out something that we are going to encounter time and time again: there is not a simple, straightforward majority opinion in *Griswold.* It is accompanied by a vast collection of concurring opinions and dissenting opinions. It is a rare thing to find a unanimous opinion in privacy cases.

It's worth spending a little bit of time trying to distinguish what these different kinds of opinions are, and why we need to know what the differences are. A majority opinion is precisely what it appears to be—an opinion that speaks for the majority of the sitting justices. In the great majority of cases, that means that a majority opinion will have anywhere between five and eight justices willing to sign that opinion. I have added the phrase "willing to sign," because, occasionally, we'll encounter a different kind of opinion called a "per curiam" opinion. A per curiam opinion represents an opinion by the bench, but it may not be attributed to any particular justice; and if you want to take the cynic's view of this, a per curiam opinion is simply an opinion that no judge is willing to attach his or her name to, so it simply says "per curiam." A majority opinion takes on the status of law; if you prefer a more sophisticated understanding, a majority opinion will achieve the status of precedent.

Sometimes we'll encounter plurality opinions. A plurality opinion is usually the most populated of opinions, but, nevertheless, falls short of the majority of the sitting justices.

We will often encounter (indeed we will encounter in *Griswold)* something known as a concurring opinion. A concurring opinion is an opinion by one justice or a collection of justices that agrees with the result that the majority has reached, but may not agree with some or all of the reasoning, or some or all of the methods of constitutional interpretation that the majority has chosen to utilize. We will see these opinions, for example, in *Griswold.* Sometimes a concurring opinion is entirely irrelevant to almost anybody who would read it, and in others, such as *Griswold,* they are fantastically significant.

Then, finally, the dissenting opinion: dissenting opinions appear, perhaps, with more frequency in privacy cases than in any other area of constitutional law. They may be written by one judge or by a collection of judges. A dissenting opinion might simply disagree about the result in the case. It might disagree about whether the case should ever have been heard in the first instance. Or it may disagree with some particular aspect of the Court's reasoning.

If we approach these opinions simply as students, and not as lawyers or as professors, we will find that dissenting opinions are often the most interesting because they are often the most vitriolic. They are the most fun to read.

Now, let's go to *Griswold* itself. I hope you will forgive me for this—*Griswold* is certainly my favorite case. We all have our favorites. *Griswold* is a case that spans a vast period of time. The *Griswold* that you have in front of you is the third effort on behalf of certain citizens in the state of Connecticut to get Connecticut's birth control statutes declared unconstitutional. The first two were dismissed for technical reasons of constitutional law. The second time the Court refused to hear the case, it refused to do so because it argued that nobody had recently been prosecuted (by "recently," I mean in the last century) under the Connecticut law. And, as a consequence, there was no real threat of harm to anyone, which led the individuals involved in *Griswold* to notify the New Haven police that they intended to violate the law on a particular day and time, and invited the police to come watch them violate the law. Eventually, the New Haven police agreed to cooperate, and the individuals were arrested and fined $100. In other words, there was not a real case here. This case is a bit fraudulent, but fascinating, nonetheless.

Now, you'll recall, as I said a few moments ago, that Justice Douglas, speaking for the majority, concluded that there is a right to privacy in the Constitution of one sort or another. I said that deliberately. I want to quote you a few things first, however.

This is how Justice Douglas opens his majority opinion: "Overtones of some arguments"—he means some arguments by the lawyers involved in the case—"suggest that *Lochner versus New York* should be our guide. But we decline that invitation." How poetic. We decline the invitation to reproduce *Lochner*.

You'll recall, when we talked about *Lochner,* that I told you that it is among the highest of insults to lay on one judge—to accuse that judge of Lochnerizing. And I suggested that, when we took up cases later, we would see that judges take great pains to deny that they're Lochnerizing. Notice where Douglas begins, "I'm not Lochnerizing," which, of course, suggests strongly, if it is not conclusive evidence, that he is, in fact, Lochnerizing.

Just to make sure we all understand, he continues: "We do not sit as a super-legislature to determine the wisdom, need, and propriety of laws that touch economic problems, business affairs, or social conditions. This law, however,"—'however' is the key—"operates directly on an intimate relation of husband and wife."

I find it fascinating. He says, "We will not Lochernize, but this case is different," and he tells you how it is different—here we have a husband and wife; that is the "how." The critical question is not how it is different, but why it is different? It appears to be self-evident, to the majority at least, that there is something categorically different about a law that touches a husband and a wife, as opposed to their business interests. If the husband and wife ran a corporation, for example, and the law regulated their corporate activity, surely Douglas would not then be saying, "Normally we don't engage in aggressive judicial scrutiny of economic legislation, but when that economic legislation touches a husband and a wife, it is somehow different." He's neglected to give us what the fundamental difference is between these two positions.

He continues, "We deal with a right of privacy older than the Bill of Rights. To allow the state to regulate the sacred precincts of the marital bedroom would be repulsive to the notions of privacy surrounding the marital relationship." Let's stop here. Why, if at all, is it relevant to the constitutional inquiry, that there is, in fact, or might be, in fact, a right of privacy that is older than the Bill of Rights? Is the assumption here that the Bill of Rights protects us insofar as it lists specific liberties? Oh, and by the way, if we can think of rights that are even older than the Bill of Rights, they suddenly become a part of our constitutional liberty? Perhaps. He doesn't say that. He simply notes that the right that we are dealing with here is, in fact, older; but one has to attach some relevance to that observation.

And then he continued, "It would be repulsive to allow the state to search or to regulate the sacred precincts of the marital bedroom." Perhaps that would be repulsive. Why is that a relevant part of the Constitution? Is the claim here that any state activity that is repulsive somehow implicates a liberty or a privacy interest? What Douglas needs to do, what the majority needs to do, in order to make any of these relevant to the constitutional inquiry, is to establish, first, that there is a constitutionally protected right to privacy. We begin with a problem—or Douglas is faced with an immediate problem—there isn't any particular provision that clearly, unequivocally, unambiguously says, "You have a right to property; you have a right to privacy."

Douglas responds to this objection, to this difficulty, in the following way: to his credit, he acknowledges that no such provision exists; instead, he argues that there is a concern for privacy manifested in several different parts of the Bill of Rights. And he alludes to the First Amendment's freedom of association. Presumably, the assumption here is that there is a kind of privacy right implicated by our freedom to associate or not to associate with whomever we choose. He references the Fourth Amendment's search and seizure provision; and again, that's not something we'll cover in this course, but the gist of the Fourth Amendment's search and seizure provision is to suggest that you have a certain kind of privacy in your physical abode, in your private property. He suggests that there is a self-incrimination dimension to privacy, which is manifested in the Fifth Amendment.

Now, I want to be careful here. I want to do justice to Douglas's opinion. He doesn't say that privacy resides necessarily in any of these specific constitutional places. He simply points out that there is an underlying concern about privacy manifested in these different provisions. He goes on to say that if you look at these provisions in total (sort of a structural argument), and that if you look at the Bill of Rights in total, you will see that they are all concerned—or many of them, at least—are concerned with protecting this more generic background kind of right; a right to privacy that exists in perhaps the most famous of constitutional phrases, in the "penumbras and emanations" of the Bill of Rights themselves.

Where does privacy reside in the Constitution? In those penumbras and emanations. It would help to know what penumbras and emanations are, or what they mean; but Douglas doesn't bother to tell us. You won't be surprised, of course, to hear that among the most prominent of criticisms of the Court's decision in *Griswold* is that the Court simply made up the right to privacy.

Another justice on the Court, Justice Black (we will spend time with his dissenting opinion a little bit later in this lecture), used to take a copy of the Constitution out of his pocket (I wish I had brought one with me); it was a 25-cent copy produced by the government printing office, and he would ostentatiously open it up (he used to do this to Bill Douglas's friend all the time), and say, "Bill, you've got to help me out here, because here's my copy of the Constitution, and I don't see anything called the right to privacy. But what really bothers me is I don't see any penumbras and emanations. They're just not here in my copy of the text."

Here's another difficulty with Douglas's opinion. He began the opinion, as you can see for yourself as you read it, by waxing eloquently about the right to privacy. He almost sounds like Justice Brandeis's grand opinion in *Olmstead*. But, at different points in the opinion, especially near the end of the opinion, he begins to talk, not about a right to privacy, but about a more narrow right to marital privacy. So, remember the quote that I gave you a few seconds ago: "To allow the state to regulate the sacred precincts of the marital bedroom," then he continues, "that would be repulsive to the notions of privacy surrounding the marriage relationship." So scholars and subsequent judges entrusted with using this precedent have asked themselves, "What kind of right did Douglas and the Court establish in *Griswold*? Some general right to privacy? Or a narrower right to marital privacy?"

An aside: Some historians have suggested that Douglas really wanted to go with a broad-based right to individualized, generalized privacy, and that the notions of marital privacy were inserted in the opinion at the request of Justice Brennan, who was concerned that a general right to privacy looked too much like Lochnerizing, and that a narrower notion of marital privacy was probably more constitutionally defensible; which provides interesting background for Justice Brennan's occurring opinion when he suggested the majority acted incorrectly by limiting privacy to the marital right, and instead should have argued for the larger privacy right more generally.

Justice Brennan's concurring opinion, as important and interesting it is, however, has largely been overshadowed by the concurring opinion of Justice Goldberg. Goldberg concurred (which is to say he agreed) that there was a right to privacy, which would be sufficiently strong to overwhelm the state, but he disagreed upon the reasoning.

Now, way back—perhaps in our first lecture, perhaps in our second—I indicated that there was some technical dispute, the kind of theological dispute that only a scholar could embrace, about whether the first eight amendments constitute the Bill of Rights or whether the first ten amendments constitute the Bill of Rights. I mention that now because Goldberg adopts a very novel form of reasoning in his concurrence. He doesn't embrace the penumbras and emanations, but instead says that, in addition to the explicit rights listed in the Bill of Rights, there must also be a set of implicit rights; and his source for this claim is the Ninth Amendment.

You'll recall that the Ninth Amendment has a reservation of rights to the individuals (the Tenth does that as well); but more importantly, the Ninth says that the enumeration of certain specific rights doesn't mean that there aren't additional constitutional liberties. In short, Goldberg argues that the very presence of the Ninth Amendment tells you that there must be additional rights beyond those specifically listed in the first eight.

Over time, occasionally, a concurring opinion will attain such validity and will be embraced by judges and scholars in a way that makes it more important than a majority opinion. That isn't what happened in this case. As a rule—not a hard and fast rule, but as a soft rule—a judge who uses the Ninth Amendment risks being assigned to obscurity. Every field of academic inquiry has certain kinds of unspoken, untested, perhaps indefensible assumptions about what is a legitimate form of inquiry and about what is an illegitimate form of inquiry; and one of those in the field of civil liberties is this: you may never use the Ninth Amendment because if you do so, you will be undoubtedly be accused of having traveled outside the boundaries of acceptable discourse.

Justice Black, in his dissenting opinion in *Griswold*, made a special effort to criticize Justice Goldberg's use of the Ninth Amendment. I think it's fair to say that Black just about became apoplectic over Goldberg's use of the Ninth Amendment. He went on to say that if

Goldberg or any judge could really use the Ninth Amendment as a source of constitutional meaning, that that would completely let loose the hounds of war; that it was worse than *Lochner,* because the Ninth Amendment was so vague, so imprecise, that any judge who wanted to could find any right imaginable in the Ninth and Tenth Amendment.

In short, the Ninth Amendment, for Black, became a vicious black hole, an expansive black hole, which, once you were drawn into it, meant you were forever untethered from the text of the Constitution itself, and untethered from the text you are left with. The easiest way to say this is, you are left with *Lochner.* You are left with a judge just making it up.

There are some appeals to what Black is saying. If the Ninth Amendment says, in layman's terms, in addition to the rights specifically listed in amendments one through eight, there are a whole bunch of other rights. You can see the temptation, can you not? The temptation is to say, "Sure, there are other rights. How about a right to education; rights to social subsistence? I'd like a right to this, that, or the other; and the Ninth Amendment tells me that such a right might, in fact, exist.

The Ninth Amendment, to use another cliché, constitutes a form of carte blanche for judges, and that scared Black to death. Black also criticized the opinion in several other ways. Here is perhaps the most famous and the most telling, succinct point of Black's dissent: he wrote, "I like my privacy as well as the next; but I am, nevertheless, compelled to admit that the government has a right to invade it, unless it is prohibited by some specific constitutional provision."

Now, let's take his position and apply it to the facts of *Griswold.* "I like my privacy as well as the next"—but the state may invade it, unless there is some specific constitutional provision that prohibits it. What specific constitutional prohibition would prevent the state from regulating access, or even forbidding the use, of contraceptives? It's difficult to know how to answer that question; so you might mentally run through the list of amendments or the list of liberties protected by the various constitutional amendments. Is there something in the First Amendment's provisions regarding speech or religion that would prohibit the state from prohibiting the use of contraceptives? I don't immediately see how there's a First Amendment objection. I can imagine one—that's what lawyers do—but one doesn't immediately suggest itself.

Perhaps the closest provision would, in fact, be the Fourth Amendment's prohibition of search and seizures. Here is where Douglas might be on the firmest ground; because if the state is, in fact, going to prohibit the use of contraceptives, at some point, presumably, it must have the investigative authority to determine whether or not that prohibition is actually being enforced or followed by citizens. But it's a small, limited protection. The Fourth Amendment doesn't prohibit searches and seizures. It prohibits unreasonable or unwarranted searches and seizures; and presumably a police officer investigating such a case would simply go to a judge, provide the same kinds of evidence that an officer of the law provides to any judge, and ask for a warrant.

Where does that leave Black? It leaves Black in the following position: the state does have the constitutional authority to prohibit the use of contraceptives, and, presumably, to regulate a wide expanse of interests or activities that would fall under the general umbrella of privacy. Black might have been uncomfortable with that individually, personally; but he stressed that his discomfort is not enough of a reason as a judge to create a new constitutional right. I use the word "create," notwithstanding what I said in a previous lecture, because here Black's position is, in fact, that the Court has simply made this right up; and making a right up is fundamentally illegitimate—or, if you prefer, is fundamentally an exercise in Lochnerizing.

If Douglas had the opportunity to respond, he would have said, "Hugo, I did not create a constitutional right to privacy. I found a constitutional right to privacy that was there. I mined it from the text. I didn't simply create it out of whole cloth."

Here is another dissent by Justice Potter Stewart. He said, "The Court's creation of the right to privacy represents an unwarranted, judicial intrusion into the powers of state legislatures." Now, part of what Stewart is referencing here is the same criticism that Black referenced—that there's no warrant for this constitutional right; the Court simply made it up. But Stewart adds to it another dimension, one that we saw repeatedly in the property cases, in which we're going to see repeatedly in the privacy cases, and that is that this is an unwarranted exercise of judicial power.

Remember, one of the recurrent themes of our course is the relationship between judicial power and democracy, or democratic theory more generally. Under what conditions, if any (and surely there are some conditions) may a Court, may a judge, displace a policy reached and reinforced through the democratic process?

It is probably worth recalling that the Connecticut statute in question in *Griswold* was then nearly 100 years old. The original birth control statute in Connecticut was passed as an obscenity statute. It was one of the very first of the so-called Comstock Laws—anti-pornography, anti-obscenity laws that swept the nation in the late 1800s. The law had survived repeated efforts at repeal by different collections of political coalitions in Connecticut. True, it hadn't been actually positively reaffirmed; but it had sat on the statute books for over a hundred years, which suggests that it represented at least part of the community's feeling about sexual behavior, even among married couples.

When, if ever, is it appropriate for the Court to say to a majority of the community, "You may not act on the basis of that moral sensibility"? Now clearly, it would be permissible for the Court to do that if the Court could have pointed to a specific provision—let's call it "Amendment Six-A"—that says there is a right to privacy, and the state may not interfere with it.

That's the easy case. We don't get easy cases. We have the difficult case. We're talking about a right that, if it exists, is an implicit right, a right inferred by judges. The Court, we will see as we continue our privacy discussion, has become more and more sensitive over time to this underlying issue of judicial power and judicial accountability to the democratic process more generally.

Now, if you'll forgive me a point that is probably trivial, but I can't resist it: Justice Stewart, perhaps not the most gifted, intellectually, of the Court's justices, was nevertheless a talented writer. Many of you will have heard the phrase, "I can't define pornography, but I know it when I see it,"—Potter Stewart. And I love that phrase, but here is an even better one, taken from his dissent in *Griswold:* "I think this is an uncommonly silly law." I'm sorry. I do hope you'll forgive me, but every time I hear it, I chuckle; and every time I hear it, I see the Keebler Elves dancing through my brain, talking about "uncommonly good cookies."

One final point about *Griswold:* the Court, the majority in *Griswold,* had to ask one final question: Is there a compelling state interest that would, nevertheless, justify the state's regulation of the privacy right? The Court's answer: No. Simply regulating the moral sensibilities surrounding birth control does not constitute a fundamental, compelling state interest that would justify the regulation of the fundamental right. As we continue to read cases in subsequent lectures, please ask yourself in every one of those cases, what interest does the state advance, and is that interest compelling?

Lecture Eleven
Roe v. Wade and Reproductive Autonomy

Scope:

Few topics in American law are as emotionally charged, and as doctrinally confused, as the discussion of abortion rights. As we shall see in this lecture, the doctrinal confusion surrounding *Roe v. Wade* (1973) is intricately caught up with the profound moral and political issues involved in abortion but equally with important questions about the role of the Supreme Court in American society. In this lecture, we explore how and why *Roe* came to the Court; the reasons offered by Justice Blackmun, writing for the Court's 7–2 majority, for finding that a right to terminate a pregnancy exists in the Constitution; and the many criticisms of the decision by the Court's dissenters, Justices White and Rehnquist. Of course, dissents to *Roe* extend well beyond the courts, and we shall explore the social and political consequences of *Roe*, as well.

Outline

I. *Roe* involved a challenge to a Texas statute that prohibited abortion at any point in a pregnancy except to save the life of the mother. In 1970, Jane Roe (a pseudonym) was 25, unmarried, and pregnant. She filed a *class action* lawsuit, asking the court to declare the statute unconstitutional as a violation of her right to privacy.

   A. The case might have been dismissed on grounds of mootness or ripeness, two important doctrines designed to promote the prudential use of judicial power.

   B. A companion case, *Doe v. Bolton*, presented a challenge to a Georgia statute that required all abortions to be approved by a "hospital abortion committee."

II. In his opinion for the majority (7–2), Justice Blackmun agreed that the right to privacy, whatever its source, is "broad enough to encompass a woman's decision whether or not to terminate a pregnancy."

   A. Note that Blackmun was not precise about where the right to privacy is located in the Constitution.

B. Equally important, Blackmun offered no support at all for his conclusion—hardly self-evident—that the right includes a decision to terminate a pregnancy. He wrote: "This right of privacy, whether it be found in the Fourteenth Amendment's concept of personal liberty, as we feel it is, or as the District Court determined, in the Ninth Amendment's reservation of rights to the people, is broad enough to encompass a woman's decision whether or not to terminate a pregnancy."

    1. This is an important point. It is not enough to establish, in this case, that the Constitution includes a right to privacy, if it does.

    2. The critical next step is to show that such a right includes this particular set of decisions or conduct—and the majority offers no support at all for the conclusion that it does.

III. Although the Court concluded that there is a right to privacy and that the right is broad enough to encompass a decision to terminate a pregnancy, the Court also denied the claim that such a right is absolute.

A. Consequently, there are times when the state's interests in regulating or prohibiting abortions will be strong enough to overcome the right.

B. Originally, the state of Texas acknowledged that one of the reasons why the state prohibited abortion was to reinforce what it called a "Victorian sense" of social morality about proper sexual conduct; however, the state refused to articulate that or to press that as a reason before the Supreme Court.

C. The state's interests are therefore two: protecting the fetus, and protecting maternal health.

D. These are interesting and important claims, and both are problematic.

    1. For example, the state's interest in protecting fetal health might lead us to address the question of when life begins. One might argue that if the fetus is a life, then it ought to be constitutionally vested with certain rights, including rights to life and liberty.

    2. The Court declined to address this question, noting that the critical question is, instead: Is the fetus a person?

  E. At some point in the pregnancy, the state's interests in protecting the fetus and protecting maternal health are sufficiently strong, or compelling, to override a woman's "fundamental" right.

    1. As regards the fetus, that point is at the moment of "viability."

    2. As regards maternal health, that moment is at the end of the second trimester.

IV. The dissents in *Roe* attacked the decision on two grounds.

  A. Justice White anticipated one of the primary criticisms of *Roe*, complaining that the Court had simply announced "a new right … with scarcely any reason or authority for its action."

  B. Justice Rehnquist similarly complained that the "privacy" right in *Roe* had little or nothing in common with the Court's earlier privacy cases.

  C. A second set of criticisms, related to the first, concerns issues of judicial power and accountability.

    1. Many critics of *Roe* think the decision is indistinguishable from *Lochner* and like cases—just another example of the majority making it up.

    2. On this understanding, *Roe* is symbolic of the dangers implicit in substantive due process, whether economic or noneconomic.

  D. *Roe* is also intensely controversial for reasons that are not essentially doctrinal in nature, in part because *Roe* touches on sensitive, complex areas of human life at the intersection of morality, faith, and law.

  E. But *Roe* is also controversial because it seems to many to highlight the dangers of a Court untethered from the actual text of the Constitution.

    1. Let's ask a counter-factual: where would we be if the Court had never decided *Roe*? Several states had already begun to liberalize their abortion laws. Would that trend have continued, or would it have been forestalled in the absence of *Roe*?

2. Some scholars suggest that the debate in the U.S. is volatile, angry, and sometimes violent precisely because, as citizens, there is nothing we can do about abortion.

Essential Reading:

Roe v. Wade (1973); *Doe v. Bolton* (1973).

Kommers, Finn, and Jacobsohn, *American Constitutional Law*, chapter 6, pp. 242–244.

John Hart Ely, "The Wages of Crying Wolf: A Comment on *Roe v. Wade*," 82 *Yale Law Journal* 920 (1973).

Supplementary Reading:

Robert H. Bork, *The Tempting of America*.

David J. Garrow, *Liberty and Sexuality: The Right to Privacy and the Making of Roe v. Wade*.

Mary Ann Glendon, *Abortion and Divorce in Western Law*.

Laurence H. Tribe, *Abortion: The Clash of Absolutes*.

Questions to Consider:

1. What right, precisely, did the majority in *Roe* claim to advance? Was it a right of self-determination? Or did the Court advance the right of women as equals to participate in the full life of the community? Is the right one of sexual liberty or lifestyle?

2. Is the issue in *Roe* less about privacy than reproductive autonomy? What difference does it make constitutionally?

3. Is the issue, ultimately, about who has the authority to decide who is and who is not a member of the community, vested with constitutional rights?

4. Is there a role for Courts to play in the resolution of such issues? Or is judicial involvement here just another instance of judges usurping popular authority in the absence of a clear constitutional command?

Lecture Eleven—Transcript
Roe v. Wade and Reproductive Autonomy

In this lecture, we take up the jurisprudence of abortion. Few topics in American law are as emotionally charged or as doctrinally confused as this one. As we shall see in this lecture, and, in particular, by our discussion of *Roe v. Wade* (decided in 1973), the doctrinal confusion surrounding *Roe* is intricately caught up with profound moral and political issues, as well as important questions about the role of the Supreme Court in American society. In this lecture, we'll explore how and why *Roe* came to the Court; the reasons the Court offered for finding that a woman's right to privacy includes the decision to terminate a pregnancy; and for the many criticisms of the decision by the Court's dissenters, especially those advanced by Justice Rehnquist. Of course, dissents to *Roe* extend well beyond the courts, and near the end of this lecture, we will want to explore the social and political consequences of *Roe,* and the controversy *Roe* has generated.

Let's begin with the case itself. *Roe* involved a challenge to a Texas statute that prohibited abortion at any point in a woman's pregnancy, except to save the life of the mother. In 1970, Jane Roe (a pseudonym) was 25; she was unmarried, and pregnant. She and her attorneys filed a class action lawsuit. A class action lawsuit is a lawsuit on behalf of herself and other individuals similarly situated. She asked the state court to declare the statute unconstitutional as a violation of her right to privacy.

Before we actually get into the terms of the Supreme Court's decision, it's important to note that the case might have been dismissed immediately on at least two grounds. First, the Court might have dismissed the case on the grounds of mootness. You'll recall from an earlier lecture, that mootness refers to those instances where the underlying controversy—in this case, it would have been the pregnancy and the collision with the statute—have expired. We haven't spent much time, if any, talking about the actual process of litigating cases, so I'm going to ask you to trust me. As a rule, getting your case from the lowest level of the judicial system to the highest, the Supreme Court, far exceeds nine months. At the end of nine months, the pregnancy would be terminated either naturally or artificially, and hence, the case would be moot.

Alternatively the Court might have dismissed the case as not being ripe. In this case, ripeness would mean that Jane Roe, or any other plaintiff, was not pregnant, and as a consequence, would only be challenging the statute as something that might interfere with her behavior at some point in the future. That's not a live conflict, to use the legal phrase; it's not a ripe conflict; and as a consequence, the Court might have stepped aside from *Roe* on the grounds of ripeness, as well as on the grounds of mootness. Please recall that these doctrines are a function of judicial evolution. They are not mandated by the Constitution itself, and as a consequence, it is fair to call them "discretionary." The Court may apply these concepts when it wants to, and it may waive them when it wants to as well.

In this case, *Roe v. Wade*, the Court chose to waive these doctrines because to enforce them strictly would mean that the underlying conflict, again, between the abortion decision and the state's statute, would never be resolved judicially.

I should add, too, that *Roe v. Wade* was accompanied by a second case, *Doe v. Bolton*, which presented a challenge to a Georgia statute that required that every abortion be approved in advance by a so-called hospital abortion committee.

Let's go right into the heart of *Roe v. Wade*. Some people seem to forget that *Roe* was not that close of a case: It was decided by a 7–2 majority. Writing for the majority, writing in really his first case (he had only been on the Court for two years), Junior Justice Blackmun agreed that a right to privacy, whatever its source, is, "broad enough to encompass a woman's decision whether or not to terminate her pregnancy."

Now you may feel that I have been somewhat unfair to Justice Blackmun when I opined that he said "the right to privacy, whatever its source, is broad enough," but I want to quote him directly here so that you can get a sense of the tenor of his argument.

Blackmun began by saying, "The Constitution does not explicitly mention any right of privacy." But we have recognized some cases of privacy, notably those concerning, "activities relating to marriage, procreation, contraception, family relationships, and child-rearing and education." He begins, in other words, by suggesting that there is a line of precedent that has indicated that there is some sort of a privacy right, a privacy right that seems to surround the activities he described; and, naturally, he cited the important case of *Griswold v. Connecticut*. But an appeal to precedent, whatever its strengths or weaknesses as a method of constitutional interpretation, does not advance or address the underlying question about where this right to privacy exists. So Blackmun continued:

> This right of privacy, whether it be found in the Fourteenth Amendment's concept of personal liberty, as we feel it is, or as the District Court determined in the Ninth Amendment's reservation of rights to the people, is broad enough to encompass a woman's decision whether or not to terminate her pregnancy.

Roe, as I mentioned before, is among the most controversial of cases in the field of civil liberties. A great deal of that controversy is located in that single paragraph.

Before I continue with the rest of the opinion, let me suggest some of what those criticisms are. "This right of privacy, whether it be found in the Fourteenth Amendment's concept of personal liberty, as we feel it is, or as the District Court determined in the Ninth Amendment..."—let's stop there for a minute. Precisely where does the right to privacy exist? There is a hint, a suggestion, that it might be in the Fourteenth Amendment; but it might also be in the Ninth. Clearly the entire flavor of this paragraph is to dismiss any real concern about where the right to privacy exists. The truth of the matter, or so it is seemed to most justices and scholars critical of Roe is this: Justice Blackmun, writing for a majority, fails in his most elementary responsibility—to articulate where a right comes from.

This is an extraordinary error. It wouldn't be quite so extraordinary if we were speaking about a right to property, because then we could all pick up our copy of the Constitution, as Justice Black was wont to do, and find it in the text. But we can't do that with privacy. Surely, Justice Blackmun knew, from having read *Griswold*, from having cited *Griswold,* that there was profound, underlying controversy about whether a right to privacy existed at all. But he passes almost directly past that question, and then reaches the heart and soul of the *Roe* decision. This right to privacy (if I may paraphrase), may be found somewhere, but wherever it is, "It is broad enough to encompass a woman's decision whether or not to terminate her pregnancy." That may or may not be an acceptable or a correct constitutional conclusion. I don't know. What I am concerned with here is that it is not an argument. It is simply an assertion.

Let me put this in another way. If I asked you to write a summary of the argument in *Roe*, I would be asking you to tell me to identify, in your paper the precise set of reasons why a right to privacy includes a decision to terminate a pregnancy. I would expect your paper to give me reason one, reason two, reason three about why a right to privacy—irrespective of its location in the text—why a right to privacy includes a decision to terminate a pregnancy.

Let me put this in another way. This is a critically important point, and I don't want to pass it until I am confident we understand it. The issue in *Roe v. Wade* is not really, does the Constitution include a right to privacy? I don't mean to belittle that or to suggest that it's insignificant, but it's not the primary issue in *Roe*. The primary issue in *Roe* is, does a right to privacy include this particular decision to terminate a pregnancy?

Please let me try yet another way. We might all agree—for purposes of argument, let's agree—that the Constitution includes a right to privacy. At best, that's half the battle. When we are faced with *Roe*, we are faced with the second part of the battle; not whether there is a right to privacy, but critically, whether the right to privacy includes this particular form of behavior.

And in every case we consider in our examination of privacy, we should ask ourselves, does the privacy right, assuming it exists at all, include a decision to terminate a pregnancy; a decision to utilize partial-birth abortions; a decision to engage in same-sex conduct; a decision to raise my child the way I would like to raise my child? On some important level, our concern with whether there is a right to privacy misleads us. It takes us down a path that it not helpful. The critical question must instead be, once we assume there is a right to privacy, what kinds of behavior will be protected under the rubric of privacy, and what kinds of behavior do not fall under that rubric?

So it is fair to ask Justice Blackmun, writing for a majority, "What reasons do you have, what reasons can you advance, to support the proposition that the right of privacy, wherever it is located, is broad enough to encompass a woman's decision to terminate a pregnancy?"

I ask you simply to read the majority opinion and to try to identify for yourself what reasons Justice Blackmun advances. On the other hand, I don't want you to spend too much time on this endeavor, because I am fairly confident of what result you will reach. There is not a single word of explanation. Not one. Please note: I am not saying that the decision is necessarily incorrect. At least at this point, I express no opinion about whether Justice Blackmun's conclusion is the correct constitutional conclusion or an incorrect one. I simply mean to point out the paucity of his reasoning.

Let's continue with the case. Assuming there is a right to privacy, and assuming that that right is broad enough, expansive enough, to include a woman's decision to terminate her pregnancy, hardly settles the issue. The plaintiffs, Jane Roe and her attorney, made a second argument. They argued that that right—the right to privacy to include the decision to terminate a pregnancy—was, in their words, absolute. What they meant by that was simply this: that there are no circumstances under which the state may regulate that decision.

We talked about absolute rights in an earlier point in the course, and you'll recall that I said there are no such things, with the possible exception of the freedom to believe whatever you would like to believe; and, presumably, if Jane Roe and her attorneys want to believe that there is an absolute right to an abortion, they are entitled to do so; but as a matter of constitutional law, they are fundamentally incorrect; and Justice Blackmun continues by saying that.

There is no such thing as an absolute right to terminate a pregnancy, which is simply the Court's way of addressing a second set of issues. That second set of issues concerns under what conditions may the state actually involve itself in this immensely private area of human life. Under what conditions may the state advance a set of interests? What kinds of interests will be sufficient for the state to involve itself in Jane Roe's decision to terminate a pregnancy? That is a profoundly important question.

In order to address it, we need to understand what interests the state advanced; and, as it turns out, at least historically, the state of Texas had three reasons why it thought it ought to be allowed to prohibit a woman from terminating her pregnancy. The first of those reasons, grounded in history, was so obsolete that the state refused to really press it or to really advance it in Court.

Originally, the state acknowledged one of the reasons why the state prohibited abortion was to reinforce what it called a "Victorian sense" of social morality about proper sexual conduct. However, the state refused to articulate that or to press that as a reason. I believe that's unfortunate. It would have been very interesting to have the Supreme Court address directly the question of whether or not a state's interest in preserving a certain kind of sexual morality would be sufficiently strong to form the basis of its abortion legislation; but, to be careful about it, the Court did not specifically address that. That left the state of Texas with two reasons for its statute. The state first claimed that it had an interest in protecting the fetus. Secondly, the state argued that it had an interest in protecting maternal health.

I want to speak about both of these briefly. The state's first interest is protecting the fetus. This interest is what opens up the question about human life in *Roe*. The Court insists that it need not resolve the difficult question of when life begins. That is a profoundly, immensely difficult and troubling question. One can appreciate, I think, why the Court would not want to open it up. The immediate objection, of course, is this: so many issues in civil liberties do not involve, simply, the right of an individual in conflict with the interests of the state. Many issues, as we shall see, involve the rights of one individual in conflict with another.

It is possible to conceptualize *Roe* in the following way: what is involved in *Roe* is a conflict of two constitutional liberties: the mother's right to privacy; or, if you prefer, autonomy, reproductive autonomy, human personality, self-determination, profoundly significant rights of great weight. But one might also say what's involved on the other side is the right of the fetus to liberty and life; and if the Court has to weigh those two interests, it won't be surprising to find that the right to liberty, the right to life, will often have to trump the privacy right. It may not always trump it, and we can imagine situations where the conflict I've described is not actually the conflict. The conflict might be between the mother's right to life and the fetus's right to life. What an extraordinary conflict to have to settle!

I believe Justice Blackmun's response, although not fully articulated in *Roe*, would go as follows: the fetus's status as a living, human being is not something we can settle as a matter of law, and it is not something we need to settle as a matter of law. The critical question isn't whether the fetus is alive, is possessed of life. The critical question is, is the fetus a person? Living things aren't necessarily invested with constitutional rights. Persons are invested with constitutional rights.

So, the critical question on this line of analysis becomes not, is the fetus alive? but, is the fetus, for purposes of constitutional inquiry, a person invested with rights? The critical question, in other words, is personhood. This is hardly much of an improvement. On an average day, I no more want to think about when are people alive than I want to think what constitutes being a person. But at least here, Justice Blackmun suggests, there is some constitutional guidance. He references the text and says there are not many references to personhood, but wherever there are references to personhood in the text, none of them suggest a prenatal suggestion of personhood.

Now, let's go back to the state's two interests. The first is protecting the fetus. The second is protecting maternal health. "At some point in a woman's pregnancy," Justice Blackmun argues, "the state's interests in these two things are sufficiently strong," or, if you'll permit me to use the jargon again, are sufficiently compelling to override a woman's "fundamental" right to privacy. As regards the fetus, the state's interest becomes compelling, sufficiently strong to regulate the right at the moment of fetal viability.

Imagine a line. One end of the line is the point of conception. At the other end of the line is the point of birth. At some point on that line, a fetus, Justice Blackmun writes, becomes "viable outside a woman's womb." At that very moment of viability, the state has a stronger interest in protecting that fetus, and may act in ways to regulate, or even to prohibit, a woman's decision to terminate the pregnancy. That's the "fetal viability" line.

Imagine the same line: the moment of conception, the moment of birth. "At some point on that line," the Court argues, "the state's interest in protecting the health of the mother also becomes sufficiently strong to allow the state to act in ways to protect the mother." We saw on the fetal viability line that the moment the state may act is at the moment of viability. As regards to the maternal health line, the Court concluded that that point, the point where the state may step in, may intervene to protect the mother is at the end of the second trimester of the pregnancy.

Now, let's just sort of step back for a second and see if we can come up with a doctrinal rule for *Roe*. I think the rule is this: a woman has a fundamental, constitutionally protected right to terminate a pregnancy up until a certain point in the pregnancy. As regards the fetus, the woman's right is nearly absolute until the moment of viability, when the state may act. As regards the maternal health issue, the state's right to act occurs at the end of the second trimester. At that point, at either of those points—conveniently, they tend to coincide—at either of those points, the state's interest becomes "compelling," and now the state may act.

This is a remarkably sophisticated, a remarkably complex set of doctrinal rules. I hope you can begin to see one of the many criticisms that will be directed to it. As aesthetically pleasing as it may be—or alternatively, as aesthetically noxious as it may be—the obvious problem is, where in the world can you get this elaborate scheme of viability in second trimesters in the Constitution? It seems a remarkable superimposition of a set of complex, medical and social-political rules that critics complain simply can't be derived in any plausible way from any single part of the Constitution, or even from any collection of parts in the Constitution. This begins to anticipate several of the criticisms that were actually filed in *Roe* itself.

Justice White anticipated one of the primary criticisms of *Roe*. He complained, "The Court had simply announced a new right...without scarcely any reason or authority for its action." Now, I've already quoted that part of the majority opinion that I think White is referring to, and you'll have to decide for yourself how persuasive you think his criticism is. Irrespective of your assessment of it, I need to tell you that the criticism is widely shared and widely voiced within the academic community.

Justice Rehnquist first advanced a similar complaint. He announced first that the "privacy" right in *Roe*, whatever its dimensions, had little or nothing in common with the Court's earlier privacy cases. Now, you'll recall that Justice Blackmun made a reference to "those activities relating to marriage, procreation, contraception, family relationships, child-rearing, and education." Justice Rehnquist's response is, our earlier privacy cases, even if they might be described in that way, simply don't have any direct relationship to the right announced in this case.

Now let's back up for a minute. What's really driving Justice Rehnquist's criticism is the ghost of Lochner. Without putting too fine a point on it, Justice Rehnquist, as so many critics later will, simply accuses the majority of making the whole thing up. By making the whole thing up, I mean making up the very existence of the right in the first instance; and, in the second instance, making up this profoundly complicated, perhaps sophisticated, system of viability, maternal health, and trimesters; and those points in a pregnancy where the state may act, and those points in a pregnancy where a woman should be free to act. On this understanding, *Roe* is genuinely indistinguishable from *Lochner*. Those individuals, those justices, those scholars, those students who want to argue that *Roe* is correct, must account for this criticism. It will not do simply to ignore *Lochner*.

Now why should you care about this criticism? This criticism suggests a larger problem with privacy cases more generally. If we can't address the claim that the Court simply made it up in *Roe*, then we are going to be in grave danger when we consider all of the Court's subsequent privacy cases; because, in all of those cases, as I suggested earlier, we are going to have to ask ourselves not so much the question, does the right to privacy exist? but rather, does the right to privacy encompass this particular set of behaviors or this particular set of interests?

Roe is controversial for an additional set of reasons as well. *Roe* is controversial because it suggests to us that the Court's use of substantive due process to protect privacy and related interests might be fundamentally illegitimate. But it's controversial, I think, for a set of other reasons, and those reasons are not essentially doctrinal in nature; perhaps, they're not even constitutional in nature. *Roe* is controversial, in part, because it touches upon a sensitive and complex area of human life—maybe the most sensitive and complex area of human life. *Roe* exists at the intersection of morality, faith, law, politics, and, perhaps only secondarily, the Constitution.

Consider for a minute what the political and social reaction to *Roe v. Wade* was. We are now some 30 years past *Roe*. And while there is certainly room for disagreement, I think—as a broad statement—it is fair to say that abortion is every bit as volatile an issue in American politics, in American life, as it was when *Roe* was decided. The fallout from *Roe* has been profound political controversy; profound constitutional controversy; controversy that, sadly, is sometimes vital. We should not pretend that some of the violence that besets America is violence that is centered around the politics of abortion. Please don't misunderstand me. I am not suggesting that the Court is directly or indirectly from abortion violence.

I want to make a different kind of claim. I want to make a kind of claim that lawyers like to call "counter-factual." Let's ask a counter-factual: Where would we be if the court had never decided *Roe*? Would there be an abortion right? Of course, this is entirely speculative, but there are some pieces of information that we should hold onto, and the first is to note that, in 1973, when *Roe* was decided, several states had already begun to liberalize their abortion laws. Would that trend have continued, or would it have been forestalled in the absence of *Roe*? We can't say.

We do know this, though: as recently as 2005—as a practical matter, not as a theoretical, constitutional matter—it is just as difficult to get an abortion in the United States (or it was just as difficult to get an abortion in the United States) as it was in 1973. And we are a society, unlike some European societies, that is in the midst of a continuing, angry, volatile debate over abortion. Some scholars suggest that that debate is volatile, angry, and sometimes violent precisely because, as citizens, there is nothing we can do about abortion.

The Supreme Court has taken over abortion politics, and whether I think abortion should be legal, on demand, illegal, prohibited, is of little ongoing significance in the same way, I am sorry to say, that your opinion is of little ongoing significance; because, in the end, you can campaign all you want, you can protest all you want, you can stand outside the Court on the anniversary of *Roe v. Wade,* but there is nothing in the constitutional system that mandates that the Court pay attention to you. The Court has carved its own course. We will see that course in greater detail in the next lecture. But understand, it is the Court's course; and perhaps the reason American politics are so violent is because the American people are fundamentally impotent when it comes to deciding abortion, or the politics of abortion, on a day-to-day basis.

Lecture Twelve
Privacy and Autonomy—From *Roe* to *Casey*

Scope:

At the end of our last lecture, we briefly considered the larger political and social reactions to *Roe*. We continue our examination of the consequences of *Roe* in this lecture by exploring litigation after *Roe*. The most recent cases involving abortion and reproductive autonomy have highlighted the issues of judicial power and accountability. As we saw last time, *Roe* did not completely prohibit the states from regulating abortion, and in the decade following *Roe*, the Court was called upon to determine the constitutionality of a great variety of such restrictions. For example, in *Planned Parenthood of Missouri v. Danforth* (1976), the Court struck down a state law requiring minors to obtain the consent of their parents and wives of their husbands before an abortion. In many of these cases, the Court began to criticize the logic of *Roe*. Some judges, notably Justice Scalia, also campaigned for the reversal of *Roe*. The Court considered a direct challenge to *Roe* in the important and controversial case of *Planned Parenthood of Southeastern Pennsylvania v. Casey* (1992), but the Court could not find a majority to overrule *Roe*. The Court's internal divisions continue to manifest themselves, as we shall see when we take up the recent decision in *Stenberg v. Carhart* (2000), in which the Court addressed Nebraska's ban on partial-birth abortions.

Outline

I. *Roe* did not settle the debate over the Constitution and abortion. Instead, it inaugurated a debate that has lasted more than 30 years and shows no sign of diminishing.

   A. This is partly because the Court acknowledged in *Roe* that there is room for state regulation in the area of abortions. The questions inevitably were redrawn to determine which state regulations could pass constitutional muster and which were unconstitutional infringements on a woman's constitutional right to privacy. Under the framework, a state may regulate an abortion when it has a compelling interest.

B. In *Planned Parenthood v. Danforth* (1976), the Court struck down a state regulation that required minors to obtain the consent of their parents and wives to obtain the consent of their husbands before an abortion.

C. In *Planned Parenthood v. Ashcroft* (1983), the Court appeared to modify its position by sustaining a parental consent statute for "unemancipated" minors, provided there was a provision that allowed some minors alternatively to obtain a judge's approval.

II. In *Akron v. Akron Center for Reproductive Heath* (1983), the Court reaffirmed its broad commitment to *Roe*. In a strongly worded dissent, Justice O'Connor argued that the "*Roe* framework … is clearly on a collision course with itself…."

A. What O'Connor refers to is a problem concerning the two "timelines" we saw in Roe. The first timeline concerned fetal viability. That point was different in 1983 than in 1973, thus illustrating a larger problem: Advances in medical technology meant that the point of viability would inevitability be pushed closer and closer to the point of conception.

B. In contrast, the second line—the line concerning maternal health—was also undergoing change driven by medical technology. Advances in technology made it safer to conduct abortions later and later in the pregnancy.

C. Thus, the state's ability to regulate a pregnancy was simultaneously being pushed back to the moment of conception and forward to the moment of birth.

D. Six years later, Chief Justice Rehnquist advanced a similar complaint [in *Webster v. Reproductive Health Services*], noting that the trimester framework adopted in *Roe* is "hardly consistent with the notion of a Constitution cast in general terms…."

E. The *Akron* Court could muster only a plurality, but the opinion is important because a plurality of justices seemed prepared to rule, in contrast to *Roe*, that a state's interest in potential life began not at the point of viability but at the point of conception.

1. Scalia, who accused the Court of acting irresponsibly by not overruling *Roe* outright, noted the significance of the potential change.
2. Justice Blackmun was equally distressed, noting that a "chill wind blows. I dissent."

III. The Court's turmoil over *Roe* continued in the significant case of *Planned Parenthood v. Casey* (1992). Again, the Court could not muster a majority opinion.

A. Justice O'Connor wrote for a three-person plurality. She rejected the government's invitation to overrule *Roe*, instead explaining at great length why the Court's reliance on precedent and concern for its own legitimacy counseled a reaffirmation of *Roe*'s central holding.

1. O'Connor began by noting:
   > Liberty finds no refuge in a jurisprudence of doubt. After considering the fundamental questions resolved by *Roe*, principles of institutional integrity and the rule of *stare decisis*, we are led to conclude this: The essential holding of *Roe v. Wade* should be retained.

2. She continued:
   > A decision to overrule *Roe* would address error, if error there was, at the cost of both profound and unnecessary damage to the Court's legitimacy and to the nation's commitment to the rule of law."

3. In response, Justice Scalia said:
   > I cannot agree with, indeed, I am appalled by, the Court's suggestion that the decision whether to stand by an erroneous constitutional decision must be strongly influenced—against overruling, no less—by the substantial and continuing public opposition the decision has generated.

4. He continued:
   > That is appalling. The Court's decision, presumably, should be governed by only one factor, and that factor should be to get the Constitution right, and if getting it right means that we acknowledge that we got it wrong once before, then so be it, because our

constitutional obligation is to the Constitution itself, not to our own constitutional integrity….*Roe* has created a national politics plagued by abortion protests, national abortion lobbying, and abortion marches on Congress.

B. Although the plurality did not overrule *Roe*, it did make potentially substantial changes in the regulatory framework governing abortions.

    1. For example, the plurality seemed to eschew the fundamental right/compelling state interest framework in favor of an important or a substantial liberty interest (a new category of liberty) and a rule that permits states to regulate abortions at any point in a pregnancy, so long as such regulations are not an "undue burden" on the woman's right.

    2. One difficulty is that the plurality did not define "undue burden."

C. Justice Blackmun, concurring in part and dissenting in part, praised the plurality opinion as an "act of personal courage and constitutional principle."

D. In contrast, Justice Scalia, dissenting, argued that to praise the plurality opinion as an act of "statesmanship" was "nothing less than Orwellian": "The issue is whether it [abortion] is a liberty protected by the Constitution of the United States. I am sure it is not."

IV. As a practical matter, one consequence of the Court's inability to muster a majority opinion in *Akron* or, later, in *Casey* is a continued and contentious role for the Court in overseeing the politics of abortion.

A. The new "undue burden" standard, for example, seems to many observers an open invitation for states to continue to test out new regulations on abortion.

B. One such recent case is *Stenberg v. Carhart* (2000), in which the Court declared unconstitutional Nebraska's ban on partial-birth abortions. Once again, however, the Court proved itself deeply divided. The case produced no less than eight separate opinions.

1. Justice Scalia wrote, "Today's decision, that the Constitution prevents the prohibition of a horrible mode of abortion, will be greeted by a firestorm · of controversy, as well it should."
2. If *Stenberg* is a guide for future cases, then we should assume, I think, that those future cases will show a Court as deeply divided as this one.
C. These are issues of politics, not necessarily or simply issues of law—and issues of politics are what it means to live in a constitutional democracy. ·

Essential Reading:

Planned Parenthood of Missouri v. Danforth (1976).

Planned Parenthood v. Ashcroft (1983).

Akron v. Akron Center for Reproductive Health (1983).

Planned Parenthood v. Casey (1992).

Stenberg v. Carhart (2000).

Kommers, Finn, and Jacobsohn, *American Constitutional Law*, chapter 6, pp. 244–248.

Supplementary Reading:

Ruth Bader Ginsburg, "Speaking in a Judicial Voice," 67 *New York University Law Review* 1185 (1993).

Questions to Consider:

1. Does the plurality in *Casey* make a more persuasive argument for the privacy right than the majority in *Roe*? How, if at all, do the arguments differ?
2. When, if ever, is it appropriate for the Court—as the plurality seemed to do—to consider its own legitimacy in resolving difficult constitutional questions?
3. Justice Scalia suggested that *Roe* is similar to *Dred Scott*. Do you agree?
4. Why did the plurality use the undue burden test and not the more familiar fundamental rights/compelling state interest test? Is there any practical consequence to the distinction?

5. Justice Blackmun wrote that the decision should be a "warning to all who have tried to turn this Court into yet another political branch." What did he mean?

Lecture Twelve—Transcript
Privacy and Autonomy—From *Roe* to *Casey*

At the end of our last lecture we briefly considered the larger political and social reactions to *Roe*. We will continue our examination of the consequences of *Roe* in this lecture, in particular, by exploring the litigation that occurred after *Roe,* and which continues to this day.

The most recent cases involving abortion and reproductive autonomy have highlighted the issues of judicial power and accountability that we saw in *Roe*. Another way to put this is simply this: *Roe* didn't settle the debate over the constitutionality of abortion; it inaugurated a debate over the constitutionality of abortion. That debate has lasted over 30 years, and there is little, if any, sign that that debate will diminish in the near future.

Part of the reason for this is because the Court acknowledged in *Roe* that there is room for state regulation in the area of abortions. So following *Roe,* the questions became important, if somewhat different in nature. The question, at least as far as litigation is concerned, wasn't, is there a constitutional right to privacy? The question, instead, became, under what precise conditions may the state act to regulate the abortion decision? You'll recall that, under the framework of *Roe,* the doctrinal test is simply this: the state may regulate an abortion when it has a "compelling" state interest to do so; and those two compelling state interests, at the level of general abstraction, are protecting fetal viability, or protecting the fetus at the point of viability, and protecting maternal health.

In subsequent cases, the Court began to elaborate upon what that would mean for specific abortion regulations. So, for example, in *Planned Parenthood v. Danforth,* decided three years later in 1976, the Supreme Court struck down a state regulation that required minors to obtain the consent of their parents, or wives, of their husbands, before an abortion.

In *Planned Parenthood v. Ashcroft,* decided in 1983, the Court appeared to modify its position a little bit, by sustaining a parental consent statute for so-called unemancipated minors, provided there was a provision in the law that would allow some minors, nevertheless, to receive an abortion by obtaining a judge's approval.

In that same year, 1983, the Court decided a very important abortion case known as *Akron v. Akron Center for Reproductive Health*. This case is important because it began to articulate—or in it, some of the justices began to articulate—fundamental discontent with the way the Court's abortion jurisprudence had proceeded. Nevertheless, the Court began in *Akron* by reaffirming its broad commitment to *Roe,* and by suggesting that the trimester framework would still hold. In response to that particular part, in a strongly worded dissent, Justice Sandra Day O'Connor argued, "the *Roe* framework…is clearly on a collision course with itself.…"

Now, the first thing I want to point out here is that this is a mere 13 years after *Roe*. What O'Connor is referring to also references a fundamental problem, or a fundamental criticism with *Roe* itself. You'll recall the two timelines: one timeline refers to fetal viability, references point of conception versus birth; the second timeline, point of conception, ends in birth, refers to maternal health. Let's just deal for a minute with the fetal viability framework.

At what point in a pregnancy is a fetus viable? I hope you can see that your answer to that question is likely to depend heavily on what time era you ask it. The point of viability in 1973 is a very different point of viability even by 1983. The point of viability now is dramatically different than it was when *Roe* was decided. Medical technology has advanced the point of viability closer and closer to the moment of conception. Now, think about what that means for a constitutional rule concerning the regulation of abortion. Because the state may regulate at the point of viability, and because the point of viability is being pushed by medical technology closer and closer to the point of conception, we are expanding that area of the pregnancy, that expanse of the pregnancy in which the state may act. That's the first timeline—fetal viability.

Consider the state's interest in maternal health. When *Roe* was decided in 1973, the Court concluded that the state of medical technology yielded a rule. The rule would be that at the end of the second trimester, abortions become such a significant threat to maternal health that the state has a legitimate interest in regulating, and perhaps even prohibiting, some abortions. Advance that time clock to now, and that same medical technology that pushes the point of viability closer and closer to the moment of conception has made abortions, as a medical procedure, safer and safer later and later during the term of the pregnancy; which means that the state's ability to regulate the abortion right, on the grounds of maternal health, is shrinking to a smaller and smaller period.

So, when Justice O'Connor says, "*Roe* is on a collision course with itself," a large measure of what she means is that these two timelines are in direct conflict. The state is simultaneously being told that it may regulate earlier and earlier during the pregnancy and later and later in the pregnancy. This points up again to a fundamental criticism with *Roe* that was only hinted at in our last lecture. If the Constitution is to be a statement of enduring principles, if it is to exist and to endure through time, then it must consist of general principles that transcend any particular moment in time.

I hope you can see the criticism here. A constitution of general principles may not be compatible with a constitution that constructs rules based on the state of medical technology, or on the state of any other kind of discourse at any particular time. So the larger point Sandra Day O'Connor wants to make is this: the trimester framework, enunciated in *Roe*, is not only on a collision course with itself, but is fundamentally inconsistent with the notion of what a constitution is intended to achieve more generally.

So, as Justice Rehnquist will say in a subsequent case, "The trimester framework adopted in *Roe* is hardly consistent with the notion of a constitution cast in general terms...." Please save this objection somewhere in your notes because we will encounter it again when we take up issues of affirmative action and racial discrimination.

To continue, the *Akron* Court also anticipated a trend that is continued to this day in the Court's abortion jurisprudence. The *Akron* Court could not find a majority voice. You'll recall, two lectures ago, we spoke about the differences between majority opinions, plurality opinions, concurrences, and dissents. The *Akron* Court could only muster a plurality. This is the first—or at least the first significant—sign of internal division in the Court over the issue of abortion. Part of the difficulty in constructing a majority opinion in *Akron* was that a majority of the justices could not agree about when the state's interest in life would become sufficiently important to justify state regulation. In other words, a plurality of justices in *Akron* seem prepared to rule in direct contrast to *Roe*—that the state's interest in potential fetal life began not at the moment of viability, but instead at the moment of conception. I want to be careful about this; please do not misunderstand me. *Akron* did not change the rule from viability to conception. Instead, *Akron* simply shows the existence of a plurality of justices who are already beginning to rethink the *Roe* framework.

In dissent, Justice Scalia accused the Court of acting irresponsibly, by which he meant simply this: he thought the *Akron* Court should have overruled *Roe* directly. Short of that, he did note that the plurality was at least suggesting a major change, and a welcome change, according to Justice Scalia, in the Court's jurisprudence. Justice Blackmun—you'll recall Justice Blackmun wrote the majority opinion in *Roe*—was profoundly distressed by the direction the Court appeared to take in *Akron*. He wrote, succinctly, "A chill wind blows. I dissent."

The Court's turmoil in *Roe,* and its continued turmoil, perhaps its exacerbated turmoil, in *Akron,* has continued. Perhaps the most dramatic example occurred in the case of *Planned Parenthood v. Casey*, decided in 1992. It's worth spending a little bit of time understanding the political context behind *Casey*. Many individuals—lawyers, citizens, government officials—began an immediate campaign after *Roe* to have the decision overturned. That campaign manifested itself in a series of cases, which included the *Akron* case; hence, Justice Scalia's sense of anger that the *Akron* Court had failed to overrule *Roe*. *Casey* represents yet another effort by governmental officials and citizen activists and attorneys to get the Court to overrule *Roe* directly.

This was a campaign that, by 1992, was nearly 20 years old and, at least in some eyes, was a campaign that was on the very verge of success. There was a widespread sense of anxiety surrounding the Court's decision in *Planned Parenthood v. Casey*. Abortion opponents thought they had good reason to find a court finally willing to overrule *Roe,* and proponents of the abortion right were fearful that they might be correct. Not surprisingly, the Court failed to muster a majority opinion. In retrospect, that may not have been completely predictable, but it shouldn't have been a surprise, given what had happened in *Akron* just 10 years earlier.

Justice O'Connor—remember O'Connor wrote that "*Roe* was on a collision course with itself" in *Akron*—Justice O'Connor wrote for a three-person plurality. In other words, Justice O'Connor wrote for herself, Justice Kennedy, and Justice Souter; and it is worth noting, in passing, that all three of those justices were appointed by presidents who were committed to the pro-life position, and had agreed to seek justices who would overturn *Roe*.

O'Connor rejected the government's invitation to overrule *Roe*, instead explaining at great length why the Court's reliance on the constitutional interpretive methods of precedent and stare decisis (respect for prior cases) as well as concern for the Court's own legitimacy, counseled a reaffirmation of *Roe's* central holding.

Now, before we actually go into the particular framework that Justice O'Connor adopted, it is worth stopping here and thinking about what she said.

Liberty finds no refuge in a jurisprudence of doubt. After considering the fundamental questions resolved by *Roe*, principles of institutional integrity and the rule of stare decisis, we are led to conclude this: The essential holding of *Roe v. Wade* should be retained. A decision to overrule *Roe* would address error, if error there was, at the cost of both profound and unnecessary damage to the Court's legitimacy and to the nation's commitment to the rule of law. Those are powerful words; they are complex words; and they point to profoundly controversial issues.

Imagine the following: she says that, "principles of institutional integrity" counsel adherence to *Roe*. What could she possibly mean by that? Please consult the opinion on your own, and I believe you will see that the plurality opinion by Justice O'Connor is overwhelmingly concerned, at least in its initial stages, with addressing the problem of the Court's appearance in the eyes of the nation at large. "Institutional integrity," in the quote I gave to you, suggests that, somehow, the very integrity of the Court as a political institution would be implicated in a decision to overrule *Roe*. How could that be so?

O'Connor goes on to note that at least one factor in considering whether to overrule *Roe* should be how the people will react to such a decision; and she is concerned, I think, that the Court teaches an unpleasant lesson every time it suggests that an earlier case was in error. That unpleasant lesson, presumably, is that the Constitution isn't necessarily always clear; that there is room for doubt about what a correct opinion or a correct decision and an incorrect decision will be; and that teaching citizens, teaching other constitutional actors, that we got it wrong the first time suggests that the Court is a fallible institution, and that the rule of law may not have the kind of certitude and consistency that most of us think it does have and should have.

Again I quote: "A decision to overrule *Roe* would address error at the cost of both profound and unnecessary damage to the Court's legitimacy." How could the Court's legitimacy be threatened by acknowledging that *Roe* might have been incorrectly decided? Perhaps by teaching that the Court doesn't always get it right; or perhaps, she means something else. Perhaps O'Connor wants to suggest that so many individuals have come to expect that there is a right to abortion that there would be a negative political fallout if the Court were to reverse its course.

Before we go any further, it is worth considering, too, Justice Scalia's response to these positions in his dissent. He said:

> I cannot agree with, indeed, I am appalled by the Court's decision that the decision whether to stand by an erroneous constitutional decision must be strongly influenced against overruling, no less, by the substantial and continuing public opposition the decision has generated.

Whether he is correct or incorrect, he is clearly accusing the Court of doing the following: he is accusing the plurality opinion of saying, "We cannot cave to political pressure to overrule *Roe,* because this Court must be an apolitical institution." If that's correct, then we have a plurality that has acted on the basis of a political position. At least, that is the position carved out by Justice Scalia; and he says again:

> That is appalling. The Court's decision, presumably, should be governed by only one factor, and that factor should be to get the Constitution right; and if getting it right means that we acknowledge that we got it wrong once before, then so be it, because our highest constitutional obligation is to the Constitution itself, not to our own institutional integrity.

I hope you can see how a seven-to-two conflict in *Roe* has transformed itself over twenty years, by the time we get to *Casey,* into a conflict that sometimes threatens, or seems to threaten, to overwhelm the Court itself. In a subsequent case, which we will consider just a little bit later on, Scalia continues this theme. He says, "*Roe* has created the national politics plagued by abortion protests, national abortion lobbying, and abortion marches on Congress."

And in *Casey*, he is concerned that that kind of national politics on abortion has begun, and I use this word deliberately, to "pollute" the decision-making of the Court itself. Now, that said, it's worth continuing to see exactly what the particular doctrinal rules are in *Roe,* because they do seem to foretell a kind of important change. The plurality made a point of saying that it would not overrule *Roe*. Nevertheless, it did make substantial changes in the overall analytical framework.

For example, the plurality, the O'Connor opinion, seemed to eschew the fundamental right/compelling state interest framework that was so prominent in *Roe*. Instead of asking, does a woman have a fundamental right to terminate a pregnancy?—and answering it, presumably, in the affirmative; and instead of then proceeding to the question, does the particular set of statutes involved in *Casey* advance a compelling state interest?—she engages in an entirely different inquiry, and comes up with an entirely different analytical framework.

She asks the following, or, I should say, recasts the doctrine into the following way. Under the *Casey* framework advanced by O'Connor, the new rule is this: a state may regulate an abortion decision at any point in the pregnancy, provided that the regulations involved are not, "an undue burden on the woman's right." What is the significance of this change? I'm not sure. I don't believe there is anybody who knows precisely what the significance of this change would be. But is it worth at least considering what the change might suggest?

Clearly, O'Connor, in order to be consistent with her earlier criticism of the trimester framework, would be searching for a way, in *Casey,* to get rid of the trimester framework; and the plurality opinion does that, by suggesting that trimesters are no longer significant points in a pregnancy. Instead, the state may, at least theoretically, regulate at any point in the pregnancy, irrespective of trimesters, viability, or the state of maternal health.

Now, the timeline isn't carved up in the way it was carved up in *Roe*. Instead, the state may act at any point. But she doesn't call the fundamental right involved "fundamental." Instead, she calls that, at different points, an important or a substantial liberty interest. What is the significance of that change? If she called the right "fundamental," then presumably, she's required to invoke the compelling state interest test. I think there is a deliberate decision here to re-categorize the right. No longer is it a fundamental right. It is now a substantial, or important, liberty interest; and because that is a new description, presumably a new category, we can now adjust what the state needs to show to regulate this important or substantial liberty. And instead of requiring the state to meet the high threshold of a compelling state interest, the state may now act when it does not impose an undue burden.

Let me try to advance this from a different direction. It seems obvious that one course of action open to O'Connor was genuinely to reaffirm *Roe,* and to adopt at least most of the *Roe* framework. She might have chosen to reject the trimester framework, but keep the language of fundamental rights and compelling state interests. She didn't do that. Alternatively, she might have said, "We were wrong in *Roe.* The right to terminate a pregnancy is not a fundamental right, and the state may regulate it whenever it has a rational reason to do so." That would be a fundamental overruling of *Roe.* She neither retains *Roe* in its pristine sense, nor does she overrule *Roe;* she appears to carve a different course, and I think we should assume that that course is a middle course.

As difficult as this may be to comprehend doctrinally, I think where we are left, with the plurality opinion, is that the fundamental right to terminate a pregnancy is no longer fundamental; it is merely substantial. But substantial is more important than non-fundamental. The state doesn't need to show that it has a compelling state interest; but on the other hand, its interest must be superior to simple rationality—it must not constitute an undue burden.

Which kinds of state regulations will constitute an undue burden? You can get some sense of that by trying to figure out in *Casey* which state regulations were ruled unconstitutional and which ones were not. But, really, we are only going to know as the Court begins to develop the undue burden test over time. The undue burden test has not enough content to it for us to say, with any kind of certainty, which state regulations will survive in the future and which ones will not.

I want to return to that point a little bit later in this lecture; but for now, I want to continue with some of the other opinions. Justice Blackmun, in a very complicated opinion—concurring in part of the opinion, dissenting in part—praised the plurality, praised O'Connor in the following way, calling it, "An act of personal courage and constitutional principle."

In contrast, Justice Scalia—angry, fitful—argued that such praise, to call it an act of statesmanship and courage, was, "nothing less than Orwellian."

Scalia also addressed the fundamental, underlying issues of judicial power involved in *Roe* and *Casey*. The note: "The issue as to whether abortion is a liberty protected by the Constitution of the United States, I am sure it is not." Continuing, he wrote that he reached this conclusion, in part, because, "The Constitution says absolutely nothing about abortion." That is as succinct a dissent as one might imagine.

Casey shows a Court, in the early 1990s, that cannot agree about what rules ought to govern the abortion decision, cannot agree about whether there is even a right to an abortion, cannot agree about what methods of constitutional interpretation are appropriate. It is a Court that is as viciously divided internally as one might imagine.

One consequence of that kind of internal division is that states, following the Court's lead, have begun to experiment with abortion rules, trying this, that, and the other with the expressed understanding that they may or may not satisfy an unarticulated undue burden test. Let me put this in another way. It would be one thing to worry about the Court as being internally divided if we are simply scholars of the Court. If we are students of the Court, or devotees of the Court, then we might worry about the Court in the same way we worry about any family that bickers among itself, and appears, sometimes at least, to be dysfunctional. But that is not our purpose here. We should be worried about a Court that cannot articulate a consistent, clear, coherent philosophy of abortion rights, because it has profound, everyday, practical consequences for the ways in which state legislatures conceptualize abortion regulations, and for the ways that men and women live their lives in this country.

The controversy shows no sign of abating. Perhaps the clearest example of this is a decision, reached in the year 2000, in a fantastically controversial case known as *Stenberg*. *Stenberg v. Carhart*, decided in 2000, involved a decision about Nebraska's ban on partial-birth abortions. Once again, the Court proved itself deeply divided. The case produced no less than eight separate opinions. Before I deal with the case in any detail, I want to give you a sense of what the language of those opinions is like.

Here is Justice Scalia in his *Stenberg* decision: "Today's decision, that the Constitution prevents the prohibition of a horrible mode of abortion, will be greeted by a firestorm of criticism, as well it should."

Now, his "horrible mode of abortion"—his so-called partial-birth abortion—the Court did, indeed, declare the Nebraska statute unconstitutional. The Nebraska statute prohibited this particular mode of abortion. The division in the eight opinions runs across a series of different fault lines. One fault line, suggested by Scalia, is the very constitutionality of all abortion regulations. Another fault line concerns whether or not this particular regulation constitutes an undue burden or not. Another fault line concerns under what conditions, again, it is appropriate for judges to displace majoritarian decisions about how to regulate abortion politics.

If *Stenberg* is a guide for future cases, then I think we can assume that most future cases will continue to crack over these same fault lines. On the other hand, this may be the place to acknowledge that close cases and sharply divided courts may be profoundly influenced by changes in Court membership.

Sometimes, students ask, "Why should I care about the internal divisions of the Court? Why do I care about whether there's really a difference between the fundamental rights, the compelling state interest test, and undue burden? And one answer to that question is because, in the end, those are issues of politics, not necessarily or simply issues of law; and issues of politics are what it means to live in a constitutional democracy. Fundamentally, those issues of politics refer to what kinds of power we possess as citizens, and what kinds of power the Court possesses as well.

Timeline of Cases Discussed in the Course

All cases were before the U.S. Supreme Court unless otherwise noted.

- Chief Justices of the U.S. Supreme Court are listed before cases during which they held office. Chief Justices who died in office are marked †.
- Winning parties are indicated in ***boldface italics***.
- A case marked with an asterisk (*) offered rulings so mixed or so complicated that the designation of an overall winner may be misleading.
- Informal names for some cases are noted in parentheses.

Chief Justice Oliver Ellsworth, March 8, 1796–December 15, 1800

1798 *Calder v. Bull*, 3 U.S. 386*

Chief Justice John Marshall, February 4, 1801–July 6, 1835†

1803 *Marbury v. Madison*, 5 U.S. 137*

1810 *Fletcher v. **Peck***, 10 U.S. 87 (Yazoo Land Fraud Case)

1825 *Eakin v. Raub*, 12 Sergeant & Rawle 330* (Pennsylvania State Supreme Court)

1833 *Barron v. **Baltimore***, 32 U.S. 243

Chief Justice Brooke Taney, March 28, 1836–October 12, 1864†

1837 *Charles River Bridge v. **Warren Bridge***, 36 U.S. 420

1857 *Dred Scott v. **Sandford***, 60 U.S. 393*

Chief Justice Salmon Portland Chase, December 15, 1864–May 7, 1873†

1873 *Butchers' Benevolent Association of New Orleans v. **Crescent City Live-Stock Landing & Slaughter-House Company***, 83 U.S. 36 (Slaughter-House Cases)

1873 *Bradwell v. **State of Illinois***, 83 U.S. 130

Chief Justice Morrison Remick Waite, March 4, 1874–March 23, 1888†

1874 *Minor v. **Happersett***, 88 U.S. 162

1877*Munn v. **Illinois***, 94 U.S. 113 (Granger Cases)

1878*Reynolds v. **United States***, 98 U.S. 145

Chief Justice Melville Weston Fuller, October 8, 1888–July 4, 1910†

1890*Davis v. **Beason, Sheriff***, 133 U.S. 333

1896*Plessy v. **Ferguson***, 163 U.S. 537

1905***Lochner*** *v. New York*, 198 U.S. 45

Chief Justice Edward Douglass White, December 19, 1910– May 19, 1921†

1919*Schenck v. **United States***, 249 U.S. 47

Chief Justice William Howard Taft, July 11, 1921–February 3, 1930

1923***Meyer*** *v. Nebraska*, 262 U.S. 390

1925*Pierce v. **Society of Sisters***, 268 U.S. 510

1925***Gitlow*** *v. New York*, 268 U.S. 652

1927*Buck v. **Bell***, 274 U.S. 200

1927*Whitney v. **California***, 274 U.S. 357

1928*Olmstead v. **United States***, 277 U.S. 438

Chief Justice Charles Evans Hughes, February 24, 1930– June 30, 1941

1937*West Coast Hotel v. **Parrish***, 300 U.S. 379

1937*Palko v. **Connecticut***, 302 U.S. 319

1938***Missouri ex rel. Gaines*** *v. Canada* 305 U.S. 337

1940***Minersville*** *v. Gobitis*, 310 U.S. 586 (Flag Salute Case I)

Chief Justice Harlan Fiske Stone, July 3, 1941–April 22, 1946†

1942*Chaplinsky v. **New Hampshire***, 315 U.S. 568

1942*Jones v. **Opelika***, 316 U.S. 584

1943*West Virginia v. **Barnette***, 319 U.S. 624 (Flag Salute Case II)

1944*Korematsu v. **United States***, 323 U.S. 214

Chief Justice Frederick Moore Vinson, June 24, 1946– September 8, 1953†

1947*Everson v. **Board of Education***, 330 U.S. 1

1948*McCollum* v. *Illinois*, 333 U.S. 203

1950*Sweatt* v. *Painter*, 339 U.S. 629

1951*Dennis* v. *United States*, 341 U.S. 494

1952*Beauharnais* v. *Illinois*, 343 U.S. 250

Chief Justice Earl Warren, October 5, 1953–June 23, 1969

1954*Brown* v. *Board of Education I*, 347 U.S. 483 (School Desegregation Case I, Brown I)

1955*Brown* v. *Board of Education II*, 349 U.S. 294

1957*Yates* v. *United States*, 354 U.S. 298

1957*Roth* v. *United States*, 354 U.S. 476

1958*Cooper* v. *Aaron*, 358 U.S. 1

1960*Talley* v. *California*, 362 U.S. 60

1961*Noto* v. *United States*, 367 U.S. 290

1961*Hoyt* v. *Florida*, 368 U.S. 57

1962*Engel* v. *Vitale*, 370 U.S. 421* (School Prayer Case)

1963*Abington Township School District* v. *Schempp*, 374 U.S. 203 (School Prayer Case)

1963*Sherbert* v. *Verner*, 374 U.S. 398

1965*Griswold* v. *Connecticut*, 381 U.S. 479

1966*Harper* v. *Virginia Board of Elections*, 383 U.S. 663

1967*Loving* v. *Virginia*, 388 U.S. 1

1968*United States* v. *O'Brien*, 391 U.S. 367 (Draft Card Case)

1969*Tinker* v. *Des Moines School District*, 393 U.S. 503

1969*Brandenburg* v. *Ohio*, 395 U.S. 444

Chief Justice Warren Earl Burger, June 23, 1969–September 26, 1986

1971*Cohen* v. *California*, 403 U.S. 15

1971*Lemon* v. *Kurtzman*, 403 U.S. 602*

1971*Reed* v. *Reed*, 404 U.S. 71

1972*Eisenstadt* v. *Baird*, 405 U.S. 438

1972*Wisconsin* v. *Yoder*, 406 U.S. 205 (Amish School Case)

1972*Furman* v. *Georgia*, 408 U.S. 238

1973*Roe* v. *Wade*, 410 U.S. 116 (Abortion Case)

1973*Doe* v. *Bolton*, 410 U.S. 179

1973*San Antonio School District* v. *Rodriguez*, 411 U.S. 1

1973 *Frontiero v. Richardson*, 411 U.S. 677

1973 *Miller v. California*, 413 U.S. 15*

1973 *Paris Adult Theatre I v. Slaton*, 413 U.S. 49

1976 *Massachusetts Board of Retirement v. Murgia*, 427 U.S. 307

1976 *Planned Parenthood of Missouri v. Danforth*, 428 U.S. 52

1976 *Gregg v. Georgia*, 428 U.S. 153*

1976 *Craig v. Boren*, 429 U.S. 190

1977 *Moore v. City of East Cleveland*, 431 U.S. 494

1977 *Trimble v. Gordon*, 430 U.S. 762

1977 *Wooley v. Maynard*, 430 U.S. 705

1978 *Regents of the University of California v. Bakke*, 438 U.S. 265*

1981 *Michael M. v. Superior Court of Sonoma County*, 450 U.S. 464

1981 *Thomas v. Review Board*, 450 U.S. 707

1982 *Mississippi University for Women v. Hogan*, 458 U.S. 718

1983 *Akron v. Akron Center for Reproductive Health*, 462 U.S. 416

1983 *Planned Parenthood v. Ashcroft*, 462 U.S. 476

1984 *Lynch v. Donnelly*, 465 U.S. 668

1984 *Clark v. Community for Creative Nonviolence*, 468 U.S. 288

1985 *Wallace v. Jaffree*, 472 U.S. 38

1985 *Cleburne v. Cleburne Living Center*, 473 U.S. 432

1985 *American Booksellers Association, Inc. v. Hudnut*, 771 F.2d 323 (U.S. Court of Appeals, 7th Circuit)

1986 *Bowers v. Hardwick*, 478 U.S. 186 (Homosexual Sodomy Case I)

Chief Justice William Hubbs Rehnquist, Sept. 26, 1986– Sept. 3, 2005†

1987 *McCleskey v. Kemp*, 481 U.S. 279

1987 *Nollan v. California Coastal Commission*, 483 U.S. 825

1989 *DeShaney v. Winnebago County*, 489 U.S. 189

1989 *Michael H. v. Gerald D.*, 491 U.S. 110

1989 *Texas v. Johnson*, 491 U.S. 397

1990 *Employment Division, Ore. Dept. of Human Resources v. Smith*, 494 U.S. 872 (Peyote Case)

1990 *Cruzan v. Director, Missouri Dept. of Health*, 497 U.S. 261

1991*Barnes v. Glen Theatre*, 501 U.S. 560

1992*RAV v. City of St. Paul*, 505 U.S. 377

1992*Lee v. Weisman*, 505 U.S. 577

1992*Planned Parenthood v. Casey*, 505 U.S. 833*

1992*Lucas v. South Carolina Coastal Council*, 505 U.S. 1003

1993*Herrera v. Collins*, 506 U.S. 390

1993*Baehr v. Lewin*, 74 Haw. 645 (Hawaii State Supreme Court)

1993*Church of the Lukumi Babalu Aye, Inc. v. Hialeah*, 508 U.S. 520

1993*Wisconsin v. Mitchell*, 508 U.S. 476

1993*Heller v. Doe*, 509 U.S. 312

1994*Callins v. Collins*, 510 U.S. 1141

1996*Romer v. Evans*, 517 U.S. 620

1996*United States v. Virginia*, 518 U.S. 515

1997*Boerne v. Flores*, 521 U.S. 507

1997*Vacco, Attorney General of New York v. Quill*, 521 U.S. 793

1997*Reno v. American Civil Liberties Union*, 521 U.S. 844

1997*Washington v. Glucksberg*, 521 U.S. 702

1999*Baker v. Vermont*, 170 Vt 194, 744 A. 2d 864 (Vermont State Supreme Court)

2000*Erie v. Pap's A.M.*, 529 U.S. 277

2000*Troxel v. Granville*, 530 U.S. 57

2000*Stenberg v. Carhart*, 530 U.S. 914 (Partial Birth Abortion Case)

2002*Ashcroft v. Free Speech Coalition*, 535 U.S. 234

2002*Tahoe-Sierra Preservation Council v. Tahoe Regional Planning Agency*, 535 U.S. 302

2002*Atkins v. Virginia*, 536 U.S. 304

2002*Zelman v. Simmons-Harris*, 536 U.S. 639

2003*Virginia v. Black*, 538 U.S. 343*

2003*Gratz v. Bollinger*, 539 U.S. 244

2003*Grutter v. Bollinger*, 539 U.S. 306

2003*Lawrence v. Texas*, 539 U.S. 558 (Sodomy Case II)

2003*Goodridge v. Mass. Dept. of Public Health*, 798 N.E.2d 241 (Massachusetts State Supreme Court)

2005*Roper v. Simmons*, 543 U.S. 551

2005*Kelo v. New London*, 545 U.S. _ _ _

2005 *McCreary County v. **ACLU*** 545 U.S. _ _ _
2005 *Van Orden v. **Perry***, 545 U.S. _ _ _

Chief Justice John Roberts, Sept. 29, 2005–

Annotated List of Cases—Alphabetical Order

---

types of opinions

Opinion of the Court: an opinion supported by a majority of the voting justices.

Judgment of the Court: a decision supported by a plurality of the justices voting; does not become a binding precedent for future courts.

Concurring opinion: an opinion by one or more justices that agrees with the result reached by the majority but disagrees with part of the reasoning.

Opinion concurring in judgment: an opinion by one or more justices that agrees with the result reached by a majority or plurality of the Court but offers a different opinion in support of that conclusion.

Dissenting opinion: an opinion by one or more justices that disagrees with the result reached by the majority.

Seriatim opinion: a judicial decision with separate opinions from each judge instead of a majority or plurality opinion announced by the Court.

Note: winning parties are indicated in ***boldface italics***, except for cases with rulings so mixed or so complicated— marked with an asterisk (*)—that the designation of an overall winner may be misleading.

*Abington Township School District v. **Schempp***, 374 U.S. 203 (1963) (School Prayer Case): Vote 7 (White, Brennan, Goldberg, Black, Warren, Douglas, Harlan II)–1 (Stewart)

> Opinion of the Court: Clark; Concurring opinions: Goldberg (Harlan II), Douglas; Dissenting opinion: Stewart

The Court upheld the school prayer decision in *Engel v. Vitale* (370 U.S. 412, 1962) by confirming that a state may not impose any sort of religious requirement in schools.

*Akron v. **Akron Center for Reproductive Health***, 462 U.S. 416 (1983): Vote 5 (Stevens, Powell, T. Marshall, Brennan, Burger)–4 (O'Connor, Rehnquist, White, Blackmun)

> Opinion of the Court: Powell; Dissenting opinion: O'Connor (Rehnquist)

The Court found that parts of the city of Akron's 1978 ordinance imposing several regulations on abortion violated a woman's reproductive rights under *Roe v. Wade*.

***American Booksellers Association, Inc.** v. Hudnut*, 771 F.2d 323 (U.S. Court of Appeals, 7th Circuit, 1985):
> Opinion of the Court: Easterbrook (Cudahy); Concurring opinion: Swygert

The 7th Circuit Court of Appeals ruled that an Indianapolis ordinance that criminalized some forms of pornography as a civil rights violation itself violated the First Amendment.

*Ashcroft v. **Free Speech Coalition***, 535 U.S. 234 (2002): Vote 6 (Stevens, Kennedy, Souter, Thomas, Ginsburg, Breyer)–3 (Rehnquist, O'Connor, Scalia)
> Opinion of the Court: Kennedy; Opinion concurring in judgment: Thomas; Dissenting opinions: Rehnquist (Scalia), O'Connor (Rehnquist, Scalia)

The Court agreed with the 9th Circuit that the provisions of the Child Pornography Prevention Act of 1996 were insufficiently related to the state's legitimate interest in prohibiting pornography that actually involved minors.

***Atkins** v. Virginia*, 536 U.S. 304 (2002): Vote 6 (Stevens, O'Connor, Kennedy, Souter, Ginsburg, Breyer)–3 (Rehnquist, Scalia, Thomas)
> Opinion of the Court: Stevens; Dissenting opinions: Rehnquist (Scalia, Thomas), Scalia (Rehnquist, Thomas)

The Court decided that the execution of a mentally retarded person would violate the Eighth Amendment's ban on cruel and unusual punishment.

***Baehr** v. Lewin*, 74 Haw. 645 (Hawaii State Supreme Court) (5 May 1993):
> Opinion of the Court: Levinson; Concurring opinion: J. Burns; Dissenting opinion: Heen

The Hawaii Supreme Court ruled that the state must show compelling reason for denying same-sex couples equal access to legal marriage.

***Baker** v. Vermont*, 170 Vt 194, 744 A. 2d 864 (Vermont State Supreme Court, 1999):
> Opinion of the Court: Amestoy; Concurring opinion: Dooley; Opinion concurring in part and dissenting in part: Johnson

In this case, the Vermont Supreme Court ruled that the exclusion of same-sex couples from the benefits and protections of marriage under state law violated the common benefits clause of the Vermont Constitution.

Barnes v. ***Glen Theatre***, 501 U.S. 560 (1991): Vote 5 (Rehnquist, O'Connor, Scalia, Kennedy, Souter)–4 (B. White, T. Marshall, Blackmun, Stevens)
> Judgment of the Court: Rehnquist; Opinions concurring in judgment: Scalia, Souter; Dissenting opinion: B. White (T. Marshall, Blackmun, Stevens)

In this case, a majority ruled that an Indiana law prohibiting nude dancing performed as entertainment did not violate the First Amendment.

Barron v. ***Baltimore***, 32 U.S. 243 (7 Pet. 243) (1833): Unanimous vote (J. Marshall, W. Johnson, Duvall, Story, Thompson, McLean, Baldwin)
> Opinion of the Court: J. Marshall

In this case, the Court ruled that the Fifth Amendment, in particular, and the Bill of Rights, more generally, did not apply to the actions of state governments.

Beauharnais v. ***Illinois***, 343 U.S. 250 (1952): Vote 5 (Vinson, Frankfurter, Burton, Clark, Minton)–4 (Black, Reed, Douglas, R. Jackson)
> Opinion of the Court: Frankfurter; Dissenting opinions: Black (Douglas), Reed (Douglas), Douglas, R. Jackson

The Court upheld a state law that prohibited libelous statements about certain groups against a claim that the statute violated the First Amendment.

Boerne v. ***Flores***, 521 U.S. 507 (1997): Vote: 6 (Ginsberg, Thomas, Scalia, Stevens, Rehnquist, Kennedy)– 3 (Souter, Breyer, O'Connor)
> Opinion of the Court: Kennedy; Concurring opinions: Stevens, Scalia; Dissenting opinions: Souter, Breyer, O'Connor

The Court ruled that Congress exceeded its Fourteenth Amendment enforcement powers by enacting the Religious Freedom Restoration Act (RFRA).

Bowers v. ***Hardwick***, 478 U.S. 186 (1986) (Homosexual Sodomy Case I): Vote 5 (Burger, B. White, Powell, Rehnquist, O'Connor)–4 (Brennan, T. Marshall, Blackmun, Stevens)

Opinion of the Court: B. White; Concurring opinions: Burger, Powell; Dissenting opinions: Blackmun (Brennan, T. Marshall, Stevens), Stevens (Brennan, T. Marshall)

The Court upheld a Georgia statute that criminalized consensual sodomy. Later overruled in *Lawrence v. Texas*.

*Bradwell v. **State of Illinois***, 83 U.S. 130 (1873): Vote 8 (Clifford, Swayne, Miller, Davis, Field, Strong, Bradley, Hunt)–1 (S. P. Chase)
Opinion of the Court: Miller; Concurring opinion: Bradley (Swayne, Field); Dissenting without opinion: S. P. Chase

The Court maintained that the right to admission to practice in the courts of a state is not a privilege or immunity of a citizen of the United States.

Brandenburg v. Ohio, 395 U.S. 444 (9 June 1969): Unanimous vote (Warren, Black, Douglas, Harlan II, Brennan, Stewart, White, T. Marshall); Did not participate: Fortas
Opinion of the Court: *Per curiam*; Concurring opinions: Black, Douglas (Black)

The Court ruled that if speech incites imminent unlawful action, it may be restricted, but the burden of proof in all speech cases rests on the state to show that action will result, rather than on the defendant to show that it will not.

***Brown** v. Board of Education I*, 347 U.S. 483 (1954) (School Desegregation Case/Brown I): Unanimous vote (Warren, Black, Reed, Frankfurter, Douglas, R. Jackson, Burton, Clark, Minton)
Opinion of the Court: Warren

The Court decided that segregation in public education is inherently unequal and, thus, a violation of the equal protection clause of the Fourteenth Amendment.

***Brown** v. Board of Education II*, 349 U.S. 294 (1955): Unanimous vote (Warren, Black, Reed, Frankfurter, Douglas, Burton, Clark, Minton, Harlan II)
Opinion of the Court: Warren

The Court ordered the states to end segregation in public elementary schools with "all deliberate speed."

*Buck v. **Bell***, 274 U.S. 200 (1927): Vote: 8 (Taft, Holmes, Van Devanter, McReynolds, Brandeis, Sutherland, Sanford, Stone)–1 (Butler)
Opinion of the Court: Holmes; Dissenting without opinion:

Butler

The Court upheld a Virginia law that permitted involuntary sterilization in some cases.

*Butchers' Benevolent Association of New Orleans v. **Crescent City Live-Stock Landing & Slaughter-House Company***, 83 U.S. 36 (1873) (Slaughter-House Cases): Vote 5 (Miller, Clifford, Strong, Hunt, Davis)–4 (Field, Chase, Swayne, Bradley)

Opinion of the Court: Miller; Dissenting opinions: Field, Bradley, Swayne

The Court ruled that the privileges and immunities clause of the Fourteenth Amendment did not make the Bill of Rights applicable to the states.

Calder v. Bull, 3 U.S. 386 (1798)*: Vote 4 (Cushing, Iredell, Paterson, S. Chase)–0

Seriatim opinions: Cushing, Iredell, Paterson, S. Chase; Did not participate: Ellsworth, Wilson

The Court held that the *ex post facto* clause in Article I applies only to *laws* that address the criminal law, not to civil matters or cases involving the right to property.

*Callins v. **Collins***, 510 U.S. 1141 (1994): No vote recorded because no overall opinion issued—just a denial of a cert petition for the case to be heard.

Concurring opinion (concurring with the denial): Scalia; Dissenting opinion: Blackmun

In this denial of a *certiorari* petition, the Supreme Court refused to accept an appeal from a defendant who had been sentenced to death by a Texas jury.

*Chaplinsky v. **New Hampshire***, 315 U.S. 568 (1942): Unanimous vote (Stone, Roberts, Black, Reed, Frankfurter, Douglas, Murphy, Byrnes, R. Jackson)

Opinion of the Court: Murphy

The Court ruled that the First Amendment does not protect fighting words. The Court also held that lewd, obscene, profane, and libelous words are not protected under the First Amendment.

*Charles River Bridge v. **Warren Bridge**,* 36 U.S. 420 (1837): Vote 4 (Taney, Baldwin, Wayne, Barbour)–3 (McLean, Story, Thompson)

Opinion of the Court: Taney; Concurring opinion: Baldwin; Dissenting opinions: McLean, Story, Thompson

In this case involving the right to property, the Taney Court stressed the authority of the state to regulate private property in the public interest by noting the states' need to respond to changing technologies and economic realities in the early 19th century.

Church of the Lukumi Babulu Aye, Inc. *v. Hialeah*, 508 U.S. 520 (1993): Unanimous vote (Rehnquist, B. White, Blackmun, Stevens, O'Connor, Scalia, Kennedy, Souter, Thomas)
> Opinion of the Court: Kennedy; Concurring opinion: Scalia (Rehnquist); Opinions concurring in judgment: Blackmun (O'Connor), Souter

The Court ruled that a city ordinance designed to prohibit certain kinds of animal sacrifice by members of the Santeria religion violated the free exercise clause.

Clark *v. Community for Creative Nonviolence*, 468 U.S. 288 (1984): Vote 7 (White, Burger, Blackmun, Powell, Rehnquist, Stevens, O'Connor)–2 (Brennan, J. Marshall)
> Opinion of the Court: White; Concurring opinion: Burger; Dissenting opinion: J. Marshall (Brennan)

The Court decided that National Park Service regulations prohibiting overnight camping did not violate the First Amendment, although it conceded that, in some circumstances, sleeping might be considered expressive conduct.

Cleburne *v. Cleburne Living Center*, 473 U.S. 432 (1985): Unanimous vote (Stevens, Powell, Rehnquist, O'Connor, T. Marshall, Brennan, Burger, White, Blackmun)
> Opinion of the Court: White; Concurring opinions: Marshall (Blackmun), Stevens (Burger)

The Court ruled that the denial of a special use permit to Cleburne Living Center, Inc., discriminated against the mentally retarded and violated the equal protection clause of the Fourteenth Amendment.

Cohen *v. California*, 403 U.S. 15 (1971): Vote 5 (Douglas, Harlan II, Brennan, Stewart, T. Marshall)–4 (Burger, Black, B. White, Blackmun)
> Opinion of the Court: Harlan II; Dissenting opinion: Blackmun (Burger, Black, B. White)

In deciding whether a state can outlaw an "offensive" word altogether, the Court decided that "the state has no right to cleanse public debate to the point where it is grammatically palatable to the most squeamish."

*Cooper v. **Aaron***, 358 U.S. 1 (1958): *Per curiam* vote (signed by all nine justices)
    Concurring opinion: Frankfurter
This case reaffirmed the Court's position in *Brown v. Board of Education*, 347 U.S. 483 (1954), and reinstated the Court's authority as the ultimate interpreter of the Constitution.

Craig *v. Boren*, 429 U.S. 190 (1976): Vote 7 (Brennan, Stewart, B. White, T. Marshall, Blackmun, Powell, Stevens)–2 (Burger, Rehnquist)
    Opinion of the Court: Brennan; Concurring opinions: Powell, Stevens, Blackmun; Opinion concurring in judgment: Stewart; Dissenting opinions: Burger, Rehnquist
The Court struck down an Oklahoma law prohibiting the sale of 3.2 percent beer to males under 21 and women under 18 as a violation of the equal protection clause.

*Cruzan v. **Director, Missouri Dept. of Health***, 497 U.S. 261 (1990): Vote 5 (Rehnquist, B. White, O'Connor, Scalia, Kennedy)–4 (Brennan, T. Marshall, Blackmun, Stevens)
    Opinion of the Court: Rehnquist; Concurring opinions: O'Connor, Scalia; Dissenting opinions: Brennan (Marshall, Blackmun), Stevens
In this case, the Court ruled that under the Fourteenth Amendment's due process clause, every person has a right to refuse medical treatment, even if that decision would lead to death. However, the Court found that this right may be limited by the state's interest in preserving life.

*Davis v. **Beason, Sheriff***, 133 U.S. 333 (1890): Unanimous vote (Fuller, Miller, Field, Bradley, Harlan I, Gray, Blatchford, L. Larmar, Brewer)
    Opinion of the Court: Field
The Court upheld an Idaho territorial law that denied the right to vote to any person who advocated or practiced polygamy or who belonged to an organization that did so.

*Dennis v. **United States***, 341 U.S. 494 (1951): Vote 7 (Vinson, Reed, Frankfurter, R. Jackson, Burton, Clark, Minton)–2 (Black, Douglas)

Opinion of the Court: Vinson; Opinion concurring in judgment: Frankfurter; Concurring opinion: R. Jackson; Dissenting opinions: Black, Douglas; Did not participate: Clark

In this case, the Court examined the constitutionality of the Smith Act as applied to 11 leaders of the Communist party. The Court concluded that the government could not only limit speech directly inciting unlawful action, or conspiring to promote such action, or teaching that such action should occur but may also penalize the act of conspiring to organize a group that would teach that such action ought to occur.

*DeShaney v. **Winnebago County**,* 489 U.S. 189 (1989): Vote 6 (Scalia, Stevens, O'Connor, Kennedy, Rehnquist, White)–3 (T. Marshall, Brennan, Blackmun)

Opinion of the Court: Rehnquist; Dissenting opinions: Brennan (T. Marshall), Blackmun

In this case, the Court ruled that a state's failure to protect an individual against private violence does not violate the Fourteenth Amendment.

*Dred Scott v. **Sandford**,* 60 U.S. 393 (1856–1857): Vote 7 (Taney, Wayne, Catron, Daniel, Nelson, Crier, Campbell)–2 (McLean, Curtis)

Opinion of the Court: Taney; Concurring opinions: Wayne, Nelson (Grier), Grier, Daniel, Campbell, Catron; Dissenting opinions: McLean, Curtis

In this case from its December 1856 term, the Court ruled in March 1857 that no person of African descent can be a citizen of the United States or any state.

Eakin v. Raub, 12 Sergeant & Rawle 330 (Pennsylvania State Supreme Court) (1825)*:

Opinion of the Court: Chief Justice Tilghman; Dissenting opinion: Gibson

In this case, the Supreme Court of Pennsylvania considered a case of adverse possession. It is important because in his well-known dissent, Justice Gibson criticized John Marshall's opinion in *Marbury v. Madison* (1803).

*Eisenstadt v. **Baird**,* 405 U.S. 438 (1972): Vote 6 (Douglas, Brennan, Stewart, B. White, T. Marshall, Blackmun)–1 (Burger)

Opinion of the Court: Brennan; Concurring opinions: Douglas, B. White (Blackmun); Dissenting opinion: Burger; Did not participate: Powell, Rehnquist

The Court decided that the Massachusetts statute that allowed only licensed physicians or pharmacists to distribute contraceptives for the purpose of preventing pregnancy to married persons violated the equal protection clause.

Employment Division, Ore. Dept. of Human Resources v. *Smith*, 494 U.S. 872 (1990): Vote 6 (Rehnquist, White, Stevens, O'Connor, Scalia, Kennedy)–3 (Brennan, Marshall, Blackmun)

Opinion of the Court: Scalia; Opinion concurring in judgment: O'Connor (Brennan, Marshall, Blackmun); Dissenting opinion: Blackmun (Brennan, Marshall)

The Court upheld a drug conviction against a claim that the use of the drug was protected by the free exercise clause. In so ruling, the Court also held that neutral state laws with an adverse impact on the free exercise clause need not be measured against the compelling state interest test.

Engel v. Vitale, 370 U.S. 421 (1962) (School Prayer Case)*: Vote 6 (Warren, Black, Douglas, Clark, Harlan II, Brennan)–1 (Stewart)

Opinion of the Court: Black; Concurring opinion: Douglas; Dissenting opinion: Stewart; Did not participate: Frankfurter, B. White

In this case, the Court ruled that a state law requiring prayers in public schools was a violation of the establishment clause of the First Amendment.

Erie v. *PAP's A.M.*, 529 U.S. 277 (2000): Vote 7 (O'Connor, Rehnquist, Kennedy, Souter, Breyer, Scalia, Thomas)–2 (Ginsberg, Stevens)

Opinion of the Court: O'Connor; Concurring opinion: Scalia (Thomas); Opinion concurring in part and dissenting in part: Souter; Dissenting opinion: Stevens (Ginsburg)

The Court held that a public indecency ordinance applied to prohibit nude dancing did not violate the First Amendment.

*Everson v. **Board of Education***, 330 U.S. 1 (1947): Vote 5 (Vinson, Black, Reed, Douglas, Murphy)–4 (Frankfurter, R. Jackson, W. Rutledge, Burton)

Opinion of the Court: Black; Dissenting opinions: R. Jackson (Frankfurter), W. Rutledge (Frankfurter, R. Jackson, Burton)

The Court affirmed that the establishment clause of the First Amendment applied to the states by incorporation through the Fourteenth Amendment and that the framers had intended the clause to create a wall of separation between church and state.

Fletcher v. Peck, 10 U.S. 87 (1810) (Yazoo Land Fraud Case): Vote 5 (J. Marshall, Washington, W. Johnson, Livingston, Todd)–0
> Opinion of the Court: J. Marshall; Concurring opinion: W. Johnson; Did not participate: Cushing, S. Chase

In this case, the Court ruled that a Georgia statute designed to set aside the Yazoo land frauds was unconstitutional because it infringed on the property rights of innocent third-party purchasers.

***Frontiero** v. Richardson*, 411 U.S. 677 (1973): Vote 8 (Burger, Douglas, Brennan, Stewart, B. White, T. Marshall, Blackmun, Powell)–1 (Rehnquist)
> Judgment of the Court: Brennan; Opinions concurring in judgment: Stewart, Powell (Burger, Blackmun); Dissenting opinion: Rehnquist

In this case, the Court ruled that discrimination on the basis of sex ought to be considered semi-suspect, not a suspect classification, like race.

***Furman** v. Georgia*, 408 U.S. 238 (1972): Vote 5 (Douglas, Brennan, Stewart, B. White, T. Marshall)–4 (Burger, Blackmun, Powell, Rehnquist)
> Opinion of the Court: *Per curiam*; Opinions concurring in judgment: Douglas, Brennan, Stewart, B. White, T. Marshall; Dissenting opinions: Burger (Blackmun, Powell, Rehnquist), Blackmun, Powell (Burger, Blackmun, Rehnquist), Rehnquist (Burger, Blackmun, Powell)

The Court held that the death penalty schemes in Georgia and Texas were cruel and unusual in violation of the Eighth Amendment, but that the death penalty itself was not, by definition, such a violation.

***Gitlow** v. New York*, 268 U.S. 652 (1925): Vote 7 (Taft, Van Devanter, McReynolds, Sutherland, Butler, Sanford, Stone)–2 (Holmes, Brandeis)
> Opinion of the Court: Sanford; Dissenting opinion: Holmes (Brandeis)

In this case, the Court for the first time put forward the doctrine of incorporation, by which the Fourteenth Amendment "incorporated" some of the liberties protected in the Bill of Rights and applied them to the states.

Goodridge v. *Mass. Dept. of Public Health*, 798 N.E. 2d 941 (Mass. State Supreme Court, 2003):
> Opinion of the Court: Marshall; Concurring opinion: Greaney; Dissenting opinions: Spina, Sosman, Cordy

The Massachusetts Supreme Court found that the state may not deny the benefits of civil marriage to two individuals of the same sex.

Gratz v. *Bollinger*, 539 U.S. 244 (2003): Vote 6 (Rehnquist, O'Connor, Scalia, Kennedy Thomas; Breyer)–3 (Stevens, Souter, Ginsburg)
> Opinion of the Court: Rehnquist; Concurring opinions: Thomas, O'Connor; Opinion concurring in judgment: Breyer; Dissenting opinions: Stevens, Ginsberg, Souter

The Court ruled that the use of racial preferences in the University of Michigan's undergraduate admissions violated the equal protection clause of the 14th Amendment.

Gregg v. *Georgia*, 428 U.S. 153 (1976)*: Vote 7 (Stewart, Powell, Stevens; B. White, Burger, Rehnquist, Blackmun)–2 (Brennan, T. Marshall)
> Judgment of the Court: Stewart; Concurring opinion: B. White (Burger, Rehnquist); Opinions concurring in judgment: White (Burger, Rehnquist), Blackmun; Dissenting opinions: Brennan, T. Marshall

The Court ruled that the death penalty does not violate the cruel and unusual punishment clause when states take steps to ensure that its application is not arbitrary and capricious.

Griswold v. *Connecticut*, 381 U.S. 479 (1965): Vote 7 (Warren, Douglas, Clark, Harlan II, Brennan, B. White, Goldberg)–2 (Black, Stewart)
> Opinion of the Court: Douglas; Concurring opinion: Goldberg (Warren, Brennan); Opinions concurring in judgment: Harlan II, B. White; Dissenting opinions: Black (Stewart), Stewart (Black)

The Court found that a Connecticut statute regulating access to information about contraceptives violated the right of marital privacy as protected by the First, Third, Fourth, Fifth, Ninth, and Fourteenth Amendments.

*Grutter v. **Bollinger***, 539 U.S. 306 (2003): Vote 5 (Ginsberg, Souter, Breyer, Stevens, O'Connor)–4 (Scalia, Thomas, Rehnquist, Kennedy)

> Opinion of the Court: O'Connor; Concurring opinion: Ginsberg; Dissenting opinions: Kennedy, Thomas, Scalia

The Court found that the University of Michigan's law school did not violate the equal protection clause by considering race as a factor in the admissions process.

***Harper** v. Virginia Board of Elections*, 383 U.S. 663 (1966): Vote 6 (Warren, Douglas, Clark, Brennan, B. White, Fortas)–3 (Black, Harlan II, Stewart)

> Opinion of the Court: Douglas; Dissenting opinions: Black, Harlan II (Stewart)

The Court declared the use of a poll tax in Virginia elections unconstitutional under the equal protection clause.

***Heller** v. Doe*, 509 U.S. 312 (1993): Vote 6 (Kennedy, O'Connor, Rehnquist, White, Scalia, Thomas)–3 (Blackmun, Souter, Stevens)

> Opinion of the Court: Kennedy; Concurring in opinion in part: O'Connor; Dissenting opinions: Blackmun, Souter (Blackmun, Stevens)

The Court ruled that Kentucky's involuntary commitment of mentally retarded persons did not violate the equal protection clause under the Fourteenth Amendment.

*Herrera v. **Collins***, 506 U.S. 390 (1993): Vote 6 (Rehnquist, B. White, O'Connor, Scalia, Kennedy, Thomas)—3 (Blackmun, Stevens, Souter)

> Opinion of the Court: Rehnquist; Concurring opinions: O'Connor (Kennedy), Scalia (Thomas); Opinion concurring in judgment: B. White; Dissenting opinion: Blackmun (Stevens, Souter)

The Court considered whether the Constitution permits the government to execute a person who claimed that new evidence had emerged that would prove him not guilty of the crime. The plaintiff filed a petition for *habeas corpus* relief, but the Court struck down his request, claming that federal *habeas corpus* relief was limited to constitutional issues only.

*Hoyt v. **Florida***, 368 U.S. 57 (1961): Unanimous vote (Warren, Black, Frankfurter, Douglas, Clark, Harlan II, Brennan, Whittaker, Stewart)

> Opinion of the Court: Harlan II; Concurring opinion: Warren, Black, Douglas

The Court upheld a Florida law that did not require women to serve on juries because Florida had no deliberate intent to exclude women from jury participation.

*Jones v. **Opelika***, 316 U.S. 584 (1942): Vote: 5 (Roberts, Reed, Frankfurter, Byrnes, R. Jackson)–4 (Stone, Black, Douglas, Murphy)

> Opinion of the Court: Reed; Dissenting opinions: Stone (Black, Douglas, Murphy), Murphy (Stone, Black, Douglas), Black, Douglas, Murphy

The Court ruled that Alabama's ordinance prohibiting the selling of books without a license did not violate the plaintiff's First Amendment rights to freedom of press and religion because by selling some of the books, the plaintiff was engaging in commercial activity.

*Kelo v. **New London***, 545 U.S. _ _ _ (2005): Vote 5 (Stevens, Kennedy, Souter, Ginsburg, Breyer)–4 (O'Connor, Rehnquist, Scalia, Thomas)

> Opinion of the Court: Stevens; Concurring opinion: Kennedy; Dissenting opinions: O'Connor (Rehnquist, Scalia, Thomas), Thomas

The Court ruled that municipal governments may take private property and transfer it to other private parties without violating the takings clause, provided that the transfer is part of an overall plan for economic development.

*Korematsu v. **United States***, 323 U.S. 214 (1944): Vote: 6 (Stone, Black, Reed, Frankfurter, Douglas, W. Rutledge)–3 (Roberts, Murphy, R. Jackson)

> Opinion of the Court: Black; Concurring opinion: Frankfurter; Dissenting opinions: Roberts, Murphy, R. Jackson

The Court held that the Executive Order for relocation that only applied to Japanese Americans did not deprive the plaintiff of his due process rights.

***Lawrence** v. Texas*, 539 U.S. 558 (2003) (Sodomy Case II): Vote 6 (Kennedy, Stevens, Souter, Ginsburg, Breyer, O'Connor)–3 (Scalia, Rehnquist, Thomas)

Opinion of the Court: Kennedy; Concurring opinion: O'Connor; Dissenting opinions: Scalia (Rehnquist, Thomas), Thomas

The Court overruled its decision in *Bowers v. Hardwick* and declared prohibition of homosexual sodomy unconstitutional in *Lawrence v. Texas*.

Lee v. Weisman, 505 U.S. 577 (1992): Vote 5 (Blackmun, Stevens, O'Connor, Kennedy, Souter)–4 (Rehnquist, B. White, Scalia, Thomas)

Opinion of the Court: Kennedy; Concurring opinions: Blackmun (Stevens, O'Connor), Souter (Stevens, O'Connor); Dissenting opinion: Scalia (Rehnquist, B. White, Thomas)

The Court upheld its decision in *Engel* by ruling that a school policy of including a prayer as part of an official school ceremony violated the establishment clause.

Lemon v. Kurtzman, 403 U.S. 602 (1971)*: Multiple votes

Opinion of the Court: Burger; Concurring opinions: Douglas (Black, T. Marshall), Brennan; Opinion concurring in judgment (Pennsylvania case): B. White; Dissenting opinion (Rhode Island cases): B. White; Did not participate (Pennsylvania case): T. Marshall

In this case, the Court developed a test for determining whether a state statue violates the establishment clause of the Constitution by aiding religion. The Court defined the three prongs of the test as follows: a state must have a secular legislative purpose; the principal or primary effect must be one that neither advances nor inhibits religion; and the statue must not foster an excessive government entanglement with religion.

Lochner v. New York, 198 U.S. 45 (1905): Vote 5 (Fuller, Brewer, Brown, Peckham, McKenna)–4 (Harlan I, E. White, Holmes, Day)

Opinion of the Court: Peckham; Dissenting opinions: Harlan I (E. White, Day), Holmes

In this case, the Court ruled that a New York law that regulated the working conditions of bakery employees violated the right of contract.

Loving v. Virginia, 388 U.S. 1 (1967): Unanimous vote (Warren, Black, Douglas, Clark, Harlan II, Brennan, Stewart, B. White, Fortas)

Opinion of the Court: Warren; Opinion concurring in judgment: Stewart

The court ruled that a Virginia law that prohibited interracial marriage was a violation of the Fourteenth Amendment's equal protection clause.

Lucas v. *South Carolina Coastal Council*, 505 U.S. 1003 (1992): Vote 6 (Rehnquist, B. White, O'Connor, Scalia, Thomas, Kennedy)–3 (Blackmun, Stevens, Souter)
> Opinion of the Court: Scalia; Concurring opinion: Kennedy; Dissenting opinions: Blackmun, Stevens, Souter

In this case, the Court ruled that a South Carolina law limiting the development of private property as a part of a coastal land preservation program was a violation of the takings clause of the Fifth Amendment.

Lynch v. *Donnelly*, 465 U.S. 668 (1984): Vote: 5 (Burger, B. White, Powell, Rehnquist, O'Connor)–4 (Brennan, T. Marshall, Blackmun, Stevens)
> Opinion of the Court: Burger; Concurring opinion: O'Connor; Dissenting opinions: Brennan (T. Marshall, Blackmun, Stevens), Blackmun (Stevens)

The Court decided that a municipal display of holiday decorations that included a crèche and some non-religious objects did not violate the First Amendment.

Marbury v. *Madison*, 5 U.S. 137 (1803)*: Vote 5 (J. Marshall, Paterson, S. Chase, Washington, Moore)–0
> Opinion of the Court: J. Marshall; Did not participate: Cushing

In this case, John Marshall concluded that the Court possesses the power of judicial review.

Massachusetts Board of Retirement v. *Murgia*, 427 U.S. 307 (1976): Vote 7 (Burger, Brennan, Stewart, B. White, Blackmun, Powell, Rehnquist)–1 (T. Marshall)
> Opinion of the Court: *Per curiam*; Dissenting opinion: T. Marshall; Did not participate: Stevens

The Court decided that the equal protection clause does not require strict scrutiny for a claim of discrimination based on age.

McCleskey v. ***Kemp***, 481 U.S. 279 (1987): Vote 5 (Rehnquist, B. White, Powell, O'Connor, Scalia)–4 (Brennan, T. Marshall, Blackmun, Stevens)

Opinion of the Court: Powell; Dissenting opinions: Brennan (T. Marshall, Blackmun, Stevens), Blackmun (Brennan, T. Marshall, Stevens), Stevens (Blackmun)

The Court rejected a claim that Georgia's system of capital punishment was unconstitutional because it discriminated on the basis of race.

McCollum *v. Illinois*, 333 U.S. 203 (1948): Vote 5 (Black, Frankfurter, R. Jackson, Rutledge, Burton)–1 (Reed)

Opinion of the Court: Black; Concurring opinions: Frankfurter, Jackson; Dissenting opinion: Reed

The Court ruled that religious instruction in public schools violates the establishment clause.

*McCreary County v. **ACLU***, 545 U.S. _ _ _ (2005): Vote 5 (Souter, Stevens, O'Connor, Ginsberg, Breyer)–4 (Scalia, Rehnquist, Thomas, Kennedy)

Opinion of the Court: Souter; Concurring opinion: O'Connor; Dissenting opinion: Scalia (Rehnquist, Thomas)

The Court ruled that the public display of the Ten Commandments in a Kentucky courtroom was unconstitutional.

Meyer *v. Nebraska*, 262 U.S. 390 (1923): Vote 7 (Taft, McKenna, Van Devanter, McReynolds, Brandeis, Butler, Sanford)–2 (Holmes, Sutherland)

Opinion of the Court: McReynolds; Dissenting opinion: Holmes, Sutherland

The Court ruled that a Nebraska statute that prohibited the teaching of languages other than English to children violated the Fourteenth Amendment.

*Michael H. v. **Gerald D.***, 491 U.S. 110 (1989): Vote 5 (Scalia, O'Connor, Kennedy, Rehnquist, Stevens)–4 (Brennan, White, Blackmun, J. Marshall)

Opinion of the Court: Scalia; Concurring opinions: O'Connor, Stevens; Dissenting opinions: Brennan (Blackmun, J. Marshall), White

The Court upheld a California law under which a child born to a married woman living with her husband was presumed to be a child of the marriage.

*Michael M. v. **Superior Court of Sonoma County***, 450 U.S. 464 (1981): Vote 5 (Burger, Stewart, Blackmun, Powell, Rehnquist)–4 (Brennan, B. White, T. Marshall, Stevens)

> Judgment of the Court: Rehnquist; Concurring opinion: Stewart; Opinion concurring in judgment: Blackmun; Dissenting opinions: Brennan (B. White, T. Marshall), Stevens

The Court sustained a California statutory rape law that punished males for sexual relations with a female under the age of 18 years but not females engaged in the same behavior with underage males.

Miller v. California, 413 U.S. 15 (1973)*: Vote 5 (Burger, B. White, Blackmun, Powell, Rehnquist)–4 (Douglas, Brennan, Stewart, T. Marshall)

> Opinion of the Court: Burger; Dissenting opinions: Douglas, Brennan (Stewart, T. Marshall)

In this case, the Court developed a three-part test for defining obscenity, which is not protected under the First Amendment. Justice Burger concluded, "At a minimum, prurient, patently offensive depiction or description of sexual conduct must have serious literary, artistic, political, or scientific value to merit First Amendment protection."

Minersville v. Gobitis, 310 U.S. 586 (1940) (Flag Salute Case I): Vote 8 (Hughes, McReynolds, Roberts, Black, Reed, Frankfurter, Douglas, Murphy)–1 (Stone)

> Opinion of the Court: Frankfurter; Concurring without opinion: McReynolds; Dissenting opinion: Stone

The Court upheld a Pennsylvania law that required all public school children to begin each day with a salute to the American flag. The Court decided that the law was not a violation of freedom of speech or religion.

*Minor v. **Happersett***, 88 U.S. 162 (21 Wall. 162) (1874): Unanimous vote (Waite, Clifford, Swayne, Miller, Davis, Field, Strong, Bradley, Hunt)

> Opinion of the Court: Waite

The Court ruled unanimously that a woman's right of suffrage was not protected by the Constitution.

*Mississippi University for Women v. **Hogan***, 458 U.S. 718 (1982): Vote 5 (Brennan, B. White, T. Marshall, Stevens, O'Connor)–4 (Burger, Blackmun, Powell, Rehnquist)

Opinion of the Court: O'Connor; Dissenting opinions: Burger, Blackmun, Powell (Rehnquist)

The Court ruled that the Mississippi University's nursing school for women violated the equal protection clause of the Fourteenth Amendment by not allowing men to attend.

Missouri ex rel. Gaines v. *Canada*, 305 U.S. 337 (1938): Vote 6 (Hughes, Brandeis, Stone, Roberts, Black, Reed)–2 (McReynolds, Butler)

Opinion of the Court: Hughes; Dissenting opinion: McReynolds (Butler)

The Court ruled that the racially discriminatory admissions policy of the all-white University of Missouri law school violated the equal protection clause.

Moore v. *City of East Cleveland*, 431 U.S. 494 (1977): Vote 5 (Brennan, T. Marshall, Blackmun, Powell, Stevens)–4 (Burger, Stewart, B. White, Rehnquist)

Judgment of the Court: Powell; Concurring opinion: Brennan (T. Marshall); Opinion concurring in judgment: Stevens; Dissenting opinions: Burger, Stewart (Rehnquist), B. White

The Court decided an East Cleveland housing ordinance that allowed only immediate family members to live together violated the due process clause of the Fourteenth Amendment.

Munn v. ***Illinois***, 94 U.S. 113 (1877) (Granger Cases): Vote 7 (Waite, Clifford, Swayne, Miller, Davis, Bradley, Hunt)–2 (Field, Strong)

Opinion of the Court: Waite; Dissenting opinion: Field (Strong)

In this case, the Court decided that state laws regulating how much railroads could charge to move goods and people was not a violation of the right to property.

Nollan v. *California Coastal Commission*, 483 U.S. 825 (1987): Vote 5 (Rehnquist, B. White, Powell, O'Connor, Scalia)–4 (Brennan, T. Marshall, Blackmun, Stevens)

Opinion of the Court: Scalia; Dissenting opinions: Brennan (T. Marshall), Blackmun, Stevens (Blackmun)

The Court ruled that a coastal development permit issued by the California Costal Commission violated the takings clause of the Fifth Amendment because it deprived the plaintiffs of the reasonable use of their property.

Noto v. *United States*, 367 U.S. 290 (1961): Vote 7 (Harlan II, Frankfurter, Whittaker, Clark, Stewart, Black, Douglas)–2 (Brennan, Warren)

> Opinion of the Court: Harlan; Concurring opinions: Black, Douglas; Remand to lower court with request to dismiss: Brennan (Warren)

In this case, the Court distinguished sharply between the advocacy of illegal action, which may be prohibited under the First Amendment, and the advocacy of ideas, which may not be prohibited.

Olmstead v. **United States**, 277 U.S. 438 (1928): Vote 5 (Taft, Van Devanter, McReynolds, Sutherland, Sanford)–4 (Holmes, Brandeis, Butler, Stone)

> Opinion of the Court: Taft; Dissenting opinions: Holmes (Stone), Brandeis (Stone), Butler (Stone), Stone

The Court ruled that the Fourth Amendment did not prohibit the use of wiretaps to monitor private telephone conversations without an actual trespass onto private property.

Palko v. **Connecticut**, 302 U.S. 319 (1937): Vote 8 (Hughes, McReynolds, Brandeis, Sutherland, Stone, Roberts, Cardozo, Black)–1 (Butler)

> Opinion of the Court: Cardozo; Dissenting without opinion: Butler

The Court ruled that the Fourteenth Amendment did not incorporate the guarantee against double jeopardy in the Fifth Amendment. Palko was executed.

Paris Adult Theatre I v. **Slaton**, 413 U.S. 49 (1973): Vote 5 (Burger, B. White, Blackmun, Powell, Rehnquist)–4 (Douglas, Brennan, Stewart, T. Marshall)

> Opinion of the Court: Burger; Dissenting opinions: Douglas, Brennan (Stewart, T. Marshall)

The Court upheld a Georgia statute that outlawed "hard-core" pornography.

Pierce v. **Society of Sisters**, 268 U.S. 510 (1925): Unanimous vote (Taft, Holmes, Van Devanter, McReynolds, Brandeis, Sutherland, Butler, Sanford, Stone)

> Opinion of the Court: McReynolds

The Court concluded that an Oregon law requiring a public school education for children ages 8 to 16 was a violation of parents' right to direct the upbringing and education of their children.

Planned Parenthood of Missouri v. *Danforth*, 428 U.S. 52 (1976):
Multiple votes

> Opinion of the Court: Blackmun; Concurring opinion: Stewart
> (Powell); Dissenting opinions: B. White (Burger, Rehnquist),
> Stevens

In this case, the Court responded to several provisions of a 1974
Missouri act passed in response to *Roe v. Wade*, including a
provision that required a married woman to obtain the consent of her
husband for an abortion.

Planned Parenthood v. ***Ashcroft***, 462 U.S. 476 (1983): Multiple
votes

> Judgment of the Court: Powell; Opinion concurring in judgment:
> O'Connor (B. White, Rehnquist); Dissenting opinion: Blackmun
> (Brennan, T, Marshall, Stevens)

The Court upheld a Missouri regulation requiring parental consent
for "unemancipated minors" to obtain an abortion, coupled with a
provision that provided, in some cases, for an alternative process for
judicial approval.

Planned Parenthood v. Casey, 505 U.S. 833 (1992)*: Vote 5
(Blackmun, Stevens, O'Connor, Kennedy, Souter)–4 (Rehnquist, B.
White, Scalia, Thomas)

> Judgment of the Court: O'Connor, Kennedy, Souter; Concurring
> opinion: Stevens; Opinion concurring in judgment: Blackmun;
> Dissenting opinions: Rehnquist (B. White, Scalia, Thomas),
> Scalia (Rehnquist, B. White, Thomas)

A plurality of the Court refused to overrule *Roe* but in the process
worked several substantial changes in the Court's abortion
jurisprudence, including eliminating the trimester and viability
framework and replacing the compelling state interest test with the
undue burden test.

Plessy v. ***Ferguson***, 163 U.S. 537 (1896): Vote 7 (Fuller, Field,
Gray, Brown, Shiras, E. White, Peckham)–1 (Harlan I)

> Opinion of the Court: Brown; Dissenting opinion: Harlan I; Did
> not participate: Brewer

In announcing the separate but equal doctrine, the Court ruled that
Louisiana's separate car law did not violate the equal protection
clause of the Fourteenth Amendment.

RAV v. City of St. Paul, 505 U.S. 377 (1992): Unanimous vote (Rehnquist, B. White, Blackmun, Stevens, O'Connor, Scalia, Kennedy, Souter, Thomas)

Opinion of the Court: Scalia; Opinions concurring in judgment: B. White (Blackmun, Stevens, O'Connor), Blackmun, Stevens (B. White, Blackmun)

In this case, the Court struck down a St. Paul ordinance that forbade placing "on public or private property a symbol or object," such as a burning cross or a Nazi swastika, "which one knows or has reasonable grounds to know arouses anger, alarm, or resentment in others on the basis of race, color, creed, religion or gender."

Reed v. Reed, 404 U.S. 71 (1971): Unanimous vote (Burger, Douglas, Brennan, Stewart, B. White, T. Marshall, Blackmun, Powell, Rehnquist)

Opinion of the Court: Burger

The Court found that an Idaho statue giving preference to males in the administration of a decedent's estate violated the equal protection clause of the Fourteenth Amendment.

Regents of the University of California v. Bakke, 438 U.S. 265 (1978)*: Multiple votes

Judgment of the Court: Powell; Opinions concurring in part and dissenting in part: Brennan, B. White, T. Marshall, Blackmun, Stevens (Burger, Stewart, Rehnquist), B. White, T. Marshall, Blackmun

A plurality of the Court held that public universities may not constitutionally use numerical quotas in their admissions programs but may use race as a criterion in admissions.

*Reno v. **American Civil Liberties Union***, 521 U.S. 844 (1997): Vote 7 (Stevens, Scalia, Kennedy, Souter, Thomas, Ginsburg, Breyer)–2 (Rehnquist, O'Connor)

Opinion of the Court: Stevens; Opinion concurring in part and dissenting in part: O'Connor (Rehnquist)

The Court ruled that a federal law prohibiting the transmission of obscene or indecent messages on the Internet to recipients younger than 18 years of age was unconstitutional because it was overbroad.

*Reynolds v. **United States***, 98 U.S. 145 (1878): Unanimous vote (Waite, Clifford, Swayne, Miller, Strong, Bradley, Hunt, Harlan I; Field)

Opinion of the Court: Day; Opinion concurring in part and
dissenting in part: Field

In this case, the Court sustained the constitutionality of a
congressional statute that forbade polygamy as applied to the
territory of Utah.

Roe v. Wade, 410 U.S. 116 (1973) (Abortion Case): Vote 7 (Burger,
Douglas, Brennan, Stewart, T. Marshall, Blackmun, Powell)–2 (B.
White, Rehnquist)

Opinion of the Court: Blackmun; Concurring opinions: Burger,
Douglas, Stewart; Dissenting opinions: B. White (Rehnquist),
Rehnquist

The Court ruled that a right to an abortion was part of the Fourteenth
Amendment's concept of personal liberty and privacy. The Court
also devised an elaborate scheme, based on the state's interests in
protecting the fetus at the point of viability and the mother's health,
that permits the state to regulate the abortion decision at certain
points in the pregnancy, provided that the state's interest is
"compelling."

Romer v. Evans, 517 U.S. 620 (1996): Vote 6 (Stevens, O'Connor,
Kennedy, Souter, Ginsburg, Breyer)–3 (Rehnquist, Scalia, Thomas)

Opinion of the Court: Kennedy; Dissenting opinion: Scalia
(Rehnquist, Thomas)

The Court invalidated a Colorado constitutional amendment that
barred local governments from enforcing any regulation or
conferring any entitlement that granted homosexuals protected
minority status.

Roper v. Simmons, 543 U.S. 551 (2005): Vote 5 (Kennedy, Stevens,
Breyer, Ginsburg, Souter)–4 (Rehnquist, Scalia, O'Connor, Thomas)

Opinion of the Court: Kennedy; Concurring opinion: Stevens
(Ginsburg); Dissenting opinions: O'Connor, Scalia (Rehnquist,
Thomas)

The Court ruled that the Eighth Amendment forbids the execution of
offenders who were under the age of 18 when their crimes were
committed.

Roth v. United States, 354 U.S. 476 (1957): Vote 6 (Warren,
Frankfurter, Burton, Clark, Brennan, Whittaker)–3 (Black, Douglas,
Harlan II)

Opinion of the Court: Brennan; Opinion concurring in judgment: Warren; Opinion concurring in part and dissenting in part: Harlan II; Dissenting opinion: Douglas (Black)

In this case, the Court established that the test for obscenity is "whether to an average person, applying contemporary community standards, the dominant theme of the material taken as a whole appeals to prurient interest."

San Antonio School District v. *Rodriguez*, 411 U.S. 1 (1973): Vote 5 (Burger, Stewart, Blackmun, Powell, Rehnquist)–4 (Douglas, Brennan, B. White, T. Marshall)

Opinion of the Court: Powell; Concurring opinion: Stewart; Dissenting opinions: Brennan, B. White (Douglas, Brennan), T. Marshall (Douglas)

The Court found that a public school education is not a fundamental right under the due process clause and that economic classifications are not entitled to strict scrutiny under the equal protection clause.

Schenck v. ***United States***, 249 U.S. 47 (1919): Unanimous vote (E. White, McKenna, Holmes, Day, Van Devanter, Pitney, McReynolds, Brandeis, Clarke)

Opinion of the Court: Holmes

In upholding the Espionage Act of 1917, the Court, speaking through Justice Holmes, established the clear and present danger test.

Sherbert v. *Verner*, 374 U.S. 398 (1963): Vote 7 (Warren, Black, Douglas, Clark, Brennan, Stewart, Goldberg)–2 (Harlan II, B. White)

Opinion of the Court: Brennan; Concurring opinion: Douglas; Opinion concurring in judgment: Stewart; Dissenting opinion: Harlan II (B. White)

In this case, the Court ruled that a secular regulation that "substantially burdens" a religious practice must be justified by a compelling state interest. Parts of this case were later overruled by *Employment Division v. Smith* (1989).

Stenberg v. ***Carhart***, 530 U.S. 914 (2000): Vote 5 (Stevens, O'Connor, Souter, Ginsburg, Breyer)–4 (Rehnquist, Scalia, Kennedy, Thomas)

Opinion of the Court: Breyer; Concurring opinions: Stevens (Ginsberg), O'Connor, Ginsberg (Stevens); Dissenting opinions: Rehnquist, Scalia, Kennedy (Rehnquist), Thomas (Rehnquist, Scalia)

The Court concluded that a Nebraska law that banned dilation and evacuation procedures during abortion procedures (or so-called partial-birth abortions) was unconstitutional because it was too broad and did not include a health exception.

Sweatt v. Painter, 339 U.S. 629 (1950): Unanimous vote (Vinson, Black, Reed, Frankfurter, Douglas, R. Jackson, Burton, Clark, Minton)
> Opinion of the Court: Vinson

The Court ordered the state of Texas to admit an African-American student to its all-white law school, even though the state did have a separate law school for African-Americans.

*Tahoe-Sierra Preservation Council v. **Tahoe Regional Planning Agency***, 535 U.S. 302 (2002): Vote 6 (Stevens, O'Connor, Kennedy, Souter, Ginsberg, Breyer)–3 (Rehnquist, Scalia, Thomas)
> Opinion of the Court: Stevens; Dissenting opinions: Rehnquist (Scalia, Thomas), Thomas (Scalia)

The Court refused to rule that a series of local statutes that placed moratoria on land development in advance of a comprehensive land-use plan necessarily constituted a "temporary taking" under the Fifth Amendment.

***Talley** v. California*, 362 U.S. 60 (1960): Vote 6 (Black, Warren, Douglas, Brennan, Stewart; Harlan II)–3 (Clark, Frankfurter, Whittaker)
> Opinion of the Court: Black; Concurring opinion: Harlan; Dissenting opinion: Clark

The Court found that a California ordinance restricting the distribution of anonymous handbills violates the First Amendment.

*Texas v. **Johnson***, 491 U.S. 397 (1989): Vote 5 (Brennan, T. Marshall, Blackmun, Scalia, Kennedy)–4 (Rehnquist, B. White, Stevens, O'Connor)
> Opinion of the Court: Brennan; Concurring opinion: Kennedy; Dissenting opinions: Rehnquist (B. White, O'Connor), Stevens

In overturning a criminal conviction for burning a U.S. flag, the Court ruled that the defendant's actions were constitutionally protected under the First Amendment because he was expressing a political viewpoint and because his actions qualified as symbolic speech.

***Thomas** v. Review Board*, 450 U.S. 707 (1981): Vote: 8 (Burger,

Brennan, Stewart, B. White, T. Marshall, Blackmun, Powell, Stevens)–1 (Rehnquist)

    Opinion of the Court: Burger; Opinion concurring in judgment: Blackmun; Dissenting opinion: Rehnquist

The Court decided that a state decision denying unemployment benefits to the plaintiff impermissibly interfered with his free exercise of religion.

Tinker v. *Des Moines School District*, 393 U.S. 503 (24 Feb. 1969): Vote 7 (Warren, Douglas, Brennan, Stewart, B. White, Fortas, T. Marshall)–2 (Black, Harlan II)

    Opinion of the Court: Fortas; Concurring opinions: Stewart, B. White; Dissenting opinions: Black, Harlan II

In this case, the Court held that the decision of school administrators to prohibit students from wearing armbands to protest the war in Vietnam was an unconstitutional infringement of symbolic speech.

Trimble v. *Gordon*, 430 U.S. 762 (1977): Vote 5 (Stevens, T. Marshall, Powell, Brennan, White)–4 (Rehnquist, Blackmun, Stewart, Burger)

    Opinion of the Court: Powell; Dissenting opinions: Rehnquist, Blackmun, Stewart, Burger

The Court struck down an Illinois inheritance statute that disadvantaged nonmarital children as a violation of the equal protection clause.

Troxel v. ***Granville***, 530 U.S. 57 (2000): Vote 6 (Rehnquist, O'Connor, Souter, Thomas, Ginsburg, Breyer)–3 (Stevens, Scalia, Kennedy)

    Judgment of the Court: O'Connor; Opinions concurring in judgment: Souter, Thomas; Dissenting opinions: Stevens, Scalia, Kennedy

In this case, the Court struck down Washington's third-party visitation statute, noting that it interfered with parents' due process right "to make decisions concerning the care, custody, and control" of their children.

United States v. *O'Brien*, 391 U.S. 367 (1968) (Draft Card Case): Vote 7 (Fortas, Stewart, White, Harlan II, Black, Warren, Brennan)–1 (Douglas)

    Opinion of the Court: Warren; Concurring opinion: Harlan II; Dissenting opinion: Douglas; Did not participate: T. Marshall

In upholding a conviction based on the burning of a draft card, the Court developed a three-part test to determine when the First Amendment protects symbolic speech or expressive conduct.

United States v. *Virginia*, 518 U.S. 515 (1996): Vote 7 (Rehnquist, Stevens, O'Connor, Kennedy, Souter, Ginsburg, Breyer)–1 (Scalia)
> Opinion of the Court: Ginsburg; Opinion concurring in judgment: Rehnquist; Dissenting opinion: Scalia; Did not participate: Thomas

In this case, the Court struck down the males-only admissions policy of the Virginia Military Institute as a violation of the equal protection clause. The Court ruled that for sex discrimination to be constitutional, the government must present an "exceedingly persuasive justification" to treat men and women differently.

Vacco, Attorney General of New York v. *Quill*, 521 U.S. 793 (1997): Unanimous vote (Ginsberg, Souter, Thomas, Breyer, Scalia, Stevens, Rehnquist, O'Connor, Kennedy)
> Opinion of the Court: Rehnquist; Concurring opinions: O'Connor, Ginsburg, Souter, Stevens, Breyer

The Court found that New York's ban on physician-assisted suicide did not violate the equal protection clause because the ban was rationally related to the state's interest in protecting medial ethics.

Van Orden v. **Perry**, 545 U.S. _ _ _ (2005): Vote 5 (Rehnquist, Scalia, Kennedy, Thomas, Breyer)–4 (Ginsberg, O'Connor, Souter, Stevens)
> Opinion of the Court: Rehnquist; Concurring opinion: Breyer (Scalia, Thomas); Dissenting opinion: Stevens (Ginsberg)

The Court ruled that a monument of the Ten Commandments on the Texas state capitol building grounds did not violate the First Amendment's establishment clause.

Virginia v. *Black*, 538 U.S. 343 (2003)*: Vote 7 (Ginsberg, Breyer, Scalia, Rehnquist, Kennedy, O'Connor, Stevens)–2 (Thomas, Scalia)
> Opinion of the Court: O'Connor; Concurring opinions: Scalia (Rehnquist), Souter (Kennedy, Ginsburg); Dissenting opinion: Thomas

The Court ruled that Virginia's cross-burning statue prohibiting the burning of a cross to intimidate any person or group did not violate the First Amendment.

*Wallace v. **Jaffree***, 472 U.S. 38 (1985): Vote 6 (Brennan, T. Marshall, Blackmun, Powell, Stevens, O'Connor)–3 (Burger, B. White, Rehnquist)

> Opinion of the Court: Stevens; Concurring opinion: Powell; Opinion concurring in judgment: O'Connor; Dissenting opinions: Burger, B. White, Rehnquist

The Court struck down an Alabama statute that requited a one-minute "moment of silence" at the beginning of the school day as a violation of the establishment clause.

***Washington** v. Glucksberg*, 521 U.S. 702 (1997): Unanimous vote (Rehnquist, Stevens, O'Connor, Scalia, Kennedy, Souter, Thomas, Ginsburg, Breyer)

> Opinion of the Court: Rehnquist; Concurring opinions: Ginsburg, Breyer, Stevens, Souter, O'Connor (Ginsburg, Breyer)

The Court decided that Washington's prohibition against physician-assisted suicide does not violate the due process clause of the Fourteenth Amendment.

*West Coast Hotel v. **Parrish***, 300 U.S. 379 (1937): Vote 5 (Hughes, Brandeis, Stone, Roberts, Cardozo)–4 (Van Devanter, McReynolds, Sutherland, Butler)

> Opinion of the Court: Hughes; Dissenting opinion: Sutherland (Van Devanter, McReynolds, Butler)

The Court upheld a wages and hours statute and, thus, overruled *Lochner v. New York*.

*West Virginia v. **Barnette***, 319 U.S. 624 (1943): Vote 6 (Stone, Black, Douglas, Murphy, R. Jackson, W. Rutledge)–3 (Roberts, Reed, Frankfurter)

> Opinion of the Court: R. Jackson; Concurring opinions: Black (Douglas), Murphy; Dissenting opinion: Frankfurter; Dissenting without opinion: Roberts, Reed

The Court ruled that a state law requiring students in public elementary schools to salute the flag violated the First Amendment. This case overruled *Minersville v. Gobitis* (1940).

*Whitney v. **California***, 274 U.S. 357 (1927): Unanimous vote (Taft, Holmes, Van Devanter, McReynolds, Brandeis, Sutherland, Butler, Sanford, Stone)

> Opinion of the Court: Sanford; Concurring opinion: Brandeis (Holmes)

The Court upheld the California Criminal Syndicalism Act of 1919, which made it a crime to organize or knowingly become a member of an organization that aims to bring about revolutionary change through the use of violence.

Wisconsin v. *Mitchell*, 508 U.S. 476 (1993): Unanimous vote (Rehnquist, B. White, Blackmun, Stevens, O'Connor, Scalia, Kennedy, Souter, Thomas)
> Opinion of the Court: Rehnquist

The Court unanimously upheld a state hate crime law that provided for up to five years' additional imprisonment for an offender who intentionally selected his or her victim because of the person's race, religion, color, disability, sexual orientation, national origin, or ancestry.

Wisconsin v. ***Yoder***, 406 U.S. 205 (1972) (Amish School Case): Vote 6 (Burger, Brennan, Stewart, B. White, T. Marshall, Blackmun)–1 (Douglas)
> Opinion of the Court: Burger; Concurring opinions: Stewart (Brennan), B. White (Brennan, Stewart); Dissenting opinion: Douglas; Did not participate: Powell, Rehnquist

The Court held that the First Amendment protected the religious rights of the Amish to withdraw their children from public schools at the age of 14.

Wooley v. ***Maynard***, 430 U.S. 705 (1977): Vote 6 (Burger, Brennan, Stewart, T. Marshall, Powell, Stevens)–3 (B. White, Blackmun, Rehnquist)
> Opinion of the Court: Burger; Dissenting opinions: B. White (Rehnquist, Blackmun), Rehnquist (Blackmun)

The Court ruled that under the First Amendment, New Hampshire could not force a citizen to display the words "Live Free or Die" on a license plate.

Yates v. *United States*, 354 U.S. 298 (1957): Vote 6 (Warren, Black, Frankfurter, Douglas, Burton, Harlan II)–1 (Clark)
> Opinion of the Court: Harlan II; Opinion concurring in judgment: Burton; Opinion concurring in part and dissenting in part: Black (Douglas); Dissenting opinion: Clark; Did not participate: Brennan, Whittaker

The Court overturned the convictions of 14 communist leaders on the grounds that the Smith Act undermined free speech.

Zelman *v. Simmons-Harris*, 536 U.S. 639 (2002): Vote: 5 (Rehnquist, O'Connor, Scalia, Kennedy, Thomas)–4 (Stevens, Souter, Ginsburg, Breyer)

> Opinion of the Court: Rehnquist; Concurring opinions: O'Connor, Thomas; Dissenting opinions: Stevens, Souter (Stevens, Ginsburg, Breyer), Breyer (Stevens, Souter)

The Court upheld an Ohio school voucher plan against a claim that the plan violated the establishment clause of the First Amendment.

Glossary

advisory opinion: A formal opinion issued by a court about a hypothetical or nonadversarial state of affairs or when no concrete case or controversy is to be decided.

affidavit: A written and signed declaration of facts made before a notary public or a similar officer.

affirm: A decision by a higher or superior court to uphold or confirm a decision by a lower or inferior court.

amicus curiae: "Friend of the court"; a person or group, not a litigant in the case, that submits a brief on an issue before the court.

appeal: A request asking a higher court to review a trial or lower-court decision to decide whether it was correct.

appellant: A person or group who appeals a judicial decision from a lower court. This is the party listed first in the title of a decision.

appellate jurisdiction: When a higher or superior court has the authority to review the judgment and proceedings of an inferior or lower court.

appellee: The person or group who won the suit in a lower court and against whom an appeal is taken. This is the party listed second in the title of a decision.

balancing: A method of constitutional interpretation in which judges weigh one set of interests or rights against another set of interests or rights. This method is often found in First Amendment cases or in cases where two or more rights are in apparent tension.

bench trial: A trial, in a lower court, by a judge and without a jury.

Brandeis brief: A lawyer's brief that utilizes not only case law and other legal materials but also a wide variety of non-legal materials, such as legislative findings, public policy documents, and data from social science. Named after Justice Louis Brandeis, who as a lawyer was among the first to use such materials.

brief: A written argument of law submitted by lawyers explaining why a case should be decided in favor of their client.

case and controversy (also "case or controversy"): A matter before a court in which the parties suffer real and direct harm and seek judicial resolution. The phrase often refers to Article III, Section 2 of the Constitution. Contrast with **advisory opinion**.

certification, writ of: Similar to an appeal, this is a process in which a lower court forwards a case to, and requests guidance from, an appellate court regarding unresolved legal questions.

***certiorari*, writ of**: This is a method of appeal to the Supreme Court and the primary means by which the Court sets its docket. Technically, it is an order issued by the Supreme Court directing the lower court to transmit records for a case the Court has accepted on appeal.

circuit court: An appellate court; in the federal judicial system, each circuit covers several states; in most states, the court's jurisdiction is by county.

comity: Courtesy, or the respect a court owes to other branches and levels of government.

common law: A type of legal system that is based primarily on judicial decisions rather than legislative action and statutory law.

complaint: A written statement by the plaintiff indicating legally and factually how he or she has been harmed by the defendant.

concurring opinion: An opinion by a judge who agrees with the result reached by the majority or plurality but disagrees with all or part of the reasoning.

constitutional court: A court with the authority to review whether governmental action conforms with the national constitution; in the United States, such courts are created under Article III.

counsel: The lawyers of record in a case.

de facto: In fact or practice.

defendant: The person named as the offender in a civil complaint or, in a criminal case, the person accused of the crime.

de jure: In law or official policy.

deposition: An oral statement, whether by a defendant or a witness, usually taken by an attorney, that may later be used at trial. See also **discovery.**

dicta (*obiter dicta*): Statements by a court that are not strictly necessary to reach the result in the case or that are not necessarily relevant to the result of the case. *Dicta* do not have the binding force of precedent.

discovery: The process before trial in which attorneys investigate what happened, often by using written interrogatories and taking oral depositions.

dissenting opinion: An opinion filed by a judge or judges who do not agree with the result reached by the majority of the court.

distinguish: To show why a case differs from another case and, thus, does not legally control the result.

diversity jurisdiction: The authority of federal courts to hear cases in which the litigants are citizens of different (or diverse) states.

docket: A full record of a court's proceedings.

doctrinalism: A method of constitutional interpretation that decides cases by appealing to specific doctrines, such as the "clear and present danger" test, and a way of organizing constitutional law more generally. This method is often found in First Amendment and equal protection cases.

doctrinal test: A set of guidelines, usually established through precedent, that the Court uses to adjudicate specific cases in specific areas of constitutional law. For example, the Court uses a three-part doctrinal test called the Miller test, first formulated in *Miller v. California* (1973), to determine whether materials are obscene. Other examples include the *Lemon v. Kurtzman* (1971) test for cases determining when a law has the effect of establishing religion, and the clear and present danger test in cases of subversive speech. Closer to terms of art than definitions, doctrinal tests typically have meanings that are much more fluid and dynamic than those of many other legal concepts: They change may from judge to judge and case to case.

due process: A requirement of fair and regular procedures; in the United States, there are two due process clauses, one in the Fifth

Amendment, which applies to the federal government, and one in the Fourteenth Amendment, which applies to the states.

en banc: "In the bench" or "full bench." Refers to cases in which all the judges of the court participate. For example, in federal circuit courts, cases are usually decided, not *en banc*, but by a smaller panel of three judges. See also **panel**.

error, writ of: A writ—or an order—sent by a higher court to a lower court instructing it to send the case to the higher court for review for possible error.

ex parte: "From one side; on one side." A hearing at which only one of the sides to a case is present.

ex post facto: "After the fact"; a law that makes something illegal that was not illegal when it was done or that increases the penalty for the act after it has occurred. In the United States, *ex post facto* applies only to the criminal law.

ex rel.: "On behalf of" (Latin: *ex relatione*); typically, when the government brings a case on behalf of a private party that has an underlying interest in the case, as in *Missouri ex rel. Gaines v. Canada* (1938).

federal question jurisdiction: A case based on, or that involves, the application of the U.S. Constitution, acts of Congress, and treaties of the United States.

habeas corpus, **writ of**: "You have the body"; a writ from a judge or a court sent to an officer or official asking him or her to explain why he has authority to detain or imprison a certain individual.

impeachment: The constitutional process in which the House of Representatives may accuse high officers of the federal government of misconduct. The trial of an impeached officer takes place in the Senate.

incorporation: In constitutional doctrine, the process by which the Supreme Court made the Bill of Rights applicable to the states through the due process clause of the Fourteenth Amendment.

injunction: A judicial order, usually temporary in duration, that prohibits or compels the performance of a specific act to prevent irreparable damage or injury.

interrogatories: Written questions, prepared by an attorney, that must be completed under oath by the other party, usually with the assistance of counsel, during the process of discovery. See also **deposition**.

issue presented: The legal issue or constitutional controversy raised by the facts of the case.

judgment: A final decision by a court. It usually determines the respective rights and claims of the parties but is subject to **appeal**.

judicial review: The authority of a court to review legislation, executive orders, and other forms of state action for their conformity with constitutional provisions.

jurisdiction: The authority of a court to entertain, or hear, a case.

jurisprudence: The study of law and legal philosophy.

justiciability: Whether a case may be heard by a court or is suitable for a judicial resolution. See also **jurisdiction**.

legislative court: A court created by Congress under its Article I powers; in contrast to Article III courts, judges on such courts generally do not receive lifetime tenure.

litigant: A party to a lawsuit, whether plaintiff, defendant, petitioner, or respondent.

majority opinion: An opinion by a majority of sitting judges or justices. Majority opinions typically have the force of law. See also **precedent.**

mandamus, **writ of**: "We command"; an order by a court to a governmental official directing that official to take a particular course of action or to comply with a judicial order.

martial law: A condition under which rule by military authorities replaces that of civilian authorities and courts martial replace civilian courts. See also **habeas corpus.**

moot: "Unsettled; undecided." A situation in which the underlying legal or constitutional controversy has been resolved or changed so that a judicial resolution is not possible or must be hypothetical.

natural law, natural rights: A system of law or rights based on "nature" or a higher law that transcends human authority.

opinion: A written explanation by a judge that sets forth the legal basis and rationale for his or her decision.

opinion of the court: An opinion by a majority of the judges or justices hearing a case. Compare with **plurality opinion**.

oral argument: Proceeding where attorneys explain their positions to a court and answer questions from the judges.

original jurisdiction: The authority of a court to hear a case in the first instance or as a trial court. Contrast with **appellate jurisdiction**.

originalism: A method of constitutional interpretation that seeks the "original" meaning of a constitutional provision or the intent of its drafters.

overrule: Where a decision by a court specifically repudiates or supersedes a statement of law made in an earlier case. Contrast with **distinguish.**

panel: A group of appellate judges, usually three, that decides cases. Also, a group of potential jurors for a trial court.

parties: The litigants in a case, including the plaintiff and the defendant, or on appeal, the appellants and appellees. The parties are typically named in the title of a case.

per curiam: "By the bench"; a collective decision issued by a court for which no individual judge or justice claims authorship or is identified by name.

per se: "In or by itself"; intrinsic, in the nature of the thing.

petitioner: The party who seeks a writ from a judge or the assistance of the court.

plaintiff: A person in a civil lawsuit who files the complaint against one or more defendants.

plurality opinion: The opinion in a case by a group of judges or justices that commands the most votes, but not an absolute majority of the court.

police powers: The powers reserved to state or local government to protect the "health, safety, welfare, and morals of the community."

political question doctrine: A rule of judicial power which holds that cases primarily involving political instead of legal issues should not be decided by courts but, instead, should be left to the other branches of government.

precedent: A court decision in an earlier case that is similar to the case at hand. Precedents are typically binding, in the sense that other courts must follow the rule established in the precedent, or explain why the rule does not apply (see **distinguish**) or why the precedent should be **overruled**.

prima facie: "At first sight"; the evidence needed to establish a case until it is contested by opposing evidence.

procedure: The code or rules that govern how a lawsuit proceeds. Different areas of law and different courts have different rules of procedure.

prudentialism: A method of constitutional interpretation that advises judges to avoid setting broad rules for future cases, as well as a particular understanding of the limited role courts should play in a constitutional democracy.

record: A full and written account of the proceedings in a lawsuit.

recuse: The process by which a judge decides not to participate in a case, usually because he or she has or appears to have a conflict of interest. A judge normally will not set forth the reasons for his or her recusal.

remand: The process by which an appellate court sends a case back to a lower court for further proceedings, often with specific instructions of law.

reserved powers: Powers, or areas of governance, that remain with the states, as confirmed by the Tenth Amendment.

respondent: The party against whom legal action is sought or taken.

reverse: When a higher court sets aside, or overrules, an erroneous decision by a lower court.

ripeness: A requirement that a case must be sufficiently developed factually before it may be heard by a court. Contrast with **moot.**

seriatim opinion: "In series"; usually a reference to a judicial decision where each judge issues a separate opinion instead of a majority opinion announced by the court.

sovereign immunity: A doctrine that holds that the government may not be sued without its consent.

standing: A doctrine requiring a plaintiff to demonstrate that he or she has a real, direct, and personal concern in a case before the court will hear the case.

stare decisis: "Let the decision stand." The practice of adhering to settled law and prior decisions. See **precedent.**

state action: Actions for which the state bears responsibility, either directly or indirectly; a requirement for a judicial remedy under the Constitution. In other words, the Constitution does not apply to private action.

statute: A law passed by a legislature. Compare with **common law**.

stay: A suspension of court proceedings.

structuralism: This method of constitutional interpretation suggests that the meaning of any particular or specific constitutional provision should be found by understanding how it relates to the constitutional text as a whole. This method is often found in separation of powers and federalism cases.

subpoena: A command to a witness to appear in a court or before a judge and give testimony.

textualism: A method of constitutional interpretation that stresses the actual wording of the constitutional provision in question, and which argues that we should read the words first for their ordinary meaning.

tort: A private civil wrong or breach of a legal duty owed to another person.

vacate: To set aside.

venue: The location or jurisdiction where a case in a lower court is tried.

verdict: A decision by a jury or a judge.

vested rights: A doctrine which holds that longstanding property rights must be respected by the government absent an urgent claim of public need.

writ: A written order by a court ordering an individual or a party to comply with its terms.

Biographical Notes

Note: Names of current justices are printed in capital letters.

ALITO, SAMUEL ANTHONY, JR. (b. 1950). Associate Justice; after an undergraduate degree from Princeton University and a J.D. from Yale Law School, he served as a law clerk for Leonard I. Garth of the United States Court of Appeals for the Third Circuit from 1976 to 1977. Thereafter he worked in several different capacities for the Department of Justice and was U.S. Attorney, District of New Jersey, from 1987 to 1990. He was appointed to the United States Court of Appeals for the Third Circuit in 1990. Nominated by President George W. Bush, he joined the Supreme Court on January 31, 2006.

Black, Hugo (1886–1971). Associate Justice; nominated by President Roosevelt. He served from 1937 until his retirement in 1971. Black had been an Alabama state judge and U.S. senator (1926–1937). He was a firm supporter of Roosevelt's New Deal programs in the Senate; his youthful membership in the Ku Klux Klan did not block his confirmation. Black was a First Amendment absolutist on the Court, strongly supporting free speech, separation of church and state, and strict textual analysis of the Constitution. His most important opinions include *Everson v. Ewing Township* (1947), *McCollum v. Board of Education* (1948), *Engel v. Vitale* (1962), and dissents in *Chambers v. Florida* (1940), *Betts v. Brady* (1942), *Adamson v. California* (1947), *Griswold v. Connecticut* (1965), and *Tinker v. Des Moines* (1969).

Blackmun, Harry (1908–1999). Associate Justice; nominated by President Nixon in 1970, he served until 1994. Blackmun attended Harvard University, where he earned his bachelor's degree in mathematics and studied law under the guidance of Felix Frankfurter. In 1959, President Eisenhower appointed Blackmun to the United States Court of Appeals for the Eighth Circuit, where his opinion in *Jackson v. Bishop* (1968) determined that physical abuse of prisoners was in violation of the Eighth Amendment. He voted to strike down laws interfering with reproductive rights and filed emotional separate opinions in *Webster v. Reproductive Health Services* (1989) and *Planned Parenthood v. Casey* (1992). His opinion in Roe was joined by six other justices, while in *Casey,* no other justice joined his opinion. Blackmun also wrote strong dissents

©2006 The Teaching Company Limited Partnership

in *Bowers v. Hardwick* (1986) and *DeShaney v. Winnebago County* (1989).

Brandeis, Louis D. (1856–1941). Associate Justice; nominated by President Wilson. He served from 1916 until his retirement in 1939 as the first Jewish justice. He argued the case of *Muller v. Oregon* in 1908, introducing the famous "Brandeis brief" and the use of social science in law. Brandeis also advocated the right to privacy in an influential law review article in 1890 and was opposed to the "bigness" in business and government. He wrote important opinions in *Whitney v. California* (1927), *Erie v. Tompkins* (1938), *Olmstead v. United States* (1928), and *New State Ice Co. v. Liebmann* (1932).

Brennan, William J., Jr. (1906–1997). Associate Justice; nominated by President Eisenhower in 1956, he served until 1990. He completed his law degree at Harvard and entered private practice in New Jersey. He authored important opinions in the areas of free expression, criminal procedure, and reapportionment. Brennan wrote the Court decision in *Cooper v. Aaron* (1958) that forced school officials to accelerate classroom integration and in *Baker v. Carr* (1962). In *United Steelworkers of America v. Weber* (1979), he wrote for the Court that federal anti-discrimination law does not bar employers from adopting race-based affirmative action programs to boost the number of blacks in the work force and management. Also, Brennan's opinion in *New York Times v. Sullivan* (1964) required public figures who sue for libel to prove "actual malice." He delivered the majority opinion in *Edwards v. Aguillard* (1987) that invalidated the required teaching of "creation science."

BREYER, STEPHEN G. (b. 1938). Associate Justice; nominated by President Clinton in 1994. Breyer graduated from Stanford University, and also received a B.A. from Magdalen College, Oxford, and a law degree from Harvard Law School, where he then taught, as well as at the Kennedy School of Government. He served as a law clerk to Justice Goldberg during the 1964 term. During 1980–1990, he served as a judge of the United States Court of Appeals for the First Circuit, and as Chief Judge during 1990–1994. Breyer wrote the plurality opinion declaring that the government may not require cable TV operators to segregate and block leased access channels that feature offensive or indecent programming in *Denver Area Consortium v. Federal Communications Commission* (1996). He dissented in the *Bush v. Gore* (2003) decision.

Burger, Warren Earl (1907–1995). Fifteenth Chief Justice; nominated by President Nixon. He served from 1969 until his retirement in 1986. Burger attended St. Paul's College of Law, now known as The William Mitchell College of Law. He went on to become a federal appeals judge. His most important opinions include *Swann v. Charlotte-Mecklenburg School District* (1971), *Milliken v. Bradley* (1974), and *Nixon v. United States* (1974), which upheld a subpoena for the Watergate tapes and resulted in Nixon's resignation. Burger's other benchmark decisions include *Miller v. California* (1973), defining obscenity, and *Lemon v. Kurtzman* (1971), concerning state establishment of religion.

Douglas, William O. (1898–1980). Associate Justice; nominated by President Cleveland in 1939, he left office in 1975, having served the Court for thirty-six years—the longest of any justice. Douglas graduated from Columbia Law School in 1925, began teaching at Yale Law School in 1927, and became a member of the Securities and Exchange Commission in 1936 (and chair in 1937). He expressed strong opinions in First Amendment rights cases, including *Terminiello v. City of Chicago* (1949) and *Dennis v. United States* (1952), and wrote the lead opinion in *Griswold v. Connecticut* (1965). Some of his other important opinions include *Skinner v. Oklahoma* (1942) and a dissent in *Roth v. United States* (1957).

Frankfurter, Felix (1882–1965). Associate Justice; nominated by President Roosevelt in 1939, he served until 1962. Frankfurter was born in Vienna; emigrated with his parents to New York, where he attended City College; and then went on to Harvard Law School, where he earned a reputation as an expert in Constitutional and federal law. He advised Woodrow Wilson during the Paris Peace Conference of 1919, maintained an active interest in Zionist causes, and helped to found the American Civil Liberties Union in 1920. In *Minersville School District. v. Gobitis* (1940) flag salute case, Frankfurter's opinion for the Court concluded that a public school was permitted to expel a student who refused, for religious reasons, to salute the American flag. His last opinion before retiring was a long dissent to *Baker v. Carr* (1962), in which he argued that legislative apportionment was a political rather than judicial matter.

GINSBURG, RUTH BADER (b. 1933). Associate Justice; nominated by President Clinton in 1993 as the first Jewish woman

Justice. Ginsburg received her undergraduate degree from Cornell University, attended Harvard Law School, and received her LL.B. from Columbia Law School. She served as a law clerk to Edmund L. Palmieri, Judge of the United States District Court for the Southern District of New York, from 1959–1961. She was a professor of law at Rutgers University School of Law (1963–1972) and Columbia Law School (1972–1980). Ginsburg also served as the ACLU's General Counsel and was on the National Board of Directors during 1974–1980. She was appointed a judge of the United States Court of Appeals for the District of Columbia Circuit in 1980. Majority opinions authored by Ginsberg include *United States v. Virginia* (1996). In *Bush v. Gore* (2000), Ginsberg dissented. She also voted against the execution of minors in *Roper v. Simmons* (2005).

Harlan, John M., II (1899–1971). Associate Justice; nominated by President Eisenhower, he served from 1955 until his death in 1971. Harlan was educated at Princeton and was a Rhodes Scholar at Oxford where he read law. He took an American law degree at New York Law School in 1925. President Eisenhower appointed Harlan to the United States Court of Appeals for the Second Circuit, where he served for ten months. Eisenhower promoted him to the High Court. He argued for a broad interpretation of the Fourteenth Amendment's due process clause, evidenced in his dissenting opinion to *Poe v. Ullman* (1961). Harlan dissented in *Mapp v. Ohio* (1961) and *Miranda v. Arizona* (1966), which expanded the protections of defendants in criminal cases, and again in *Reynolds v. Sims* (1964).

Holmes, Oliver Wendell, Jr. (1841–1933). Associate Justice; nominated by President Taft in 1902, he served until his retirement in 1932 at age 90. He was a Harvard law professor, edited the *American Law Review*, and was Chief Justice of the Massachusetts Supreme Court. Holmes played an important role in shaping Legal Realism. His benchmark opinions include *Schenck v. United States* (1919) and the opinion for the Court in *Buck v. Bell* (1927). His dissents in *Northern Securities Co. v. U. S.* (1904), *Lochner v. New York* (1905), *Dr. Miles Medical v. J. D. Park & Sons* (1911), *American Column & Lumber v. U. S.* (1921), and *Abrams v. United States* (1919) earned him the reputation "The Great Dissenter."

Hughes, Charles Evan (1962–1948). Eleventh Chief Justice; nominated by President Hoover in 1930, Hughes served until his retirement in 1941. Hughes was governor of New York (1907–1910), appointed to the Supreme Court as an associate justice in 1910 by President Taft, resigned in 1916 to run a losing race against Democratic candidate Woodrow Wilson in 1918, and later became Secretary of State (1921–1925). Hughes's *West Coast Hotel* (1937) decision abandoned a line of cases that had read the due process clauses of the Fifth and Fourteenth amendments as providing expansive protection for freedom of contract and the right of property.

Jackson, Robert (1892–1954). Associate Justice; nominated by Franklin Roosevelt, he served from 1941 until 1954, taking a leave of absence during 1945–46 to serve as the chief prosecutor of the Nuremburg Trials. Jackson formulated a three-tier test for evaluating claims of presidential power in *Youngstown Sheet & Tube Co. v. Sawyer* (1952), which remains one of the most widely-cited opinions in Supreme Court history. He also wrote the majority opinion in *West Virginia State Board of Education v. Barnette* (1943), which overturned mandatory saluting of the American flag. He dissented in *Korematsu v. United States* (1944).

KENNEDY, ANTHONY (b. 1936). Associate Justice; nominated by President Reagan in 1988. Kennedy received his B.A. in Political Science from Stanford University, and an LL.B. from Harvard Law School. He was Professor of Constitutional Law at McGeorge School of Law, University of the Pacific. In 1975, he was appointed to the United States Court of Appeals for the Ninth Circuit by President Ford. Kennedy joined the opinion of *Atkins v. Virginia* (2002), declaring execution of the mentally ill unconstitutional. He also wrote the opinion of the court in *Roper v. Simmons* (2005), invalidating the execution of felons. Kennedy joined the opinion of O'Connor and Souter in *Planned Parenthood v. Casey* (1993) but dissented in *Stenberg v. Carhart* (2002), which supported partial-birth abortions. He authored the Court's opinion in *Lawrence v. Texas* (2003).

Marshall, John (1755–1835). Fourth Chief Justice; nominated by President Adams. He served from 1801 until his death in 1835. Marshall had been a Virginia state legislator, U.S. envoy to France, a U.S. representative from Virginia, and U.S. Secretary of State under Adams. Marshall established that the courts were entitled to exercise judicial review, or the power to strike down laws that violated the Constitution. Thus, Marshall has been credited with cementing the position of the judiciary as an independent and influential branch of government. His most important opinions include *Marbury v. Madison* (1803), *McCulloch v. Maryland* (1819), *Dartmouth College v. Woodward* (1819), and *Gibbons v. Ogden* (1824).

Marshall, Thurgood (1908–1993). Associate Justice; nominated by President Johnson. He served from 1967 until his retirement in 1991 and was the first black justice on the Court. He headed the NAACP legal staff from 1938 until 1961 and argued many benchmark civil rights cases before the Court. Of the thirty-two cases he argued before the Supreme Court, Marshall won twenty-nine. These cases include *Dong v. Florida* (1940), *Smith v. Allwright* (1944), *Shelley v. Kraemer* (1948), *Sweatt v. Painter* (1950), and *McLaurin v. Oklahoma State Regents* (1950). His most famous case as a lawyer was *Brown v. Board of Education of Topeka* (1954). His most important opinions include *Stanley v. Georgia* (1969), *Furman v. Georgia* (concurrence, 1972), and *San Antonio School District v. Rodriguez* (1973).

Murphy, Frank (1890–1949). Associate Justice; nominated by President Roosevelt in 1939, he served from 1940 through 1949. Murphy was elected Governor of Michigan in 1936; his settlement of the automobile strike (1937) in Flint, Michigan, made him a national figure. While serving the Court, his decisions protected citizens against discrimination in *Falbo v. United States* (1944)*, West Virginia State Board of Education v. Barnette* (1943), and *Korematsu v. United States* (1944). He sought to protect labor workers picketing in *Thornhill v. Alabama,* (1940). He worked to uphold the Fourth Amendment, dissenting in *Wolf v. Colorado* (1949).

O'Connor, Sandra Day (b. 1930). The Supreme Court's 102nd Justice and first female Justice; nominated by President Reagan in 1985, she retired in 2006. O'Connor received her B.A. and LL.B. from Stanford University. She was appointed to the Arizona State Senate in 1969 and was subsequently reelected to two two-year terms. In 1975, she was elected Judge of the Maricopa County Superior Court and served until 1979, when she was appointed to the Arizona Court of Appeals. In *Grutter v. Bollinger* (2003), she maintained that the state's legitimate interest in using race as a factor for admission had gradually declined over the past 25 years as minority test scores improved, and that the Court should continue to monitor the strength of that interest until it decided that it was no longer sufficient to merit racial distinctions. O'Connor was instrumental in the Court's refashioning of its position on the right to abortion in 1992. In *Planned Parenthood v. Casey* (1992), O'Connor wrote the decision with Justices Kennedy and Souter that reaffirmed the constitutionally protected right to abortion established in *Roe v. Wade* (1973) but also lowered the standard that legal restrictions on abortion must meet in order to pass constitutional muster.

Powell, Lewis (1907–1998). Associate Justice; nominated by President Nixon in 1971, after turning down a nomination two years before. Often the swing vote, Powell's opinion in *Regents of the University of California v. Bakke* (1978) and *Bowers v. Hardwick* (1986); concerning the latter, he stated he had never met a homosexual person. After his retirement from the Court in 1987, he expressed remorse for his majority opinion in *McCleskey v. Kemp* (1987), where he voted to uphold the death penalty despite a study purporting to confirm that the penalty was applied disproportionately to African-Americans. Powell dissented in *Furman v. Georgia* (1972) but also helped rewrite the opinion in the compromise four years later in *Gregg v. Georgia* (1976).

Rehnquist, William H. (1924–2005). Sixteenth Chief Justice; nominated by President Nixon in 1972, he served for fourteen years until President Reagan appointed him Chief Justice in 1986, replacing Chief Justice Burger. Rehnquist served on the Supreme Court until his death in 2005. He received a B.A., M.A., and LL.B. from Stanford University and an M.A. from Harvard University. He served as a law clerk for Justice Robert H. Jackson during the 1951 and 1952 terms, practiced law in Phoenix, Arizona (1953–1969), and served as Assistant Attorney General, Office of Legal Counsel (1969–1971). Rehnquist wrote many important opinions, including dissents in *Roe v. Wade* (1972) and *Wallace v. Jaffree* (1985). He joined the majority in *Bowers v. Hardwick* (1986). Rehnquist presided over the Clinton impeachment hearings.

ROBERTS, JOHN G., JR. (b. 1955). Seventeenth Chief Justice; nominated by President George W. Bush in 2005. Roberts graduated from Harvard where he earned his undergraduate and law degrees. He then clerked for Henry Friendly of the United States Court of Appeals for the Second Circuit (1979–1980), and then-Associate Justice Rehnquist. He served as Associate Counsel to President

Reagan, White House Counsel's Office (1982–1986), and Principal Deputy Solicitor General, U.S. Department of Justice (1989–1993). He was appointed to the United States Court of Appeals for the District of Columbia Circuit in 2003. Roberts joined Justice Scalia's dissent in *Gonzales v. Oregon* (2006), where the Court decided that an Oregon state law permitting physician-assisted suicide did not conflict with the Controlled Substances Act. Roberts also wrote the unanimous decision in *Rumsfeld v. Forum for Academic and Institutional Rights* (2006).

SCALIA, ANTONIN (b. 1936). Associate Justice; nominated by President Reagan in 1986. He received his B.A from Georgetown University and the University of Fribourg, Switzerland, and his law degree from Harvard Law School. He was in private practice in Cleveland, Ohio (1961–1967), and then served as a professor of law at the University of Virginia and the University of Chicago. In 1982, President Reagan appointed him to the United States Court of Appeals for the District of Columbia Circuit. His most notable decisions include preventing personal property form being searched without a warrant in *Kyllo v. United States* (2001). Scalia also wrote strongly worded dissents in *Lawrence v. Texas* (2003), *Webster v. Reproductive Health Services* (1999), and *Planned Parenthood v. Casey* (1992).

SOUTER, DAVID H. (b. 1939). Associate Justice; nominated by President George W. Bush in 1990. Souter graduated from Harvard College, earned a B.A. in jurisprudence from Oxford University, and received his law degree from Harvard in 1966. In 1983, he was appointed an Associate Justice to the Supreme Court of New Hampshire. He became a judge of the United States Court of Appeals for the First Circuit in 1990. Souter joined the plurality opinion of *Planned Parenthood v. Casey* (1992), along with Kennedy and O'Connor. He dissented in *Bush v. Gore* (2000). Souter voted to affirm a state ban on nude dancing in *Barnes v. Glen Theatre* (1991) and concurred in *Lee v. Weisman* (1992).

STEVENS, JOHN PAUL (b. 1920). Associate Justice; nominated by President Ford in 1975. Previously, Stevens served as a judge of the United States Court of Appeals for the Seventh Circuit, nominated by President Nixon. He voted to reinstate capital punishment in the United States, opposed the affirmative action program at issue in *Regents of the University of California v. Bakke*

(1978), and refused to recognize a right to burn the flag as a speech act in *Texas v. Johnson* (1994). Later, Stevens supported a different affirmative program at the University of Michigan Law School, challenged in *Grutter v. Bollinger* (2003). In *Cleburne v. Cleburne Living Center* (1985), Stevens argued against the Supreme Court's famous "strict scrutiny" doctrine for laws involving "suspect classifications."

Stewart, Potter (1915–1985). Associate Justice; nominated by President Eisenhower in 1958, he served until his retirement in 1981. In 1954, Stewart was appointed to the United States Court of Appeals for the Sixth Circuit. Stewart dissented from the Court's decision in *Griswold v. Connecticut* (1965), but he changed his views and joined the Court's decision in *Roe v. Wade* (1973). Stewart is known for his views in the obscenity case of *Jacobellis v. Ohio* (1964), where he wrote in his short concurrence that "hard-core pornography" was hard to define, but that "I know it when I see it."

Story, Joseph (1779–1845). Associate Justice; nominated in 1811 by President Madison, he served until his death. In 1829, Story also accepted a newly-created position as Dane Professor of Law at Harvard University. Story devoted his efforts to equity jurisprudence and contributed significantly to patent law. In 1819, he attracted attention by his vigorous denunciation of the slave trade, and in 1820, he called on his fellow members of the Massachusetts Convention to revise the state constitution. He is also remembered for his ruling in *Amistad* (1841) in favor of kidnapped Africans.

Taney, Roger (1777–1864). Fifth Chief Justice; nominated by President Jackson in 1836, he served until 1864 as the first Roman Catholic to hold this position. Educated at Dickinson College before a law degree was required, Taney practiced law in Maryland was elected to the Maryland State Senate, and served as Attorney General of the United States. The Taney Court overturned the Marshall Court's decision in the *Dartmouth College v. Woodward* (1819) that had limited the power of the states to regulate corporations and reversed the Marshall Court's previous holding that states could not charter banks. In the *Charles River Bridge v. Warren Bridge* (1837) Taney declared that a state charter of a private business conferred only privileges expressly granted and that any ambiguity must be decided in favor of the state. He is also known for the benchmark decision of *Dred Scott v. Stanford* (1857).

THOMAS, CLARENCE (b. 1948). Associate Justice; nominated by President George W. Bush in 1991. Thomas attended Conception Seminary, graduated from Holy Cross College, and received his law degree from Yale University. He served as Assistant Secretary for Civil Rights in the U.S. Department of Education (1981–1982) and as Chairman of the U.S. Equal Employment Opportunity Commission (1982–1990). He became a judge of the United States Court of Appeals for the District of Columbia Circuit in 1990. In *McIntyre v. Ohio Elections Commission* (1995), Thomas wrote a concurring opinion agreeing with a majority of the Court that a law banning anonymous campaign literature violated the First Amendment. He concurred with the Court's decision in *United States v. Lopez* (1995) invalidating a federal law prohibiting possession of a firearm in a school zone, and he voted to expand personal gun rights under the Second Amendment in *Printz v. United States* (1997). Thomas also voted to uphold the school voucher program in *Zelman v. Simmons-Harris* (2002). He was the only Justice to side with the government in *United States v. Hubbell* (2000) and dissented with a divided court in *Lawrence v. Texas* (2003).

Vinson, Frederick (1890–1953). Thirteenth Chief Justice; nominated by President Truman. He served from 1946 until his death in 1953. Vinson served in the U.S. House of Representatives, became an associate justice of the U.S. Court of Appeals for the District of Columbia, and later became chief justice of the U.S. Emergency Court of Appeals. He made several significant decisions concerning internal security legislation. In *American Communications* v. *Douds* (1950), he found the requirement that members of labor unions swear to their non-membership in the Communist party unconstitutional; in *Dennis* v. *United States* (1951), he upheld the conviction of eleven leaders of the Communist party for violations of the Smith Act. His important opinions include *Sweatt v. Painter* (1948) and *Shelley v. Kraemer* (1948).

Warren, Earl (1891–1974). Fourteenth Chief Justice; nominated by President Eisenhower in 1953, and served until his retirement in 1969. Warren attended the University of California at Berkeley, where he earned his undergraduate and law degrees. In 1942, Warren was elected Governor of California, and he was twice re-elected. In 1948, he was the Republican nominee for Vice President of the

United States, and in 1952, he sought the Republican Party's nomination for President. Among his most important opinions is his unanimous decision for the Court in *Brown v. Board of Education* (1954).

Bibliography

The cases we read throughout this course are available in many places and formats. Full copies of the cases are available at most public libraries and there are several sites on the Internet, including the official site of the U.S. Supreme Court, which has most of the cases. However, the cases are often extremely long and include information not directly relevant to our inquiry. For this reason, I advise students to purchase a casebook, or a collection of edited cases. Many such collections are available. The readings and cases I have recommended are from Donald P. Kommers, John E. Finn, and Gary J. Jacobsohn, *American Constitutional Law: Essays, Cases, and Comparative Notes,* Volume 2, 2nd edition (Lantham, MD: Rowman & Littlefield Publishers: 2004), but any casebook will have most of the cases.

Essential Reading:

Amar, Akhil Reed. "Did the Fourteenth Amendment Incorporate the Bill of Rights Against States?" 19 *Harvard Journal of Law and Public Policy* 443 (1999). This important article discusses whether the Fourteenth Amendment should make the Bill of Rights applicable to state governments.

Banner, Stuart. *The Death Penalty: An American History.* Cambridge: Harvard University Press, 2003. A comprehensive history of the death penalty in the United States.

Berlin, Isiah. *Four Essays on Liberty.* 2nd ed. New York: Oxford University Press, 2002. The classic treatise on the differences between positive and negative liberties.

Burt, Robert A. "The Constitution of the Family." 1979 *Supreme Court Review* 329. Provides a comprehensive account of the role of the family in constitutional law.

Chafee, Zechariah, Jr. *Free Speech in the United States.* Cambridge: Harvard University Press, 1948. A classic history of freedom of speech in America.

Cooper, Phillip J., and Howard Ball. *The United States Supreme Court: From the Inside Out.* Englewood Cliffs, NJ: Prentice Hall College Division, 1995. Provides an excellent window into the structure and operation of the U.S. Supreme Court.

Ely, John Hart. "The Wages of Crying Wolf: A Comment on *Roe v. Wade*." 82 *Yale Law Journal* 920 (1973). This classic article marshals a series of criticisms about the Court's decision in *Roe v. Wade*.

————. *Democracy and Distrust*. Cambridge: Harvard University Press, 1981. Outlines an important theory about the proper role of the Court and the limits of judicial review in a constitutional democracy.

Greenawalt, Kent. *Fighting Words*. Princeton: Princeton University Press, 1995. Makes a set of arguments about the fighting words doctrine and the meaning of the First Amendment.

Hamburger, Phillip. *Separation of Church and State*. Cambridge: Harvard University Press, 2002. Examines the history and meaning of the establishment clause, tracing it from the 1840s.

Howe, Mark De Wolfe. *The Garden and the Wilderness*. Chicago: University of Chicago Press, 1965. This important book argues that religious freedoms are as much to protect religion from the state as the state from religion.

Hutson, James H. *Religion and the New Republic: Faith in the Founding of America*. Littleton, CO: Rowman & Littlefield Publishers, 2000. A collection of essays that explores the importance of religious faith at the Founding.

Kalven, Harry, Jr. *A Worthy Tradition: Freedom of Speech in America*. New York: Harper & Row, 1988. A comprehensive history of freedom of speech in the United States.

Ketcham, Ralph, ed. *The Federalist Papers*. New York: Signet Classics, 2003. This collection of essays on the Constitution is mandatory reading.

Kluger, Richard. *Simple Justice: The History of "Brown v. Board of Education" and Black America's Struggle for Equality*. New York: Vintage, 2004. The leading account of the facts and issues in *Brown. v. Board of Education*.

Kommers, Donald P., John E. Finn, and Gary Jacobsohn. *American Constitutional Law: Essays, Cases and Comparative Notes*. Vol. 2. Littleton, CO: Rowman & Littlefield, 2004. This casebook covers the major topics and issues in civil liberties and includes edited versions of the Court's most important cases.

Levinson, Sanford. *Constitutional Faith*. Princeton: Princeton University Press, 1989. Explores issues basic to the constitutional order, including questions about why and when the Constitution ought to be reaffirmed by individual citizens.

Phillips, Michael J. *The Lochner Court, Myth and Reality: Substantive Due Process from the 1890s to the 1930s*. Westport, CT: Praeger Publishers, 2000. This important book situates the Lochner decision against the Court's general treatment of substantive due process, arguing that the decision in Lochner is not representative of the Court's general approach.

Rubenfeld, Jed. "The Right of Privacy." 102 *Harvard Law Review* 737 (1989). Offers a comprehensive set of arguments about the origins, meanings, and limits of privacy as a constitutional concept.

Sunstein, Cass R. *Democracy and the Problem of Free Speech*. New York: Free Press, 1995. Examines the relationship between democratic theory and the First Amendment, calling for a New Deal vision of the First Amendment, in which political speech is more fully protected than commercial speech.

Weschler, Herbert. "Toward Neutral Principles of Constitutional Law." 73 *Harvard Law Review* 1 (1959). An important article on the necessity of neutral principles in constitutional interpretation.

Whittington, Keith. *Constitutional Interpretation: Textual Meaning, Original Intent, and Judicial Review*. Lawrence, KS: University Press of Kansas, 2001. Examines and evaluates various methods of constitutional interpretation and how they influence our understanding of judicial review.

Supplementary Reading:

Abel, Richard. *Speech and Respect*. London: Sweet & Maxwell, 1994. Discusses the relationship among speech, respect, and human dignity.

Ackerman, Bruce. *Private Property and the Constitution*. New Haven: Yale University Press, 1978. A comprehensive account of the importance of property to the constitutional order.

Baer, Judith A. *Equality under the Constitution: Reclaiming the Fourteenth Amendment*. Ithaca, NY: Cornell University Press, 1983. Argues for a reinvigorated and more expansive conception of equal protection of the laws.

Barber, Sotirios A. *Welfare and the Constitution*. Princeton: Princeton University Press, 2003. This important book argues for a broader understanding of welfare rights as basic constitutional rights.

Beard, Charles. *An Economic Interpretation of the Constitution*. Reissue ed. New York: Free Press, 1986. A classic treatise that argues that the Founders meant for the Constitution to protect the propertied classes.

Becker, Theodore. *The Declaration of Independence: A Study in the History of Political Ideas*. New York: Vintage, 1958. A classic examination of the political philosophy behind the Declaration of Independence.

Bedau, Hugo Adam. *The Death Penalty in America: Current Controversies*. Reprint ed. Oxford: Oxford University Press, 1998. A wide-ranging overview of various aspects of the death penalty.

Berns, Walter. *For Capital Punishment: Crime and the Morality of the Death Penalty*. Reprint ed. Lanham, MD: University Press of America, 1991. This book is still one of the best defenses of the constitutionality and sensibility of the death penalty.

————. *The First Amendment and the Future of American Democracy*. Reprint ed. Washington, DC: Regnery Publishing, 1976. Examines the argument that speech is a critical component of democracy.

Bernstein, Anita. "For and Against Marriage: A Revision," 102 *Michigan Law Review* 129 (2003). In this article, Bernstein provides an important and comprehensive overview of the arguments for and against marriage as an institution.

Bickel, Alexander M. *The Least Dangerous Branch: The Supreme Court at the Bar of Politics*. 2nd ed. New Haven: Yale University Press, 1986. Provides an excellent account of when and why the Supreme Court should defer to the democratic process.

Black, Charles L. *Capital Punishment: The Inevitability of Caprice and Mistake*. 2nd ed. New York: W.W. Norton & Co., 1981. Provides a set of arguments about why the death penalty is flawed and should be unconstitutional.

Bollinger, Lee C. *The Tolerant Society*. Reprint ed. New York: Oxford University Press, 1995. Argues that the First Amendment is critical to the development of a tolerant and informed society.

Bork, Robert H. "Neutral Principles and Some First Amendment Problems." 47 *Indiana Law Journal* 1 (1971). In this classic article, Judge Bork examines a number of critical problems raised by the Court's First Amendment jurisprudence.

———. *The Tempting of America.* New York: Free Press, 1997. In this influential book, Judge Bork argues in favor of a method of constitutional interpretation called "originalism" or "original understanding."

Brill, Alida. *Nobody's Businesses: Paradoxes of Privacy.* Reprint ed. Redwood City, CA: Addison-Wesley, 1991. Provides a comprehensive overview of privacy as a legal concept and the difficulties that inhere in it, arguing that privacy issues are related to prenatal rights, the right to die, and the AIDS crisis.

Carter, Lief. *Constitutional Interpretation: Cases in Law and Religion.* New York: Longman Publishing Group, 1991. This primer introduces readers to the religion clauses and addresses a set of cases and interpretive problems generated by the religion clauses.

Carter, Stephen L. *The Culture of Disbelief: How American Law and Politics Trivialize Religious Devotion.* Garden City, NY: Anchor, 1994. Argues that American law and culture tend to devalue the importance of religious faith.

———. *Reflections of an Affirmative Action Baby.* Reprint ed. New York: Basic Books, 1992. Examines the arguments surrounding affirmative action.

Cogan, Neal. *The Complete Bill of Rights: The Drafts, Debates, Sources, and Origins.* New York: Oxford University Press, 1997. Contains a complete history and a collection of documents relating to the Bill of Rights.

Cord, Robert. *Separation of Church and State: Historical Fact and Current Fiction.* Brooklyn, NY: Carlson Publishing, 1982. Examines the history of the establishment clause.

Cortner, Richard C. *The Supreme Court and the Second Bill of Rights: The Fourteenth Amendment and the Nationalization of the Bill of Rights.* Madison, WI: University of Wisconsin Press, 1980. Traces the rise of the incorporation doctrine through the Fourteenth Amendment.

Curtis, Michael Kent. *No State Shall Abridge: The Fourteenth Amendment and the Bill of Rights.* Durham, NC: Duke University

Press, 1986. An excellent history of the relationship between the Fourteenth Amendment and the Bill of Rights.

Downs, Donald A. *The New Politics of Pornography*. Chicago: University of Chicago Press, 1989. Provides an overview of pornography as a political and constitutional issue.

―――. *Nazis in Skokie: Freedom, Community, and the First Amendment*. Notre Dame: University of Notre Dame Press, 1986. A compelling account of the Nazi march in Skokie, Illinois.

Davidson, Kenneth M., Ruth Bader Ginsburg, and Herma Hill Kay. *Text, Cases, and Materials on Constitutional Aspects of Sex-Based Discrimination*. St. Paul, West Publishing Company, 1974. This is an edited collection of materials, including Supreme Court and lower court cases, that address the constitutional issues surrounding sex discrimination.

Dworkin, Ronald. *Life's Dominion*. Reprint ed. New York: Vintage, 1994. Addresses human life values and the role they play in the constitutional order.

―――. *Sovereign Virtue: The Theory and Practice of Equality*. Cambridge: Harvard University Press, 2002. Presents a series of arguments about the meaning and importance of equality in the legal system.

Ely, Richard. *The Guardian of Every Other Right: The Constitutional History of Property Rights*. New York: Oxford University Press, 1992. Provides a complete history of the right to private property in the American constitutional system.

Emerson, Thomas. *The System of Freedom of Expression*. New York: Vintage Books, 1971. Covers an important theory of freedom of speech.

Epstein, Richard. *Takings: Private Property and the Power of Eminent Domain*. Reprint ed. Cambridge: Harvard University Press, 1989. Provides a comprehensive account of the takings clause and argues for its reinvigoration.

Farber, Daniel. *Lincoln's Constitution*. Chicago: University of Chicago Press, 2003. This important new book examines the constitutional philosophy of President Lincoln as forged by the Civil War.

Fehrenbacher, Donald E. *The Dred Scott Case*. New York: Oxford University Press, 2001. The complete account of the facts and issues in *Dred Scott*.

Finkelman, Paul. *An Imperfect Union: Slavery, Federalism, and Comity*. Chapel Hill, NC: University of North Carolina Press, 1981. Examines the role of slavery and Federalism in the formation of the Union.

Fisher, Louis. *Religious Liberty in America: Political Safeguards*. Lawrence, KS: University Press of Kansas, 2002. Examines the role of religious liberty in the political system and how it is protected by political as much as judicial institutions.

Fishkin, James S. *Justice, Equal Opportunity, and the Family*. New Haven: Yale University Press, 1983. Explores the relationship between the family and the constitutional values of merit and equality.

Formicola, Jo Renee, and Hubert Morken. *Everson Revisited: Religion, Education, and Law at the Crossroads*. Littleton, CO: Rowman & Littlefield Publishers, 1997. A complete history of the facts and issues in the case of *Everson v. School Board* (1947).

Garrow, David J. *Liberty and Sexuality: The Right to Privacy and the Making of Roe v. Wade*. Updated ed. Berkeley: University of California Press, 1998. A complete history of the facts and issues in *Roe v. Wade* (1973).

Gerstmann, Evan. *The Constitutional Underclass: Gays, Lesbians and the Failure of Class-Based Equal Protection*. Chicago: University of Chicago Press, 1999. Argues that current equal protection doctrines fail to protect gays and lesbians.

————. *Same-Sex Marriage and the Constitution*. Cambridge University Press, 2003. In this provocative book, Gerstmann argues that the right to marry must be fundamental, and should extend to same sex couples.

Gillman, Howard. *The Constitution Besieged*. Durham, NC: Duke University Press, 1995. Argues that *Lochner* was not motivated by laissez-faire market views but, instead, was an effort to preserve a conception of the police power that held that it could be used only in a neutral manner to benefit the general welfare.

Ginsburg, Ruth B. "Speaking in a Judicial Voice." 67 *New York University Law Review* 1185 (1993). Justice Ginsburg defends intermediate scrutiny.

Glendon, Mary Ann. *Abortion and Divorce in Western Law*. Reprint ed. Cambridge: Harvard University Press, 1989. A comprehensive and comparative account of abortion and divorce policies in Western democracies.

Gordon, Sarah Barringer. *The Mormon Question: Polygamy and Constitutional Conflict in Nineteenth-Century America*. Chapel Hill: University of North Carolina Press, 2002. A history of polygamy and the Mormon conflict in the United States.

Harvie, J. Wilkinson, III. *From Brown to Bakke*. New York: Oxford University Press, 1993. Examines the Court's work on race and affirmative action up to the *Bakke* case.

Horwitz, Morton. *The Transformation of American Law, 1780–1860*. Cambridge: Harvard University Press, 1979. This classic book traces the transformation of property as a constitutional right from the Founding to the Civil War.

Hull, Elizabeth. *Without Justice for All: The Constitutional Rights of Aliens*. Westport, CT: Greenwood Press, 1985. Examines the constitutional rights of aliens.

Irons, Peter. *The Courage of Their Convictions: Sixteen Americans Who Fought Their Way to the Supreme Court*. Reprint ed. New York: Penguin, 1990. Each of the 16 chapters in this book explores the personalities and issues involved in a famous Supreme Court case.

Kauper, Thomas. "Penumbras, Peripheries, Things Fundamental and Things Forgotten." 64 *Michigan Law Review* 235 (1965). Explores the doctrine of fundamental rights advanced in *Griswold v. Connecticut*.

Kirp, David L., Mark G. Yudof, and Marlene Strong Franks. *Gender Justice*. Reprint ed. Chicago: University of Chicago Press, 1986. Examines the relationship among gender, justice, and equality.

Lahav, Pnina. "Holmes and Brandeis: Libertarian and Republican Justifications of Free Speech." 4 *Journal of Law and Politics* 451 (1987). Explores the philosophical arguments behind the Holmes-Brandeis understanding of freedom of speech.

Law, Sylvia. "Rethinking Sex and the Constitution." 132 *University of Pennsylvania Law Review* 955 (1984). Explores the relationship between gender and basic constitutional rules and principles.

Lawrence, Charles, and Mari J. Matsuda. *We Won't Go Back: Making the Case for Affirmative Action*. Boston: Houghton Mifflin, 1997. Advances a series of arguments in favor of affirmative action.

Lessig, Lawrence. "Reading the Constitution in Cyberspace." 45 *Emory Law Journal* 869 (1996). A pioneering article about the Constitution and its role in cyberspace.

Leuchtenberg, William. *The Supreme Court Reborn: The Constitutional Revolution in the Age of Roosevelt*. Oxford University Press, 1995. This is an important collection of essays that explores the Roosevelt Court, with particular emphasis upon how the various social and political movements of the 1930s influenced the Court and its relationship with the Roosevelt administration.

Levy, Leonard. *Origins of the Bill of Rights*. New Haven: Yale University Press, 2001. An important history of the origins of the Bill of Rights.

———. *The Emergence of a Free Press*. Chicago: Ivan R. Dee, Publisher, 2004. A history of freedom of the press and its meaning at the Founding.

———. *The Establishment Clause: Religion and the First Amendment*. 2nd/rev. ed. Chapel Hill, NC: University of North Carolina Press, 1994. This important book provides a complete history of the origins and original purposes of the establishment clause.

Low, Susan Bloch, and Thomas Krattenmaker, eds. *Supreme Court Politics: The Institution and Its Procedures*. Minneapolis, MN: West Publishing Company, 1994. Offers detailed information about the Court, its internal operation, and its procedures.

MacKinnon, Catherine A. *Only Words*. Reprint ed. Cambridge: Harvard University Press, 1996. Makes an important argument that certain kinds of speech, including pornography, should be limited because they can harm.

Malbin, Michael. *Religion and Politics*. Washington, DC: American Enterprise Institute Press, 1978. Examines the religion clauses and what they meant at the Founding.

Marilley, Suzanne M. *Woman Suffrage and the Origins of Liberal Feminism in the United States*. Cambridge: Harvard University Press, 1996. A history of the right to vote for women and the rise of liberal feminism as a political movement.

McConnell, Michael. "Free Exercise and the *Smith* Decision." 57 *University of Chicago Law Review* 1109 (1990). This important article examines and criticizes the Court's decision in the celebrated Peyote case (*Employment Division v. Smith*), decided in 1990.

———. "The Right to Die and the Jurisprudence of Tradition," *Utah Law Review* 665 (1997). In this important law review article, McConnell rejects the claim that there should be a constitutionally recognized right to privacy.

McGrath, C. Peter. *Yazoo:Law and Politics in the New Republic: The Case of Fletcher v. Peck*. New York: W.W. Norton, 1966. A complete account of the Yazoo land fraud and the case of *Fletcher v. Peck*.

Meisel, Alan. *The Right to Die,* 2nd ed. New York: John Wiley, 1995. Although it is somewhat dated, this book provides a comprehensive overview of the legal and constitutional issues that surround the right to die, including an overview of various right to die statutes and cases.

Mill, John Stuart. *On Liberty*. New York: Penguin Books, 1975. Presents a classic argument about the meaning of liberty and the conditions under which it can be limited.

Miller , John C. *Crisis in Freedom*: *The Alien and Sedition Acts*. Mattituck, NY: Amereon Ltd., 2002. A complete history of the Alien and Sedition Acts.

Myrdal, Gunnar. *An American Dilemma: The Negro Problem and American Democracy*. Reprint ed. New Brunswick, NJ: Transaction Publishers, 1996. The classic account of race in the United States.

Nieman, Donald G. *Promises to Keep: African-Americans and the Constitutional Order, 1776 to the Present*. New York: Oxford University Press, 1991. An overview of the role that race has played in American constitutional history.

Noonan, John T., Jr. *The Luster of Our Country: The American Experience of Religious Freedom*. Berkeley: University of California Press, 2000. Examines the history and role of religious freedom in American constitutional history.

Okin, Susan Moller. *Justice, Gender, and the Family*. Reprint ed. New York: Basic Books, 1991. Explores the relationship between the family and gender in the legal order and how current conceptions fail to promote the ideal of justice.

Paul, Ellen Frankel, and Howard Dickman, eds. *Liberty, Property, and the Foundations of the American Constitution*. Albany, NY: State University of New York Press, 1989. Examines the centrality of liberty and property to the constitutional order and provides a history of property as a constitutional right.

Posner, Richard. *Sex and Reason*. Cambridge: Harvard University Press, 1992. Explores the relationship among sex, public policy, and the Constitution, often through the use of economic analysis.

Rabban, David. *Free Speech in Its Forgotten Years*. New York and Cambridge: Cambridge University Press, 1999. Explores the meaning of free speech before the First World War.

Ravitch, Frank S. *School Prayer and Discrimination: The Civil Rights of Minorities and Dissenters*. Boston: Northeastern University Press, 1999. Boston: Northeastern University Press, 2001. Ravitch argues that treating the prayer in schools controversy as a First Amendment problem only is insufficient to protect the rights of religious minorities.

Rehnquist, William H. *The Supreme Court: How It Was, How It Is*. Revised and updated ed. New York: Vintage, 2002. Examines the history and functions of the Supreme Court.

Sarat, Austin. *When the State Kills: Capital Punishment and the American Condition*. Princeton: Princeton University Press, 2001. Argues that the death penalty plays a "major and dangerous role in the modern economy of power."

Scalia, Antonin. *A Matter of Interpretation: Federal Courts and the Law*. Princeton: Princeton University Press, 1998. Justice Scalia sketches a theory about the role of courts in a democratic society.

Siegan, Bernard. *Economic Liberties and the Constitution*. Chicago: University of Chicago Press, 1981. A classic account of property rights and economic liberties.

Siegel, Reva B. "Text in Contest: Gender and the Constitution from a Social Movement Perspective." 150 *University of Pennsylvania Law Review* 297 (2001). Examines the politics of gender and constitutional law.

Smith, James Morton. *Freedom's Fetters: The Alien and Sedition Laws and American Civil Liberties.* Ithaca, NY: Cornell University Press, 1966. A comprehensive history of the Alien and Sedition Acts.

Smith, Rogers. "The Constitution and Autonomy." 60 *Texas Law Review* 175 (1982). This important article examines autonomy as a constitutional interest.

Smith, Steven D. *Foreordained Failure: The Quest for a Constitutional Principle of Religious Freedom.* New York: Oxford University Press, 1999. Argues that no single principle can adequately account for the complexity of the religion clauses.

Sorauf, Frank. *The Wall of Separation: The Constitutional Politics of Church and State.* Princeton: Princeton University Press, 1976. An outstanding though dated account of the establishment clause and the constitutional politics surrounding it.

Strasser, Mark. *On Same-Sex Marriage, Civil Unions, and the Rule of Law: Constitutional Interpretation at the Crossroads.* Praeger, 2002. Strasser argues that the right of same sex couples to marry is indistinguishabele from other constitutional protections afforded to the family more generally.

Strossen, Nadine. *Defending Pornography: Free Speech, Sex, and the Fight for Women's Rights.* New York: New York University Press, 2000. Argues that a commitment to free speech, as well as to women's rights, must mean that pornography will sometimes be protected under the First Amendment.

Sunstein, Cass R. "*Lochner*'s Legacy." 87 *Columbia Law Review* 873 (1987). Undertakes a critical review of *Lochner v. New York.*

———. *One Case at a Time: Judicial Minimalism on the Supreme Court.* Cambridge: Harvard University Press, 2001. This important book argues that a correct understanding of the role of judicial review in a democracy calls for a restrained Court.

———. "The Right to Marry," 26 *Cardozo Law Review* 2081 (2005). Sunstein provides an excellent overview of the right to marry as a constitutional liberty.

———. *The Second Bill of Rights: FDR'S Unfinished Revolution and Why We Need It More Than Ever.* New York: Basic Books, 2004. Builds on a speech by Roosevelt to argue for a "second" bill of rights.

Thayer, James Bradley. "The Origin and Scope of the American Doctrine of Judicial Review." 7 *Harvard Law Review* (1883). The classic statement on behalf of judicial restraint in constitutional law.

Tribe, Laurence H. *Abortion: The Clash of Absolutes.* Updated/revised ed. New York: W.W. Norton & Company, 1992. Examines the constitutional issues surrounding abortion.

Tushnet, Mark. *Taking the Constitution away from the Courts.* Princeton: Princeton University Press, 1999. This book rejects judicial supremacy in constitutional interpretation and argues for the importance of extrajudicial constitutional interpretation.

Van Alstyne, William. "A Critical Guide to *Marbury v. Madison.*" *Duke Law Journal* 1 (1969). One of the leading studies of *Marbury v. Madison* (1803).

Van Burkleo, Sandra F. *Belonging to the World: Women's Rights and American Constitutional Culture.* New York: Oxford University Press, 2000. This comprehensive book examines the role of women's rights in the American constitutional order.

Warren, Samuel D., and Louis D. Brandeis. "The Right to Privacy." 4 *Harvard Law Review* 193 (1890). This article is the classic argument in favor of a right to privacy in the American legal order.

West, Robin. *Progressive Constitutionalism: Reconstructing the Fourteenth Amendment.* Durham, NC: Duke University Press, 1994. Argues for a more progressive account of the Fourteenth Amendment and the equal protection clause.

Whittington, Keith. "Extrajudicial Constitutional Interpretation: Three Objections and Responses." 80 *North Carolina Law Review* 773 (2002). Examines constitutional interpretation by nonjudicial actors.

Wildenthal, Bryan H. "The Lost Compromise: Reassessing the Early Understanding in Court and Congress on Incorporation of the Bill of Rights in the Fourteenth Amendment." 61 *Ohio Law Journal* 1051 (2000). Reexamines the history of the Fourteenth Amendment and the process of incorporation.

Wolters, Raymond. *The Burden of Brown.* Nashville: University of Tennessee Press, 1984. An examination of *Brown v. Board of Education* and its aftermath, both politically and constitutionally.

Woodward, C. Vann. *The Strange Career of Jim Crow.* Commemorative ed. New York: Oxford University Press, 2001. An important history and analysis of Jim Crow laws in the United States.

Zipursky, Benjamin C. "*DeShaney* and the Jurisprudence of Compassion." 65 *New York University Law Review* 1101 (1990). Examines the Court's decision in *DeShaney* and the role of compassion in the various opinions.

Internet References:

Cases

http://www.law.cornell.edu/supct/index.html. Cornell Law School's Legal Information Institute archive contains all opinions of the court issued since May of 1990. In addition, a collection of 610 of the most important historical decisions of the Court is available on CD-ROM and (with reduced functionality) over the Internet.

http://www.findlaw.com/casecode/. This is an excellent source for finding cases, both at the federal level and the state level. Searches Supreme Court cases by name or year from 1893 to the present; however, retrieves even earlier cases if searched by case number.

http://www.landmarkcases.org/. This useful site includes a wide range of materials about landmark cases, including secondary sources and a helpful glossary.

The Supreme Court and the Justices

http://www.supremecourtus.gov/. This is the official site of the Supreme Court. It has information about the history and operation of the Court and links to cases, as well as biographical information about the justices.

http://www.supremecourthistory.org/. The official site for the Historical Society of the Supreme Court, it is an excellent resource for information about the Court. It includes a timeline, biographies of the justices, and information about landmark cases.

http://www.oyez.org/oyez/frontpage. This is a superb multimedia site. It includes audio transcripts of oral arguments in major cases and a virtual tour of the Court, as well as biographical information for sitting justices, information about pending cases, and news items about the Court.

News and Press Coverage

http://news.findlaw.com/legalnews/us/sc/. This site carries news about the Supreme Court and other federal courts.

http://www.law.com/jsp/scm/index.jsp. Provides news and commentary about the Supreme Court.

http://jurist.law.pitt.edu/currentawareness/ussupremes.php. This comprehensive site includes news about the Supreme Court, as well as links to blogs and others sources of information and commentary about the Court.

Academic Centers/Journals

http://stu.findlaw.com/journals/. A comprehensive database of academic journals and law reviews.

http://www.lawreview.org/. This site allows students to do full text searches of online law reviews.

http://www.loc.gov/law/guide/lawreviews.html. A list of online law reviews.

Blogs

http://www.scotusblog.com/movabletype/. This well-established blog is dedicated to discussions about the Court and its cases.

http://scotus.blogspot.com/. This blog includes information about pending cases.

http://supremecourtwatch.tpmcafe.com/. This blog has commentary about current cases and Supreme Court news.

U.S. Constitution and Other Founding Documents

http://memory.loc.gov/ammem/help/constRedir.html. Hyperlinks to the Declaration of Independence, the Constitution, the Bill of Rights, later amendments, *The Federalist Papers*, and other materials.

http://www.law.indiana.edu/uslawdocs/declaration.html. The Declaration of Independence.

http://www.usconstitution.net/. A comprehensive, annotated online guide to the Constitution.

http://www.constitution.org/. Includes secondary information about the Constitution.

http://www.law.ou.edu/hist/federalist/. *The Federalist Papers*.

http://www.yale.edu/lawweb/avalon/federal/fed.htm. *The Federalist Papers*, annotated.

http://confinder.richmond.edu/. Links to other constitutions.

The Bill of Rights (Amendments I-X)

Transmitted October 2, 1789.
Ratified by three-fourths of the states, December 15, 1791.

The Conventions of a number of the States having, at the time of adopting the Constitution, expressed a desire, in order to prevent misconstruction or abuse of its powers, that further declaratory and restrictive clauses should be added, and as extending the ground of public confidence in the Government will best insure the beneficent ends of its institution;

Resolved, by the Senate and House of Representatives of the United States of America, in Congress assembled, two-thirds of both Houses concurring, that the following articles be proposed to the Legislatures of the several States, as amendments to the Constitution of the United States; all or any of which articles, when ratified by three-fourths of the said Legislatures, to be valid to all intents and purposes as part of the said Constitution, namely:

Amendment I

Congress shall make no law respecting an establishment of religion, or prohibiting the free exercise thereof; or abridging the freedom of speech, or of the press; or the right of the people peaceably to assemble, and to petition the government for a redress of grievances.

Amendment II

A well regulated militia, being necessary to the security of a free state, the right of the people to keep and bear arms, shall not be infringed.

Amendment III

No soldier shall, in time of peace be quartered in any house, without the consent of the owner, nor in time of war, but in a manner to be prescribed by law.

Amendment IV

The right of the people to be secure in their persons, houses, papers, and effects, against unreasonable searches and seizures, shall not be violated, and no warrants shall issue, but upon probable cause, supported by oath or affirmation, and particularly describing the place to be searched, and the persons or things to be seized.

Amendment V

No person shall be held to answer for a capital, or otherwise infamous crime, unless on a presentment or indictment of a grand jury, except in cases arising in the land or naval forces, or in the militia, when in actual service in time of war or public danger; nor shall any person be subject for the same offense to be twice put in jeopardy of life or limb; nor shall be compelled in any criminal case to be a witness against himself, nor be deprived of life, liberty, or property, without due process of law; nor shall private property be taken for public use, without just compensation.

Amendment VI

In all criminal prosecutions, the accused shall enjoy the right to a speedy and public trial, by an impartial jury of the state and district wherein the crime shall have been committed, which district shall have been previously ascertained by law, and to be informed of the nature and cause of the accusation; to be confronted with the witnesses against him; to have compulsory process for obtaining witnesses in his favor, and to have the assistance of counsel for his defense.

Amendment VII

In suits at common law, where the value in controversy shall exceed twenty dollars, the right of trial by jury shall be preserved, and no fact tried by a jury, shall be otherwise reexamined in any court of the United States, than according to the rules of the common law.

Amendment VIII

Excessive bail shall not be required, nor excessive fines imposed, nor cruel and unusual punishments inflicted.

Amendment IX

The enumeration in the Constitution, of certain rights, shall not be construed to deny or disparage others retained by the people.

Amendment X

The powers not delegated to the United States by the Constitution, nor prohibited by it to the states, are reserved to the states respectively, or to the people.